HARDTACK AND COFFEE

GENERAL GRANT REPRIMANDED BY A LIEUTENANT.

HARDTACK AND COFFEE

INCLUDING CHAPTERS ON

ENLISTING, LIFE IN TENTS AND LOG HUTS, JONAHS AND BEATS,
OFFENCES AND PUNISHMENTS, RAW RECRUITS, FORAGING,
CORPS AND CORPS BADGES, THE WAGON TRAINS,
THE ARMY MULE, THE ENGINEER
CORPS, THE SIGNAL
CORPS, ETC.

By JOHN D. BILLINGS

AUTHOR OF "THE TENTH MASSACHUSETTS BATTERY"; PAST DEPARTMENT COMMANDER
MASSACHUSETTS G. A. R.; FORMERLY OF SICKLES' THIRD AND HANCOCK'S
SECOND CORPS, ARMY OF THE POTOMAC

𝕴llustrated

CHARLES W. REED

MEMBER OF NINTH MASSACHUSETTS BATTERY; ALSO, TOPOGRAPHICAL
ENGINEER ON GENERAL WARREN'S STAFF, FIFTH
CORPS, ARMY OF THE POTOMAC

KONECKY&KONECKY

KONECKY & KONECKY
72 AYERS POINT RD.
OLD SAYBROOK, CT 06475

ISBN: 1-56852-443-9

Printed and bound in Colombia by Imprelibros S.A.

DEDICATION.

To my comrades of the Army of the Potomac who, it is believed, will find rehearsed in these pages much that has not before appeared in print, and which it is hoped will secure to their children in permanent form valuable information about a soldier's life in detail that has thus far been only partially written, this work is most affectionately dedicated by their friend,

THE AUTHOR.

PREFACE.

DURING the summer of 1881 I was a sojourner for a few weeks at a popular hotel in the White Mountains. Among the two hundred or more guests who were enjoying its retirement and good cheer were from twelve to twenty lads, varying in age from ten to fifteen years. When tea had been disposed of, and darkness had put an end to their daily romp and hurrah without, they were wont to take in charge a gentleman from Chicago, formerly a gallant soldier in the Army of the Cumberland, and in a quiet corner of the spacious hotel parlor, or a remote part of the piazza, would listen with eager attention as he related chapters of his personal experience in the Civil War.

Less than two days elapsed before they pried out of the writer the acknowledgment that he too had served Uncle Sam; and immediately followed up this bit of information by requesting me to alternate evenings with the veteran from the West in entertaining them with stories of the war as I saw it. I assented to the plan readily enough, and a more interested or interesting audience of its size could not be desired than that knot of boys who clustered around us on alternate nights, while we related to them in an offhand way many facts regarded as too commonplace for the general histories of the war.

This trifling piece of personal experience led to the preparation of these sketches, and will largely account for the didactic manner in which they are written. They are far from complete. Many topics of interest are left untreated — they will readily suggest themselves to veterans; but it was thought best not to expand this volume beyond its present proportions. It is believed that what is herein written will appeal largely to a common experience among soldiers. In full faith that such is the case, they are now presented to veterans, their children, and the public as an important contribution of warp to the more majestic woof which comprises the history of the Great Civil War already written. That history, to date, is a history of battles, of campaigns and of generals. This is the first attempt to record comprehensively army life in detail; in which both text and illustrations aim to permanently record information which the history of no other war has preserved with equal accuracy and completeness.

I am under obligations to many veterans for kindly suggestions and criticisms during the progress of this work, to Houghton & Mifflin for the use of Holmes' "Sweet Little Man," and especially to Comrade Charles W. Reed, for his many truthful and spirited illustrations. The large number of sketches which he brought from the field in 1865 has enabled him to reproduce with telling effect many sights and scenes once very familiar to the veterans of the Union armies, which cannot fail to recall stirring experiences in their soldier's life.

Believing they will do this, and that these pages will appeal to a large number to whom the Civil War is yet something more than a myth, they are confidently put forth, the pleasant labor of spare hours, with no claim for their literary excellence, but with the full assurance that they will partially meet a want hitherto unsupplied.

CAMBRIDGEPORT, Mass., March 30, 1887.

CONTENTS.

CHAPTER I.

THE TOCSIN OF WAR.

CHAPTER II.

ENLISTING.

CHAPTER III.

HOW THE SOLDIERS WERE SHELTERED.

CHAPTER IV.

LIFE IN TENTS.

CHAPTER V.

LIFE IN LOG HUTS.

CHAPTER VI.

JONAHS AND BEATS.

CHAPTER VII.

ARMY RATIONS.

CHAPTER VIII.

OFFENCES AND PUNISHMENTS.

CHAPTER IX.

A DAY IN CAMP. "ASSEMBLY OF BUGLERS." "TURN OUT !" "ASSEMBLY."

4 *CONTENTS.*

CHAPTER XIII.

CORPS AND CORPS BADGES.

CHAPTER XIV.

SOME INVENTIONS AND DEVICES OF THE WAR.

CHAPTER XV.

THE ARMY MULE.

CHAPTER XVI.

HOSPITALS AND AMBULANCES.

CHAPTER XVII.

SCATTERING SHOTS. THE CLOTHING.

CHAPTER XVIII.

BREAKING CAMP. ON THE MARCH.

CHAPTER XIX.

ARMY WAGON TRAINS.

CHAPTER XX.

ARMY ROAD AND BRIDGE BUILDERS.

CHAPTER XXI.

TALKING FLAGS AND TORCHES.

LIST OF ILLUSTRATIONS.

HARD TACK AND COFFEE.

CHAPTER I.

THE TOCSIN OF WAR.

A score of millions hear the cry
And herald it abroad,
To arms they fly to do or die
For liberty and God.
E. P. Dyer.

And yet they keep gathering and marching away!
Has the nation turned soldier — and all in a day ?
There's the father and son!
While the miller takes gun
With the dust of the wheat still whitening his hair ;
Pray where are they going with this martial air ?
F. E. Brooks.

On the 6th of November, 1860, Abraham Lincoln, the candidate of the Republican party, was elected President of the United States, over three opponents. The autumn of that year witnessed the most exciting political canvass this country had ever seen. The Democratic party, which had been in power for several years in succession, split into factions and nominated two candidates. The northern Democrats nominated Stephen A. Douglas, of Illinois, who was an advocate of the doctrine of *Squatter Sovereignty*, that is, the right of the people living in a Territory which wanted admission into the Union as a State to decide for themselves whether they would or would not have slavery.

The southern Democrats nominated John C. Breckenridge, of Kentucky, at that time Vice-President of the United States. The doctrine which he and his party advocated was the right to carry their slaves into every State and Territory in the Union without any hindrance whatever. Then there was still another party, called by some the *Peace Party,*

A BELL AND EVERETT CAM-
PAIGNER.

which pointed to the Constitution of the country as its guide, but had nothing to say on the great question of slavery, which was so prominent with the other parties. It took for its standard-bearer John Bell, of Tennessee; and Edward Everett, of Massachusetts, was nominated as Vice-President. This party drew its membership from both of the others, but largely from the Democrats.

Owing to these divisions the Republican party, which had not been in existence many years, was enabled to elect its candidate. The Republicans did not intend to meddle with slavery where it then was, but opposed its extension into any *new* States and Territories. This latter fact was very well known to the slave-holders, and so they voted almost solidly for John C. Breckenridge. But it was very evident to them, after the Democratic party divided, that the Republicans would succeed, and so, long before the election actually took place, they began to make threats of seceding from the Union if Lincoln was elected. Freedom of speech was not tolerated in these States, and northern people who were down South for business or pleasure, if they expressed opinions in opposition to the popular political sentiments of that section, were at once warned to leave. Hundreds came North immediately to seek personal safety, often leaving possessions of great value behind them. Even native southerners who

A GROUP OF SOUTHERNERS DISCUSSING THE SITUATION.

believed thoroughly in the Union — and there were hundreds of such — were not allowed to say so. This class of people suffered great indignities during the war, on account of their loyalty to the old flag. Many of them were driven by insult and abuse to take up arms for a cause with which they did not sympathize, deserting it at the

earliest opportunity, while others held out to the bitter
end, or sought a refuge from such persecution in the
Union lines.

As early as the 25th of October, several southerners who
were or had been prominent in politics met in South Carolina, and decided by a unanimous vote that the State
should withdraw from the Union in the event of Lincoln's
election, which then seemed almost certain. Some other
States held similar meetings about the same date. Thus
early did the traitor leaders prepare the South for dis-
union. These men were better known at that time as
" Fire-eaters."

As soon as Lincoln's election was announced, without
waiting to see what his policy towards the slave States was
going to be, the impetuous leaders at the South addressed
themselves at once to the carrying out of their threats; and
South Carolina, followed, at intervals more or less brief,
by Georgia, Alabama, Mississippi, Louisiana, Florida, and
Texas, seceded from the Union, and organized what was
known as the Southern Confederacy. Virginia, North Carolina, Arkansas, and Tennessee seceded later. The people at
the North stood amazed at the rapidity with which treason
against the government was spreading, and the loyal Union-
loving men began to inquire where President Buchanan was
at this time, whose duty it was to see that all such upris-
ings were crushed out; and " Oh for one hour of Andrew
Jackson in the President's chair ! " was the common exclamation, because that decided and unyielding soldier-Presi-
dent had so promptly stamped out threatened rebellion in
South Carolina, when she had refused to allow the duties
to be collected at Charleston. But that outbreak in its
proportions was to this one as an infant to a giant, and it
is quite doubtful if Old Hickory himself, with his promptness to act in an emergency, could have stayed the angry
billows of rebellion which seemed just ready to break over
the nation. But at any rate he would have attempted it,

even if he had gone down in the fight, — at least so thought the people.

The very opposite of such a President was James Buchanan, who seemed anxious only for his term of office to expire, making little effort to save the country, nor even willing, at first, that others should do so. With a traitor for his Secretary of War, the South had been well supplied with arms under the very nose of the old man. With a traitor for his Secretary of the Navy, our vessels — not many in number, it is true — had been sent into foreign waters, where they could not be immediately recalled. With a traitor as Secretary of the Treasury, the public treasury had been emptied. Then, too, there began the seizure of arsenals, mints, custom-houses, post-offices, and fortifications within the limits of the seceding States, and still the President did nothing, or worse than nothing, claiming that the South was wrong in its acts, but that he had no right to prevent treason and secession, or, in the phraseology of that day, "no right to coerce a sovereign State." And so at last he left the office a disgraced old man, for whom few had or have a kind word to offer.

Such, briefly, was the condition of affairs when Abraham Lincoln, fearful of his life, which had been threatened, entered Washington under cover of darkness, and quietly assumed the duties of his office. Never before were the people of this country in such a state of excitement. At the North there were a large number who boldly denounced the "Long-heeled Abolitionists" and "Black Republicans" for having stirred up this trouble. I was not a voter at the time of Lincoln's election, but I had taken an active part in the torchlight parades of the "Wide-awakes" and "Rail-splitters," as the political clubs of the Republicans were called, and so came in for a share of the abuse showered upon the followers of the new President. As fresh deeds of violence or new aggressions against the government were reported from the daily papers in the shop where I was then employed, some one who was not a "Lincolnite" would exclaim, in an angry tone; "I hope you fellows are satisfied now. I don't blame the South an atom. They have been driven to desperation by such lunatics as Garrison and Phillips, and these men ought to be hung for it." . . . "If there is a war, I hope you and every other Black Republican will be made to go and fight for the niggers all you want to." . . . "You like the niggers so well you'll marry

A LINCOLN WIDE AWAKE.

one of them yet." . . . And, "I want to see those hot-headed Abolitionists put into the front rank, and shot first." These are mild quotations from the daily conversations, had not only where I was employed, but in every other shop and factory in the North. Such wordy contests were by no means one-sided affairs; for the assailed, while not anxious for war, were not afraid of it, and were amply supplied with arguments with which they answered and enraged their antagonists; and if they did not always silence them, they drove them into making just such ridiculous remarks as the foregoing. If I were asked who these men were, I should not call them by name. They were my neighbors and my friends, but they are changed men to-day. There is not one of them who, in the light of later experiences, is not heartily ashamed of his attitude at that time. Many of them afterwards went to the field, and, sad to say, are there yet. But this was the period of the most intemperate and abusive language. Those who sympathized with the South were, some months later, called Copperheads. Lincoln and his party were reviled by these men without any restraint except such as personal shame and self-respect might impose; and these qualities were conspicuously absent. Nothing was too harsh to utter against Republicans. No fate was too evil for their political opponents to wish them.

Of course all of these revilers were not sincere in their ill-wishes, but the effect of their utterances on the community was just as evil; and the situation of the new President, at its best a perplexing and critical one, was thus made all the harder, by leading him to believe that a multitude of the citizens at the North would obstruct instead of supporting him. It also gave the slave-holders the impression that a very considerable number of northern men were ready to aid them in prosecuting their treasonable schemes. But now the rapid march of events wrought a change in the opinions of the people in both sections.

"NAYTHER AV US."

The leading Abolitionists had argued that the South was too cowardly to fight for slavery; and the South had been told by the "Fire-eaters" and its northern friends that the North could not be kicked into fighting; that in case war should arise she would have her hands full to keep her enemies *at home* in check. Alas! how little did either party understand the temper of the other! How much like that story of the two Irishmen. — Meeting one day in the army, one says, "How are you, Mike?" "How are you, Pat?" says the other. "But my name is not Pat," said the first speaker. "Nather is mine Mike," said the

second. " Faix, thin," said the first, " it musht be nayther
of us."

Nothing could better illustrate the attitude of the North
and South towards each other than this anecdote. Nothing
could have been more perfect than this mutual misunder-
standing each displayed of the temper of the other, as the
stride of events soon showed.

The story of how Major Anderson removed his little
band of United States troops from Fort Moultrie to Fort
Sumter, in Charleston Harbor, for reasons of greater safety,
is a familiar one; likewise how the rebels fired upon a
vessel sent by the President with supplies intended for
it; and, finally, after a severe bombardment of several
days, how they compelled the fort to surrender. It was
these events which opened the eyes of the " Northern
Doughfaces," as those who sympathized with the South
were often called, to the real intent of the Seceders. A
change came over the spirit of their dreams. Patriotism,
love of the Union, at last came uppermost. They had
heard it proposed to divide the old flag, giving a part to
each section. They had seen a picture of the emblem thus
rent, and it was not a pleasing one. Soon the greater portion of them ceased their sneers and ill-wishes, and joined
in the general demand that something be done at once to
assert the majesty and power of the national government.
Even President Lincoln, who, in his inaugural address, had
counselled his " countrymen, one and all, to take time and
think calmly and well upon this whole subject," had come
to feel that further forbearance was no virtue, and that a
decent respect for this great nation and for his office as President demanded that something should be done speedily.
So on the 15th of April he issued a proclamation calling
out 75,000 militia, for three months, to suppress the Rebellion, and to cause the laws to be executed.

Having been a Massachusetts soldier, it is but natural
that I should refer occasionally to her part in the opening

of this momentous crisis in the country's history, as being
more familiar to me than the record of any other State.
Yet, proud as I am of her conspicuous services in the early
war period, I have no desire to extol them at the expense of
Pennsylvania, New York, and Rhode Island, who so promptly
pressed forward and touched elbows with her in this emergency; nor of those other great Western States, whose sturdy
patriots so promptly crossed Mason's
and Dixon's line in such serried
ranks at the summons of Father
Abraham.

It has often been asked how Massachusetts, so much farther from the
National Capital than any of the
other States, should have been so
prompt in coming to its assistance.
Let me give some idea of how it
happened. In December, 1860, Adjutant-General Schouler of that
State, in his annual report, suggested to Governor (afterwards
General) N. P. Banks, that as
events were then occurring which
might require that the militia of
Massachusetts should be increased
in number, it would be well for
commanders of companies to for-

THE MINUTE MAN OF '61.

ward to head-quarters a complete roll of each company,
with their names and residence, and that companies not
full should be recruited to the limit fixed by law, which
was then one hundred and one for infantry. Shortly afterwards John A. Andrew, now known in history as the *Great
War Governor* of Massachusetts, assumed the duties of his
office. He was not only a leading Republican before the
war, but an Abolitionist as well. He seemed to clearly
foresee that the time for threats and arguments had gone

by, and that the time for action was at hand. So on the
16th of January he issued an order (No. 4) which had for
its object to ascertain exactly how many of the officers and
men in the militia would hold themselves ready to respond
immediately to any call which might be made upon their
services by the President. All who were not ready to do
so were discharged at once, and their places filled by others.
Thus it was that Massachusetts for the second time in her
history prepared her " Minute Men " to take the field at a
minute's notice.

This general order of the Governor's, although a very
wise one as it proved, carried dismay into the ranks of the
militia, for there were in Massachusetts, as in other States,
very many men who had made valiant and well disciplined
peace soldiers, who, now that one of the real needs of a
well organized militia was upon us, were not at all thirsty
for further military glory. But pride stood in the way of
their frankness. They were ashamed in this hour of their
country's peril to withdraw from the militia, for they feared
to face public opinion. Yet there were men who had good
and sufficient reasons for declining to pledge themselves for
instant military service, at least until there was a more
general demand for troops. They were loyal and worthy
citizens, and could not in a moment cast aside or turn their
back on their business or domestic responsibilities, and in
a season of calmer reflection it would not have been expected of them. But the public pulse was then at fever-
heat, and reason was having a vacation.

General Order No. 4 was, I believe, the first important
step taken by the State in preparing for the crisis. The
next was the passage of a bill by the Legislature, which was
approved by the Governor April 3, appropriating $25,000
for " overcoats, blankets, knapsacks, 200,000 ball cartridges,
etc., for two thousand troops." These supplies were soon
ready. The militiamen then owned their uniforms, and, as
no particular kind was prescribed, no two companies of the

same regiment were of necessity uniformed alike. It is only a few years since uniformity of dress has been required of the militia in Massachusetts.

But to return to that memorable 15th of April. War, that much talked-of, much dreaded calamity was at last upon us. Could it really be so? We would not believe it; and yet daily happenings forced the unwelcome conclusion upon us. It seemed so strange. We had nothing in our experience to compare it with. True, some of us had dim remembrances of a Mexican war in our early childhood, but as Massachusetts sent only one regiment to that war, and that saw no fighting, and, besides, did not receive the sympathy and support of the people in the State generally, we only remembered that there was a Scott, and a Taylor, and a Santa Aña, from the colored prints we had seen displayed of these worthies; so that we could only run back in memory to the stories and traditions of the wars of the Revolution and 1812, in which our ancestry had served, for anything like a vivid picture of what was about to occur, and this, of course, was utterly inadequate to do the subject justice.

I have already stated that General Order No. 4 carried dismay into many hearts, causing the more timid to withdraw from military service at once. A great many more would have withdrawn at the same time had they not been restrained by pride and the lingering hope that there would be no war after all; but this very day (the 15th) came Special Order No. 14, from Governor Andrew, ordering the Third, Fourth, Sixth, and Eighth Regiments to assemble on Boston Common forthwith. This was the final test of the militiamen's actual courage and thirst for glory, and a severe one it proved to many of them, for at this eleventh hour there was another falling-out along the line. But the moment a man's declination for further service was made known, unless his reasons were of the very best, straightway he was hooted at for his cowardice, and for a time his existence was made quite unpleasant in his own immediate neighborhood. If he had been a commissioned officer, his face was likely to appear in an illustrated paper, accompanied by the statement that he had "shown the white feather," — another term for cowardice. A reference to any file of illustrated papers of those days will show a large number of such persons. Such gratuitous advertising by a generally loyal, though not always discreet press did some men gross injustice; for, as already intimated, many of the men thus publicly sketched and denounced were among the most worthy and loyal of citizens. A little later than the period of which I am treating, Oliver Wendell Holmes wrote the following poem, hitting off a certain limited class in the community : —

THE SWEET LITTLE MAN.

Dedicated to the Stay-at-Home Rangers.

Now while our soldiers are fighting our battles,
    Each at his post to do all that he can,
Down among Rebels and contraband chattels,
    What are you doing, my sweet little man?

All the brave boys under canvas are sleeping;
    All of them pressing to march with the van,
Far from the home where their sweethearts are weeping;
    What are you waiting for, sweet little man?

You with the terrible warlike moustaches,
    Fit for a colonel or chief of a clan,
You with the waist made for sword-belts and sashes,
    Where are your shoulder-straps, sweet little man?

Bring him the buttonless garment of woman!
    Cover his face lest it freckle and tan;
Muster the Apron-string Guards on the Common, —
    That is the corps for the sweet little man!

Give him for escort a file of young misses,
    Each of them armed with a deadly rattan;
They shall defend him from laughter and hisses,
    Aimed by low boys at the sweet little man.

All the fair maidens about him shall cluster,
　　Pluck the white feather from bonnet and fan,
Make him a plume like a turkey-wing duster,—
　　That is the crest for the sweet little man.

Oh, but the Apron-string Guards are the fellows!
　　Drilling each day since our trouble began, —
"Handle your walking-sticks!"　"Shoulder umbrellas!"
　　That is the style for the sweet little man.

SWEET LITTLE MEN OF '61.

Have we a nation to save? In the first place
　　Saving ourselves is the sensible plan.
Surely, the spot where there's shooting's the worst place
　　Where I can stand, says the sweet little man.

Catch me confiding my person with strangers,
　　Think how the cowardly Bull-Runners ran!
In the brigade of the Stay-at-home Rangers
　　Marches my corps, says the sweet little man.

Such was the stuff of the Malakoff takers,
    Such were the soldiers that scaled the Redan;
Truculent housemaids and bloodthirsty Quakers
    Brave not the wrath of the sweet little man!

Yield him the sidewalk, ye nursery maidens!
    Sauve qui peut! Bridget, and Right about! **Ann;—**
Fierce as a shark in a school of menhadens,
    See him advancing, the sweet little man!

When the red flails of the battlefield's threshers
    Beat out the continent's wheat from its bran,
While the wind scatters the chaffy seceshers,
    What will become of our sweet little man?

When the brown soldiers come back from the borders,
    How will he look while his features they scan?
How will he feel when he gets marching orders,
    Signed by his lady love ? sweet little man.

Fear not for him though the Rebels expect him, —
    Life is too precious to shorten its span;
Woman her broomstick shall raise to protect him,
    Will she not fight for the sweet little man!

Now, then, nine cheers for the Stay-at-home Ranger!
    Blow the great fish-horn and beat the big pan!
First in the field, that is farthest from danger,
    Take your white feather plume, sweet little man!

The 16th of April was a memorable day in the history of
the Old Bay State, — a day made more uncomfortable by the
rain and sleet which were falling with disagreeable constancy.
Well do I remember the day.   Possessing an average amount
of the fire and enthusiasm of youth, I had asked my father's
consent to go out with Company A of the old Fourth Regiment, which belonged to my native town.   But he would
not give ear to any such "nonsense," and, having been
brought up to obey his orders, although of military age
(18), I did not enter the service in the first rally.   This
company did not go with full ranks.   There were few that
did.   Several of my shopmates were in its membership.   As

those of us who remained gathered at the windows that stormy forenoon to see the company go by, the sight filled us with the most gloomy forebodings.

So the troops went forth from the towns in the shore counties of Massachusetts. Most of the companies in the regiments that were called reported for duty at Boston this

ADJUTANT HINKS NOTIFYING CAPTAIN KNOTT V. MARTIN.

very 16th — two companies from Marblehead being the first to arrive. One of these companies was commanded by Captain Knott V. Martin, who was engaged in slaughtering hogs when Adjutant (now Major-General) E. W. Hinks rode up and instructed him to report on Boston Common in the morning. Drawing the knife from the throat of a hog, the Captain uttered an exclamation which has passed into history, threw the knife with a light toss to the floor, went im-

mediately and notified his Orderly Sergeant, and then returned to his butchering. In the morning he and his company were ready for business.

But their relatives who remained at home could not look
calmly on the departure of these dear ones, who were going
no one knew just where, and would return — perhaps never ;
so there were many touching scenes witnessed at the various
railway stations, as the men boarded the trains for Boston.
When these Marblehead companies arrived at that city the
enthusiasm was something unprecedented, and as a new detachment appeared in the streets it was cheered to the echo
all along its line of march. The early months of the war
were stirring ones for Boston ; for not only did the most of
the Massachusetts regiments march through her streets *en
route* for the seat of war, but also the troops from Maine
and New Hampshire as well, so that a regiment halted
for rest on the Common, or marching to the strain of
martial music to some railway station, was at times a daily
occurrence.

It has always seemed to me that the " Three months
men " have never received half the credit which the worth
of their services to the country deserved. The fact of their
having been called out for so short a time as compared with
the troops that came after them, and of their having seen
little or no fighting, places them at a disadvantage. But to
have so suddenly left all, and gone to the defence of the
Capital City, with no knowledge of what was in store for
them, and impelled by no other than the most patriotic of
motives, seems to me fully as praiseworthy as to have gone
later under the pressure of urgent need, when the full stress
of war was upon us, and when its realities were better
known, and the inducements to enlist greater in some other
respects. There is no doubt whatever but what the prompt
appearance of these short-term men not only saved the Capital, but that it served also to show the Rebels that the
North at short call could send a large and comparatively

CAPTAIN KNOTT V. MARTIN'S COMPANY ON ITS WAY TO FANEUIL HALL.

well equipped force into the field, and was ready to back its words by deeds. Furthermore, these soldiers gave the government time to catch its breath, as it were, and, looking the issue squarely in the face, to decide upon some settled plan of action.

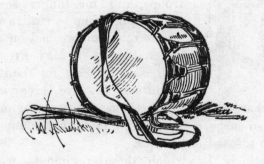

CHAPTER II.

ENLISTING.

O, did you see him in the street dressed up in army blue,
When drums and trumpets into town their storm of music threw —
A louder tune than all the winds could muster in the air,
The Rebel winds that tried so hard our flag in strips to tear?

LUCY LARCOM.

 ARDLY had the "Three months men" reached the field before it was discovered that a mistake had been made in not calling out a larger number of troops, and for longer service; — it took a long time to realize what a gigantic rebellion we had on our hands. So on the 3d of May President Lincoln issued a call for United States volunteers to serve three years, unless sooner discharged. At once thousands of loyal men sprang to arms — so large a number, in fact, that many regiments raised were refused until later.

The methods by which these regiments were raised were various. In 1861 a common way was for some one who had been in the regular army, or perhaps who had been prominent in the militia, to take the initiative and circulate an enlistment paper for signatures. His chances were pretty good for obtaining a commission as its captain, for his active interest, and men who had been prominent in assisting him, if they were popular, would secure the lieutenancies. On the return of the "Three months" troops many of the companies immediately re-enlisted in a body for three years, sometimes under their old officers. A large

34

number of these short-term veterans, through influence at
the various State capitals, secured commissions in new regiments that were organizing.   In country towns too small to
furnish a company, the men would post off to a neighboring
town or city, and there enlist.

In 1862, men who had seen a year's active service were
selected to receive a part of the commissions issued to new
organizations, and should in justice have received *all* within
the bestowal of governors.   But the recruiting of troops
soon resolved itself into individual enlistments or this programme ; — twenty, thirty, fifty or more men would go in a
body to some recruiting station, and signify their readiness
to enlist in a certain regiment *provided* a certain specified
member of their number should be commissioned captain.
Sometimes they would compromise, if the outlook was not
promising, and take a lieutenancy, but equally often it was
necessary to accept their terms, or count them out.   In the
rivalry for men to fill up regiments, the result often was
officers who were diamonds in the rough, but liberally intermingled with *veritable clod-hoppers* whom a brief experience
in active service soon sent to the rear.

This year the War Department was working on a more
systematic basis, and when a call was made for additional
troops each State was immediately assigned its quota, and
with marked promptness each city and town was informed
by the State authorities how many men it was to furnish
under that call.   The war fever was not at such a fervid heat
in '62 as in the year before, and so recruiting offices were
multiplied in cities and large towns.   These offices were of
two kinds, *viz.:* those which were opened to secure recruits
for regiments and batteries already in the field, and those
which solicited enlistments in *new* organizations.   Unquestionably, at this time the latter were more popular.

The former office was presided over by a line officer directly from the front, attended by one or two subordinates,
all of whom had smelled powder.   The latter office might

be in charge of an experienced soldier recently commissioned, or of a man ambitious for such preferment.

The flaming advertisements with which the newspapers of the day teemed, and the posters pasted on the bill-boards or the country fence, were the decoys which brought patronage to these fishers of men. Here is a sample : —

More Massachusetts Volunteers Accepted ! ! !

Three Regiments to be Immediately Recruited !

GEN. WILSON'S REGIMENT,

To which CAPT. FOLLETT'S BATTERY is attached;

COL. JONES' GALLANT SIXTH REGIMENT,

WHICH WENT "THROUGH BALTIMORE";

THE N. E. GUARDS REGIMENT, commanded by that excellent officer, MAJOR J. T. STEVENSON.

The undersigned has this day been authorized and directed to fill up the ranks of these regiments forthwith. A grand opportunity is afforded for patriotic persons to enlist in the service of their country under the command of as able officers as the country has yet furnished. Pay and rations will begin immediately on enlistment.

UNIFORMS ALSO PROVIDED !

Citizens of Massachusetts should feel pride in attaching themselves to regiments from their own State, in order to maintain the proud supremacy which the Old Bay State now enjoys in the contest for the Union and the Constitution. The people of many of the towns and cities of the Commonwealth have made ample provision for those joining the ranks of the army. If any person enlists in a Company or Regiment out of the Commonwealth, he cannot share in the bounty which has been thus liberally voted. Wherever any town or city has assumed the privilege of supporting the families of Volunteers, the Commonwealth reimburses such place to the amount of $12 per month for families of three persons.

Patriots desiring to serve the country will bear in mind that

THE GENERAL RECRUITING STATION

IS AT

No. 14 PITTS STREET, BOSTON !

WILLIAM W. BULLOCK,
General Recruiting Officer, Massachusetts Volunteers.

[*Boston Journal* of Sept. 12, 1861.]

Here is a call to a war meeting held out-of-doors: —

TO ARMS!   TO ARMS!!

GREAT WAR MEETING
IN ROXBURY.

Another meeting of the citizens of Roxbury, to re-enforce their brothers in the field, will be held in

ELIOT SQUARE, ROXBURY,

THIS EVENING AT EIGHT O'CLOCK.

SPEECHES FROM

Paul Willard, Rev. J. O. Means, Judge Russell,

And other eloquent advocates.

The **Brigade Band** will be on hand early. **Come one, come all!**

God and your Country Call!!

Per Order.

[*Boston Journal* of July 30, 1862.]

Here are two which look quite business-like: —

GENERAL POPE'S ARMY.

"Lynch Law for Guerillas and No Rebel Property Guarded!"

IS THE MOTTO OF THE

SECOND MASSACHUSETTS REGIMENT.

$578.50 for 21 months' service.
$252.00 State aid for families of four.
$830.50 and short service.
$125.00 cash in hand.

This Regiment, although second in number, is second to none in regard to discipline and efficiency, and is in the healthiest and most delightful country.

Office at Coolidge House, Bowdoin Square.

CAPT. C. R. MUDGE.
LIEUT. A. D. SAWYER.

$100 BOUNTY!

CADET REGIMENT,

Company D,

NINE MONTHS' SERVICE.

O. W. PEABODY . . . . Recruiting Officer.

Headquarters, 113 Washington Street, Boston.

[*Boston Journal*, Sept. 17, 1862.]

War meetings similar to the one called in Roxbury were designed to stir lagging enthusiasm. Musicians and orators blew themselves red in the face with their windy efforts. Choirs improvised for the occasion, sang "Red, White, and Blue" and "Rallied 'Round the Flag" till too hoarse for further endeavor. The old veteran soldier of 1812 was trotted out, and worked for all he was worth, and an occasional Mexican War veteran would air his nonchalance at grim-visaged war. At proper intervals the enlistment roll would be presented for signatures. There was generally one old fellow present who upon slight provocation would yell like a hyena, and declare his readiness to shoulder his musket and go, if he wasn't so old, while his staid and half-fearful consort would pull violently at his coat-tails to repress his unseasonable effervescence ere it assumed more dangerous proportions. Then there was a patriotic maiden lady who kept a flag or a handkerchief waving with only the rarest and briefest of intervals, who "would go in a minute if she was a man." Besides these there was usually a man who would make one of fifty (or some other safe number) to enlist, when he well understood that such a number could not be obtained. And there was one more often found present who when challenged to sign would agree to, *provided* that A or B (men of wealth) would put down *their* names. I saw a man at a war meeting promise, with a bombastic flourishment, to enlist if a certain number (which

A WAR MEETING.

I do not now remember) of the citizens would do the same. The number was obtained; but the small-sized patriot, who was willing to sacrifice his *wife's* relations on the altar of his country, crawled away amid the sneers of his townsmen.

Sometimes the patriotism of such a gathering would be wrought up so intensely by waving banners, martial and vocal music, and burning eloquence, that a town's quota would be filled in less than an hour. It needed only the first man to step forward, put down his name, be patted on the back, placed upon the platform, and cheered to the echo as the hero of the hour, when a second, a third, a fourth would follow, and at last a perfect stampede set in to sign the enlistment roll, and a frenzy of enthusiasm would take possession of the meeting. The complete intoxication of such excitement, like intoxication from liquor, left some of its victims on the following day, especially if the fathers of families, with the sober second thought to wrestle with; but Pride, that tyrannical master, rarely let them turn back.

The next step was a medical examination to determine physical fitness for service. Each town had its physician for this work. The candidate for admission into the army must first divest himself of all clothing, and his soundness or unsoundness was then decided by causing him to jump, bend over, kick, receive sundry thumps in the chest and back, and such other laying-on of hands as was thought necessary. The teeth had also to be examined, and the eyesight tested, after which, if the candidate passed, he received a certificate to that effect.

His next move was toward a recruiting station. There he would enter, signify his errand, sign the roll of the company or regiment into which he was going, leave his description, including height, complexion, and occupation, and then accompany a guard to the examining surgeon, where he was again subjected to a critical examination as to soundness.

Those men who, on deciding to "go to war," went directly to a recruiting office and enlisted, had but this simple examination to pass, the other being then unnecessary. It is interesting to note that in 1861 and '62 men were mainly examined to establish their *fitness* for service; in 1863 and '64 the tide had changed, and they were then only anxious to prove their *un*fitness.

After the citizen in question had become a soldier, he was usually sent at once to camp or the seat of war, but if he wanted a short furlough it was generally granted. If he had enlisted in a new regiment, he might remain weeks before being ordered to the front; if in an old regiment, he might find himself in a fight at short notice. Hundreds of the men who enlisted under the call issued by President Lincoln July 2, 1862, were killed or wounded before they had been in the field a week.

Any man or woman who lived in those thrilling early war days will never forget them. The spirit of patriotism was at fever-heat, and animated both sexes of all ages. Such a display of the national colors had never been seen before. Flag-raisings were the order of the day in public and private grounds. The trinity of red, white, and blue colors was to be seen in all directions. Shopkeepers decked their windows and counters with them. Men wore them in neck-ties, or in a rosette pinned on the breast, or tied in the button-hole. The women wore them conspicuously also. The bands played only patriotic airs, and "Yankee Doodle," "Red, White, and Blue," and the "Star-Spangled Banner" would have been worn threadbare if possible. Then other patriotic songs and marches were composed, many of which had only a short-lived existence; and the poetry of this period, some of it excellent, would fill a large volume.

CHAPTER III.

HOW THE SOLDIERS WERE SHELTERED.

The heath this night must be my bed,
The bracken curtain for my head,
My lullaby the warder's tread,
　　Far, far from love and thee, **Mary**.
To-morrow eve, more stilly laid,
My couch may be my bloody plaid,
My vesper song, thy wail, sweet maid.
　　It will not waken me, Mary.

LADY OF THE LAKE.

FTER enlistment, what? This deed done, the responsibility of the citizen for himself ceased in a measure, and Uncle Sam took him in charge. A word here to make clear to the uninformed the distinction between the militia and the volunteers. The militia are the soldiers of the State, and their duties lie wholly within its limits, unless called out by the President of the United States in an emergency. Such an emergency occurred when President Lincoln made his call for 75,000 militia, already alluded to. The volunteers, on the other hand, enlist directly into the service of the United States, and it becomes the duty of the national government to provide for them from the very date of their enlistment.

Before leaving the State these volunteers were *mustered into service*. This often occurred soon after their enlistment, before they had been provided with the garb of Union soldiers.

43

The oath of muster, which they took with uplifted hand ran as follows : —

"I, A—— B——, do solemnly swear that I will bear true allegiance to the United States of America, and that I will serve them honestly and faithfully against all their enemies and opposers whatsoever, and observe and obey the orders of the President of the United States, and the orders of the officers appointed over me according to the rules and articles for the government of the armies of the United States."

MUSTERING IN RECRUITS.

The provision made for the shelter of these troops before they took the field was varied. Some of them were quartered at Forts Warren and Independence while making ready to depart. But the most of the Massachusetts volunteers were quartered at camps established in different parts of the State. Among the earliest of these were Camp Andrew, in West Roxbury, and Camp Cameron, in North Cambridge. Afterwards camps were laid out at Lynnfield, Pittsfield, Boxford, Readville, Worcester, Lowell, Long Island, and a few other places. The "Three-months militia" required no provision for their shelter, as they were ordered away soon after reporting for duty. Faneuil Hall furnished quarters for a part of them one night. The First Massachusetts Regiment of Infantry quartered for a week in Faneuil Hall; but, this not being a suitable place for so large a body of men to remain, "on the first day of June the regiment marched out to Cambridge, and took possession of an old ice-house on the borders of Fresh Pond, which had been procured by the State authorities and partially fitted up for barracks, and

READVILLE (MASS.) BARRACKS.
From a Photograph.

established their first camp." But this was not the first camp established in the State, for three years' troops had already been ordered into camp on Long Island and at Fort Warren.

Owing to the unhealthiness of the location selected for the First Regiment, their stay in it was brief, and a removal was soon had to North Cambridge, where, on a well-chosen site, some new barracks had been built, and, in honor of President Lincoln's Secretary of War, had been named "Camp Cameron."

Barracks then, it will be observed, served to shelter some of the troops. To such as are not familiar with these structures, I will simply say that they were generally a long one-storied building not unlike a bowling-alley in proportions, having the entrance at one end, a broad aisle running through the centre, and a double row of bunks, one above the other, on either side. They were calculated to hold one company of a hundred men. Some of these buildings are still to be seen at Readville, Mass., near the old camp-grounds. But while barracks were desirable quarters in

SIBLEY TENTS.

the cooler weather of this latitude, and sheltered many regiments during their stay in the State, a still larger number found shelter in tents prior to their departure for the field. These tents were of various patterns, but the principal varieties used were the *Sibley*, the *A* or *Wedge Tent*, and the *Hospital* or *Wall Tent*.

The Sibley tent was invented by Henry Sibley, in 1857. He was a graduate of the United States military academy at West Point, and accompanied Capt. John C. Fremont on one of his exploring expeditions. He evidently got his idea from the *Tepee* or *Tepar*, — the Indian wigwam, of poles covered with skins, and having a fire in the centre, — which he saw on the plains. When the Rebellion broke out, Sibley cast in his fortune with the South. He afterwards attained the rank of brigadier-general, but performed no services so likely to hand down his name as the invention of this tent. It has recently been stated that Sibley was not the actual inventor, the credit being assigned to some private soldier in his command. On account of its resemblance to a huge bell, it has sometimes been called a *Bell Tent*. It is eighteen feet in diameter and twelve feet high, and is supported by a single pole, which rests on an iron tripod. This pole is the exact radius of the circle covered by the tent. By means of the tripod the tent can be tightened or slackened at pleasure. At the top is a circular opening, perhaps a foot in diameter, which serves the double purpose of ventilation and of passing a stove-pipe through in cool weather. This stove-pipe connected with a cone-shaped stove suited to this shape of tent, which stood beneath the tripod. A small piece of canvas, called a *cap*, to which were attached two long guys, covered the opening at the top in stormy weather. It was not an unusual sight in the service to see the top of one of these tents in a blaze caused by some one having drawn the cap too near an over-heated stove-pipe. A chain depended from the fork of the tripod, with a hook, on which a kettle could be hung ; when the stove was wanting the fire was built on the ground.

These tents are comfortably capacious for a dozen men. In cold or rainy weather, when every opening is closed, they are most unwholesome tenements, and to enter one of them of a rainy morning from the outer air, and encounter the night's accumulation of nauseating exhalations from the bodies of twelve men (differing widely in their habits of personal cleanliness) was an experience which no old soldier has ever been known to recall with any great enthusiasm.

Of course the air was of the vilest sort, and it is surprising to see how men endured it as they did. In the daytime these tents were ventilated by lifting them up at the bottom. Sibley tents went out of field service in 1862, partly because they were too expensive, but principally on account of being so cumbrous. They increased the amount of impedimenta too largely, for they required many wagons for their transportation, and so were afterwards used only in camps of instruction. I believe they are still used to some extent by the militia of the various States. I remember having seen these tents raised on a stockade four feet high by some regiments during the war, and thus arranged they made very spacious and comfortable winter quarters.

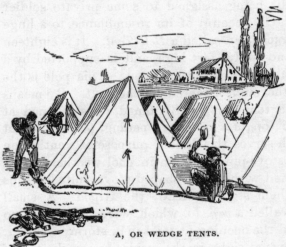

A, OR WEDGE TENTS.

When thus raised they accommodated twenty men. The camp for convalescents near Alexandria, Va., comprised this variety of tent stockaded.

The A or Wedge tents are yet quite common. The origin of this tent is not known, so far as I can learn. It seems to be about as old as history itself. A German historian, who wrote in 1751, represents the Amalekites as using them. Nothing simpler for a shelter could suggest itself to campers than some sort of awning stretched over a horizontal pole or bar. The setting-up of branches on an incline against a low horizontal branch of a tree to form a rude shelter may have been its earliest suggestion. But, whatever its origin, it is *now* a canvas tent stretched over a horizontal bar, perhaps six feet long, which is supported on two upright posts of about the same length. It covers, when pitched, an area nearly seven feet square. The name of these tents is undoubtedly derived from the fact of the ends having the proportions of the Roman letter A, and because of their resemblance to a wedge.

SPOONING TOGETHER.

Four men was the number usually assigned to one of them; but they were often occupied by five, and sometimes six. When so occupied at night, it was rather necessary to comfort that all should turn over at the same time, for six or even five men were a tight fit in the space enclosed, unless "spooned" together. These tents when stockaded were quite spacious and comfortable. A word or two just here with regard to stockading. A stockade proper is an enclosure made with posts set close together. In stockading a tent the posts were split in halves, and the cleft sides all turned inward so as to make a clean and comely inside to the hut. But by far the most common way of logging up a tent was to build the walls "cob-fashion," notching them together at the corners. This method took much less time and material than the other. But whenever I use the word stockade or stockading in any descriptions I include either method. I shall speak further of stockading by and by.

The A tents were in quite general use by the State and also by the general government the first two years of the war, but, like the Sibley, they required too much wagon transportation to take along for use in the field, and so they also were turned over to camps of instruction and to troops permanently located in or near important military centres or stations.

The Hospital or Wall tent is distinguished from those already described by having four upright sides or walls. To

THE HOSPITAL OR WALL TENT.

this fact it probably owes the latter name, and it doubtless gets the former from being used for hospital purposes in the field. These tents, also, are not of modern origin. They were certainly used by Napoleon, and probably long before his day. On account of their walls they are much more comfortable and convenient to occupy than the two preceding, as one can stand erect or move about in them with tolerable freedom. They are made of different sizes. Those used as field hospitals were quite large, accommodating from six to twenty patients, according to circumstances. It was a common occurrence to see two or more of these joined, being connected by ripping the central seam in the two ends that came in contact. By looping back the flaps thus liberated, the tents were thrown together, and quite a commodious hospital was in that way opened with a central corridor running its entire length between a double row of cots. The smaller size of wall tent was in general use as the tent of commissioned officers, and so far as I now recall, was used by no one else.

While the Army of the Potomac was at Harrison's Landing, under McClellan, he issued a General Order (Aug. 10, 1862) prescribing among other things wall tents for general field and staff officers, and a single shelter tent for each line officer; and the same order was reissued by his successors. But in some way many of these line officers

OFFICER'S WALL TENT WITH FLY.

managed to smuggle a wall tent into the wagon train, so that when a settled camp was entered upon they were provided with those luxurious shelters instead of the shelter tent.

Over the top an extra piece of canvas, called a *fly*, was stretched as additional protection against sun and rain. These tents are generally familiar. Massachusetts now provides her militia with them, I believe, without distinction of rank.

The tents thus far described I have referred to as used largely by the troops before they left the State. But there was another tent, the most interesting of all, which was used exclusively in the field, and that was *Tente d'Abri* — the *Dog* or *Shelter Tent*.

Just why it is called the shelter tent I cannot say, unless on the principle stated by the Rev. George Ellis for calling the pond on Boston Common a Frog Pond, *viz :* because there are no frogs there. So there is little shelter in this variety of tent. But about that later. I can imagine no other reason for calling it a dog tent than this, that when one is pitched it would only comfortably accommodate a dog, and a small one at that. This tent was invented late in 1861 or early in 1862. I am told it was made of light duck at first, then of rubber, and afterwards of duck again, but *I* never saw one made of anything heavier than cotton drilling. This was *the* tent of the rank and file. It did not come into general

THE DOG OR SHELTER TENT.

use till after the Peninsular Campaign. Each man was provided with a *half-shelter*, as a single piece was called, which he was expected to carry on the march if he wanted a tent to sleep under. I will describe these more fully. One I recently measured is five feet two inches long by four feet eight inches wide, and is provided with a single row of buttons and button-holes on three sides, and a pair of holes for stake loops at each corner. A single half-shelter, it can be seen, would make a very contracted and uncomfortable abode for a man; but every soldier was expected to join his resources for shelter with some other fellow. It was only rarely that a soldier was met with who was so crooked a stick that no one would chum with him, or that he cared for no chum, although I have seen a few such cases in my experience. But the rule in the army was similar to that in civil life. Every man had his chum or friend, with whom he associated when off duty, and these tented together. By mutual agreement one was the "old woman," the other the "old man" of the concern. A Marblehead man called his chum his "chicken," more especially if the latter was a *young* soldier.

By means of the buttons and button-holes two or more of these half-shelters could be buttoned together, making a very complete roofing. There are hundreds of men that came from different sections of the same State, or from different States, who joined their resources in this manner, and to-day through this accidental association they are the warmest of personal friends, and will continue so while they live. It was not usual to pitch these tents every night when the army was on the march. The soldiers did not waste their time and strength much in that way. If the night was clear and pleasant, they lay down without roof-shelter of any kind; but if it was stormy or a storm was threatening when the order came to go into camp for the night, the shelters were then quite generally pitched.

This operation was performed by the infantry in the

SHELTERS AS SOMETIMES PITCHED IN SUMMER.

following simple way : two muskets with bayonets fixed were stuck erect into the ground the width of a half shelter apart. A guy rope which went with every half-shelter was stretched between the trigger-guards of the muskets, and over this as a ridge-pole the tent was pitched in a twinkling. Artillery men pitched theirs over a horizontal bar supported by two uprights. This framework was split out of fence-rails, if fence-rails were to be had conveniently ; otherwise, saplings were cut for the purpose. It often happened that men would throw away their shelters during the day, and take their chances with the weather, or of finding cover in some barn, or under the brow of some overhanging rock, rather than be burdened with them. In summer, when the army was not in proximity to the enemy, or was lying

off recuperating, as the Army of the Potomac did a few
weeks after the Gettysburg campaign, they would pitch
their shelters high enough to get a free circulation of air
beneath, and to enable them to build bunks or cots a foot
or two above the ground. If the camp was not in the

woods, it was com-
mon to build a bow-
er of branches over
the tents, to ward
off the sun.

When cold weath-
er came on, the sol-
diers built the stock-
ades to which I have
already referred.
The walls of these
structures were

SHADED SHELTERS.

raised from two to five feet, according to the taste or working inclination of the intended occupants. Oftentimes an
excavation was made one or two feet deep. When such
was the case, the walls were not built so high. Such
a hut was warmer than one built entirely above ground.
The size depended upon the number of the proposed
mess. If the hut was to be occupied by two, it was
built nearly square, and covered by two half-shelters.
Such a stockade would and often *did* accommodate three
men, the third using his half-shelter to stop up one
gable. When four men occupied a stockade, it was built
accordingly, and covered by four half-shelters. In each
case these were stretched over a framework of light
rafters raised on the walls of the stockade. Sometimes
the gables were built up to the ridge-poles with smaller
logs, but just as often they were filled by an extra half-
shelter, a rubber blanket, or an old *poncho*. An army
poncho, I may here say, is specified as made of unbleached
muslin coated with vulcanized India-rubber, sixty inches

wide and seventy-one inches long, having an opening in
the centre lengthwise of the poncho, through which the
head passes, with a lap three inches wide and sixteen
inches long. This garment is derived from the *woollen*
poncho worn by the Spanish-Americans, but is of different
proportions, these being four feet by
seven. The army poncho was used in
lieu of the gum blanket.

The chinks between the logs were
filled with mud, worked to a viscous
consistency, which adhered more or less
tenaciously according to the amount of
clay in the mixture. It usually needed
renewing after a severe storm. The
chimney was built outside, after the
southern fashion. It stood sometimes
at the end and sometimes in the middle
of one side of the stockade. It started
from a fire-place which was fashioned
with more or less skill, according to the
taste or mechanical genius of the work-
man, or the tools and materials used,
or both. In my own company there
were two masons who had opportuni-

A PONCHO ON.

ties, whenever a winter camp was pitched, to practise
their trade far more than they were inclined to do.
The fire-places were built of brick, of stone, or of wood.
If there was a deserted house in the neighborhood of the
camp which boasted brick chimneys, they were sure to be
brought low to serve the Union cause in the manner indicated, unless the house was used by some general officer
as headquarters. When built of wood, the chimneys were
lined with a very thick coating of mud. They were generally continued above the fireplace with split wood built
cob-fashion, which was filled between and lined with the red
clayey soil of Virginia; but stones were used when abundant.

Very frequently pork and beef barrels were secured to
serve this purpose, being put one above another, and now
and then a lively hurrah would run through the camp

A CHIMNEY ON FIRE.

when one of these was discovered on fire. It is hardly
necessary to remark that not
all these chimneys were mon-
uments of success. Too often the draught was down instead
of up, and the inside of some stockades resembled smoke-
houses. Still, it was "all in the three years," as the boys
used to say. It was all the same to the average soldier,
who rarely saw fit to tear down and build anew more

scientifically.   The smoke of his camp-fires in warm weather was an excellent preparative for the smoking fireplace of winter-quarters.

Many of these huts were deemed incomplete until a sign appeared over the door.   Here and there some one would make an attempt at having a door-plate of wood suitably inscribed ; but the more common sight was a sign over the entrance bearing such inscriptions, rudely cut or marked with charcoal, as: "Parker House," "Hole in the Wall," "Mose Pearson's," "Astor House," "Willard's Hotel," "Five Points," and other titles equally absurd, expressing in this ridiculous way the vagaries of the inmates.

The last kind of shelter I shall mention as used in the field, but not the least in importance, was the *Bomb-proofs* used by both

A COMMON BOMB-PROOF.

Union and Rebel armies in the war.   Probably there were more of these erected in the vicinity of Petersburg and Richmond than in all the rest of the South combined, if I except Vicksburg, as here the opposing armies established themselves — the one in defence, the other in siege of the two cities.   These bomb-proofs were built just inside the fortifications.   Their walls were made of logs heavily banked with earth and having a door or wider opening on the side away from the enemy.   The roof was also made of heavy logs covered with several feet of earth.

The interior of these structures varied in size with the number that occupied them.   Some were built on the surface of the ground, to keep them drier and more comfortable ;

others were dug down after the manner of a cellar kitchen;
but all of them were at best damp and unwholesome habi-
tations — even where fireplaces were introduced, which they
were in cool weather. For these reasons they were occupied
only when the enemy was engaged in sending over his iron
compliments in the shape of mortar-shells. For all other
hostile missiles the breastworks were ample protection, and
under their walls the men stretched their half-shelters and
passed most of their time in the summer and fall of 1864,

A 13-INCH MORTAR.

when their lot was
cast in that part of
the lines nearest the
enemy in front of
Petersburg.

A mortar is a short,
stout cannon design-
ed to throw shells *into*
fortifications. This is
accomplished by ele-
vating the muzzle a
great deal. But the
higher the elevation
the greater the strain

upon the gun. For this reason it is that they are made so
short and thick. They can be elevated so as to drop a shell
just inside a fort, whereas a cannon-ball would either strike
it on the outside, or pass over it far to the rear.

Mortars were used very little as compared with cannon.
In the siege of Petersburg, I think, they were used more at
night than in the daytime. This was due to the exceeding
watchfulness of the pickets of both armies. At some periods
in the siege each side was in nightly expectation of an attack
from the other, and so the least provocation — an accidental
shot, or a strange and unusual sound after dark — would
draw the fire of the pickets, which would extend from the
point of disturbance all along the line in both directions.

Then the main lines, both infantry and artillery, thinking it might possibly be a night attack, would join in the fire, while the familiar Rebel yell, responded to by the Union cheer, would swell louder as the din and roar increased. But soon the yelling, the cheering, the artillery, the musketry would subside, and the mortar batteries with which each fort was supplied would continue the contest, and the

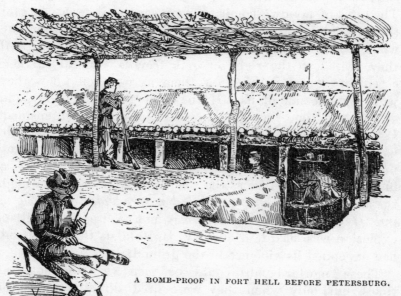

A BOMB-PROOF IN FORT HELL BEFORE PETERSBURG.

sky would become brilliant with the fiery arches of these lofty-soaring and more dignified projectiles. As the mortar-shells described their majestic curves across the heavens every other sound was hushed, and the two armies seemed to stand in mute and mutual admiration of these magnificent messengers of destruction and woe.

Sometimes a single shell could be seen climbing the sky from a Rebel mortar, but ere it had reached its destination as many as half a dozen from Union mortars would appear as if chasing each other through the air, anxious to be foremost in resenting such temerity on the part of the enemy. In this arm of the service, as in the artillery, the Union army was greatly superior to the enemy.

These evening fusillades rarely did any damage. So harmless were they considered that President Lincoln and other officials frequently came down to the trenches to be a witness of them. But, harmless as they usually were to our side, they yet often enlisted our warm personal interest. The guns of my own company were several times a mark for their particular attentions by daylight. At such times we would watch the shells closely as they mounted the sky. If they veered to the right or left from a vertical in their ascent, we cared nothing for them as we then knew they would go one side of us. If they rose perpendicularly, and at the same time increased in size, our interest intensified. If they soon began to descend we lost interest, for that told us they would fall short; but if they continued climbing until much nearer the zenith, and we could hear the creaking whistle of the fuse as the shell slowly revolved through the air, *business of a very pressing nature suddenly called us into the bomb-proofs;* and it was not transacted until an explosion was heard, or a heavy jar told us that the bomb had expended its violence in the ground.

These mortar-bombs could be seen very distinctly at times, but only when they were fired directly toward or from us. They can be seen immediately after they leave the gun if they come against the sky. Coming towards one they appear first as a black speck, increasing in size as stated. Besides mortar-shells I have seen the shot and shell from twelve-pounders in transit, but never from rifled pieces, as their flight is much more rapid.

CHAPTER IV.

LIFE IN TENTS.

"Sir, he made a chimney in my father's house, and the bricks are alive at this day to testify it."   KING HENRY VI.

N the last chapter I described quite fully the principal varieties of shelter that our troops used in the war. In this I wish to detail their daily life in those tents when they settled down in camp. Enter with me into a Sibley tent which is not stockaded. If it is cold weather, we shall find the cone-shaped stove, which I have already mentioned, setting in the centre. These stoves were useless for cooking purposes, and the men were likely to burn their blankets on them in the night, so that many of the troops utilized them by building a small brick or stone oven below, in which they did their cooking, setting the stove on top as a part of the flue. The length of pipe furnished by the government was not sufficient to reach the opening at the top, and the result was that unless the inmates bought more to piece it out, the upper part of such tents was as black and sooty as a chimney flue.

The dozen men occupying a Sibley tent slept with their feet towards the centre. The choice place to occupy was that portion opposite the door, as one was not then in the way of passers in and out, although he was himself more or less of a nuisance to others when he came in. The tent was most crowded at meal times, for, owing to its shape, there can be no standing or sitting erect except about the centre.

But while there was more or less growling **at accidents** by
some, there was much forbearance by others, and, aside from
the vexations arising from the constitutional blundering of
the Jonahs and the Beats, whom I shall describe later, these
little knots were quite family-like and sociable.

The manner in which the time was spent in these tents —
and, for that matter, in all tents — varied with the disposition

SIBLEY TENT. — INSIDE VIEW.

of the inmates. It was not always practicable for men of
kindred tastes to band themselves under the same canvas,
and so just as they differed in their avocations as citizens,
they differed in their social life, and many kinds of pastimes
went on simultaneously. Of course, all wrote letters more
or less, but there were a few men who seemed to spend the
most of their spare time in this occupation. Especially was

this so in the earlier part of a man's war experience. The side or end strip of a hardtack box, held on the knees, constituted the writing-desk on which this operation was performed. It is well remembered that in the early months of the war silver money disappeared, as it commanded a premium, so that, change being scarce, postage stamps were used instead. This was before scrip was issued by the government to take the place of silver; and although the use of stamps as change was not authorized by the national government, yet everybody took them, and the soldiers in particular just about to leave for the war carried

WRITING HOME.

large quantities away with them — not all in the best of condition. This could hardly be expected when they had been through so many hands. They were passed about in little envelopes, containing twenty-five and fifty cents in value.

Many an old soldier can recall his disgust on finding what a mess his stamps were in either from rain, perspiration, or compression, as he attempted, after a hot march, to get one for a letter. If he could split off one from a welded mass of perhaps a hundred or more, he counted himself fortunate. Of course they could be soaked out after a while, but he would need to dry them on a griddle afterwards, they were so sticky. It was later than this that the postmaster-general issued an order allowing soldiers to send letters without pre-payment; but, if I recollect right, it was necessary to write on the outside " Soldier's Letter." I recall in this connection a verse that was said to have appeared on a letter of this kind. It ran as follows : —

> Soldier's letter, nary red,
> Hardtack and no soft bread,
> Postmaster, please put it through,
> I've nary cent, but six months due.

There were a large number of fanciful envelopes got up during the war. I heard of a young man who had a collection of more than seven thousand such, all of different designs. I have several in my possession which I found among the numerous letters written home during war-time. One is bordered by thirty-four red stars — the number of States then in the Union — each star bearing the abbreviated name of a State. At the left end of the envelope hovers an eagle holding a shield and streamer, with this motto, " *Love one another.*" Another one bears a representation of the earth in space, with " United States " marked on it in large letters, and the American eagle above it. Enclosing all is the inscription, " *What God has joined, let no man put asunder.*" A third has a medallion portrait of Washington, under which is, " A Southern Man with Union Principles." A fourth displays a man sitting among money-bags, on horseback, and driving at headlong speed. Underneath is the inscription, " Floyd off for the South. *All that the Seceding States ask is to be let alone.*" Another has a negro standing grinning, a hoe in his hand. He is represented as saying, " Massa can't have dis chile, dat's what's de matter "; and beneath is the title, " *The latest contraband of war.*" Then there are many bearing the portraits of early Union generals. On others Jeff Davis is represented as hanged ; while the national colors appear in a hundred or more ways on a number — all of which, in a degree at least, expressed some phase of the sentiments popular at the North. The Christian Commission also furnished envelopes gratuitously to the armies, bearing their stamp and "Soldier's letter" in one corner.

Besides letter-writing the various games of cards were freely engaged in. Many men played for money. Cribbage and euchre were favorite games. Reading was a pastime quite generally indulged in, and there was no novel so dull, trashy, or sensational as not to find some one so bored with nothing to do that he would wade through it. I, certainly, never read so many such before or since. The mind was hungry for something, and took husks when it could get nothing better. A great deal of good might have been done by the Christian Commission or some other organization planned to furnish the soldiers with good literature, for in that way many might have acquired a taste for the works of the best authors who would not have been likely to acquire it except under just such a condition as they were then in, viz.: a want of some entertaining pastime. There would then have been much less gambling and sleeping away of daylight than there was. Religious tracts were scattered among the soldiers by thousands, it is true, and probably did some good. I heard a Massachusetts soldier say, not long ago, that when his regiment arrived in New York *en route* for the seat of war, the men were presented with "a plate of thin soup and a Testament." This remark to me was very suggestive. It reminded me of the vast amount of mistaken or misguided philanthropy that was expended upon the army by good Christian men and women, who, with the best of motives urging them forward no doubt, often labored under the delusion that the army was composed entirely of men thoroughly bad, and governed their actions accordingly. That there were bad men in the army is too well known to be denied if one cared to deny it; and, while I may forgive, I cannot forget a war governor who granted pardon to several criminals that were serving out sentences in prison, if they would enlist. But the morally bad soldiers were in the minority. The good men should have received some consideration, and the tolerably good even more. Men are only children of an older growth; they like to be appreciated at their worth at least, and the nature of many of the tracts was such that they defeated the object aimed at in their distribution.

Chequers was a popular game among the soldiers, back-gammon less so, and it was only rarely that the statelier and

STOCKADED A TENTS.

less familiar game of chess was to be observed on the board. There were some soldiers who rarely joined in any games. In this class were to be found the illiterate members of a company. Of course they did not read or write, and they rarely played cards. They were usually satisfied to lie on their blankets, and talk with one another, or watch the playing. Yes, they did have one pastime — the proverbial soldier's pastime of smoking. A pipe was their omni-present companion, and seemed to make up to them in sociability for whatsoever they lacked of entertainment in other directions.

Then there were a few men in every organization who engaged in no pastimes and joined in no social intercourse. These men were irreproachable as soldiers, it may have been, doing without grumbling everything that was expected of them in the line of military or fatigue duty; but they seemed shut up within an impenetrable shell, and would lie on their blankets silent while all others joined in the social round; or, perhaps, would get up and go out of the tent as if its lively social atmosphere was uncongenial, and walk up and down the parade or company street alone. Should you address them, they would answer pleasantly, but in monosyllables; and if the conversation was continued, it must be done in the same way. They could not be drawn out. They would cook by themselves, eat by themselves, camp by themselves on the march, — in fact, keep by themselves at all times as much as possible. Guard duty was the one occupation which seemed most suited to their natures, for it provided them with the exclusiveness and comparative solitude that their peculiar mental condition craved. But these men were the exceptions. They were few in number, and the more noticeable on that account. They only served to emphasize the fact that the average soldier was a sociable being.

One branch of business which was carried on quite extensively was the making of pipes and rings as mementos of a camp or battle-field. The pipes were made from the root of the mountain laurel when it could be had, and often ornamented with the badges of the various corps, either in relief or inlaid. The rings were made sometimes of dried horn or hoof, very often of bone, and some were fashioned out of large gutta-percha buttons which were sent from home.

The evenings in camp were less occupied in game-playing, I should say, than the hours off duty in the daytime; partly, perhaps, because the tents were rather dimly lighted, and partly because of a surfeit of such recreations by daylight. But, whatever the cause, I think old soldiers will generally agree in the statement that the evenings were the time of sociability and reminiscence. It was then quite a visiting time among soldiers of the same organization. It was then that men from the same town or neighborhood got together

DRAFTING.

and exchanged home gossip. Each one would produce recent letters giving interesting information about mutual friends or acquaintances, telling that such a girl or old schoolmate was married; that such a man had enlisted in such a regiment; that another was wounded and at home on furlough; that such another had been exempted from the forthcoming draft, because he had lost teeth; that yet another had suddenly gone to Canada on important business — which was a favorite refuge for all those who were afraid of being forced into the service.

And when the draft finally was ordered, such chucklings as these old schoolmates or fellow-townsmen would exchange as they again compared notes; first, to think that they themselves had voluntarily responded to their country's appeal, and, second, to hope that some of the croakers they left at home might be drafted and sent to the front at the point of the bayonet, interchanging sentiments of the following character: " There's A——, he was always urging others to go, and declaring he would himself make one of the next quota." . . . " I want to see him out here with a government suit on." . . . " Yes, and there's B——, who has lots of money. If he's drafted, he'll send a substitute. The government ought not to allow any able-bodied man, even if he has got money, to send a substitute." . . . " Then there's C——, who declared he'd die on his doorstep rather than be forced into the service. I only hope that his courage will be put to the test."— Such are fair samples of the remarks these fellow-soldiers would exchange with one another during an evening visitation.

Then, there were many men not so fortunate as to have enlisted with acquaintances, or to be near them in the army. These were wont to lie on their blankets, and join in the general conversation, or exchange ante-war experiences, and find much of interest in common ; but, whatever the number or variety of the evening diversions, there is not the slightest doubt that home, its inmates, and surroundings were more thought of and talked of then than in all the rest of the twenty-four hours.

In some tents vocal or instrumental music was a feature of the evening. There was probably not a regiment in the service that did not boast at least one violinist, one banjoist, and a bone player in its ranks — not to mention other instruments generally found associated with these — and one or all of them could be heard in operation, either inside or in a company street, most any pleasant evening. However unskilful the artists, they were sure to be the centre

of an interested audience. The usual medley of comic
songs and negro melodies comprised the greater part of
the entertainment, and, if the space admitted, a jig or clog
dance was stepped out on a hard-tack box or other crude
platform. Sometimes a real negro was brought in to
enliven the occasion by patting and dancing " Juba,"
or singing his quaint music. There were always plenty

of them in or near
camp ready to fill
any gap, for they
asked nothing bet-
ter than to be with
" Massa Linkum's

THE CAMP MINSTRELS.

Sojers." But the men played tricks of all descriptions on
them, descending at times to most shameful abuse until some
one interfered. There were a few of the soldiers who were
not satisfied to play a reasonable practical joke, but must
bear down with all that the good-natured Ethiopians could
stand, and, having the fullest confidence in the friendship
of the soldiers, these poor fellows stood much more than
human nature should be called to endure without a murmur.
Of course they were on the lookout a second time.

There was one song which the boys of the old Third Corps used to sing in the fall of 1863, to the tune of " When Johnny comes marching home," which is an amusing jingle of historical facts. I have not heard it sung since that time, but it ran substantially as follows : —

> We are the boys of Potomac's ranks,
> >   Hurrah! Hurrah!
> We are the boys of Potomac's ranks,
> We ran with McDowell, retreated with Banks,
> >   And we'll all drink stone blind —
> >   Johnny, fill up the bowl.
>
> We fought with McClellan, the Rebs, shakes and fever,
> >   Hurrah! Hurrah!
> Then we fought with McClellan, the Rebs, shakes and fever,
> But Mac joined the navy on reaching James River,
> >   And we'll all drink, etc.
>
> Then they gave us John Pope, our patience to tax,
> >   Hurrah! Hurrah!
> Then they gave us John Pope our patience to tax,
> Who said that out West he'd seen naught but Gray *backs.**
>
> He said his headquarters were in the saddle,
> >   Hurrah! Hurrah!
> He said his headquarters were in the saddle,
> But Stonewall Jackson made him skedaddle.
>
> Then Mac was recalled, but after Antietam,
> >   Hurrah! Hurrah!
> Then Mac was recalled, but after Antietam
> Abe gave him a rest, he was too slow to beat 'em.
>
> Oh, Burnside then he tried his luck,
> >   Hurrah! Hurrah!
> Oh, Burnside then he tried his luck,
> But in the mud so fast got stuck.
>
> Then Hooker was taken to fill the bill,
> >   Hurrah! Hurrah!
> Then Hooker was taken to fill the bill,
> But he got a black eye at Chancellorsville.

---

* An allusion to a statement in the address made by Pope, on taking command of the Army of Virginia, " I have come to you from the West where we have always seen the *backs* of our enemies."

> Next came General Meade, a slow old plug,
>   Hurrah! Hurrah!
> Next came General Meade, a slow old plug,
> For he let them away at Gettysburg.

I think that there were other verses, and some of the above may have got distorted with the lapse of time. But they are essentially correct.

Here is the revised prayer of the soldier while on the celebrated " Mud March " of Burnside : —

> " Now I lay me down to sleep
>   In mud that's many fathoms deep;
>   If I'm not here when you awake,
>   Just hunt me up with an oyster rake."

It was rather interesting to walk through a company street of an evening, and listen to a few words of the conversation in progress in the tents — all lighted up, unless some one was saving or had consumed his allowance of candle. It would read much like a chapter from the telephone — noted down by a listener from one end of the line only. Then to peer into the tents, as one went along, just time enough to see what was going on, and excite the curiosity of the inmates as to the identity of the intruder, was a feature of such a walk.

While the description I have been giving applies in some particulars to life in Sibley tents, yet, so far as much of it is concerned, it describes equally well the life of the private soldier in any tent. But *the* tent of the army was the shelter or dog tent; and the life of the private soldier in log huts under these tents requires treatment by itself in many respects. I shall therefore leave it for consideration in another chapter.

CHAPTER V.

LIFE IN LOG HUTS.

Then he built him a hut,
And in it he put
The carcass of Robinson Crusoe.
                                    OLD SONG.

HE camp of a regiment or battery was supposed to be laid out in regular order as definitely prescribed by Army Regulations. These, I may state in a general way, provided that each company of a regiment should pitch its tents in two files, facing on a street which was at right angles with the color-line of the regiment. This color-line was the assigned place for regimental formation. Then, without going into details, I will add that the company officers' tents were pitched in rear of their respective companies, and the field officers, in rear of these. Cavalry had something of the same plan, but with one row of tents to a company, while the artillery had three files of tents, one to each section.

All of this is preliminary to saying that while there was in Army Regulations this prescribed plan for laying out camps, yet the soldiers were more distinguished for their breach than their observance of this plan. Army Regulations were adopted for the guidance of the regular standing army; but this same regular army was now only a very small fraction of the Union forces, the largest portion by far — "the biggest half," to use a Hibernianism — were volunteers, who could not or would not all be bound by Army

73

Regulations.   In the establishing of camps, therefore, there
was much of the go-as-you-please order of procedure.   It
is true that regiments commanded by strict disciplinarians
were likely to and did keep pretty close to regulations.
Many others approximated this standard, but still there
then remained a large residuum who suited themselves, or,
rather, perhaps did not attempt to suit anybody unless
compelled to by superior authority; so that in entering
some camps one might find everything betokening the
supervision of a critical military spirit, while others were
such a hurly-burly lack of plan that a mere pl ugh-jogger
might have been, and perhaps was, the controlling genius
of the camp.   When troops located in the woods, as they
always did for their winter cantonments, this lack of system
in the arrangement was likely to be deviated from on
account of trees.   But to the promised topic of the chapter.

Come with me into one of the log huts.   I have already
spoken of its walls, its roof, its chimney, its fire-place.   The
door we are to enter may be cut in the same end with the
fire-place.   Such was often the case, as there was just about
unoccupied space enough for that purpose.   But where four
or more soldiers located together it was oftener put in the
centre of one side.   In that case the fire-place was in the
opposite side as a rule.   In entering a door at the end one
would usually observe two bunks across the opposite end,
one near the ground (or floor, when there was such a luxury,
which was rarely), and the other well up towards the top of
the walls.   I say, *usually*.   It depended upon circumstances.
When two men only occupied the hut there was one bunk.
Sometimes when four occupied it there was but one, and
that one running lengthwise.   There are other exceptions
which I need not mention; but the average hut contained
two bunks.

The construction of these bunks was varied in character.
Some were built of boards from hardtack boxes; some of
barrel-staves laid crosswise on two poles; some men impro-

vised a spring-bed of slender saplings, and padded them
with a cushion of hay, oak or pine leaves; others obtained
coarse grain sacks from an artillery or cavalry camp, or from
some wagon train, and by making a hammock-like arrangement of them thus devised to make repose a little sweeter.
At the head of each bunk were the knapsacks or bundles
which contained what each soldier boasted of personal

INSIDE VIEW OF A LOG HUT.

effects. These were likely to be under-clothes, socks, thread,
needles, buttons, letters, stationery, photographs, etc. The
number of such articles was fewer among infantry than
among artillerymen, who, on the march, had their effects
carried for them on the gun-carriages and caissons. But in
winter-quarters both accumulated a large assortment of conveniences from home, sent on in the boxes which so glad-
dened the soldier's heart.

The haversacks, and canteens, and the equipments usually hung on pegs inserted in the logs. The muskets had no regular abiding-place. Some stood them in a corner, some hung them on pegs by the slings.

Domestic conveniences were not entirely wanting in the best ordered of these rude establishments. A hardtack box nailed end upwards against the logs with its cover on leather hinges serving as a door, and having suitable shelves inserted, made a very passable dish-closet; another such box put upside down on legs, did duty as a table — small, but large enough for the family, and useful. Over the fire-place one or more shelves were sometimes put to catch the *bric à brac* of the hut; and three- or four-legged stools enough were manufactured for the inmates. But such a hut as this one I have been describing was rather *high-toned*. There were many huts without any of these conveniences.

A soldier's table-furnishings were his tin dipper, tin plate, knife, fork, and spoon. When he had finished his meal, he did not in many cases stand on ceremony, and his dishes were tossed under the bunk to await the next meal. Or, if he condescended to do a little dish-cleaning, it was not of an æsthetic kind. Sometimes he was satisfied to scrape his plate out with his knife, and let it go at that. Another time he would take a wisp of straw or a handful of leaves from his bunk, and wipe it out. When the soft bread was abundant, a piece of that made a convenient and serviceable dish-cloth and towel. Now and then a man would pour a little of his hot coffee into his plate to cleanse it. While here and there one, with neither pride, nor shame, nor squeamishness would take his plate out just as he last used it, to get his ration, offering no other remark to the comment of the cook than this, that he guessed the plate was a fit receptacle for the ration. As to the knife and fork, when they got too black to be tolerated — and they had to be of a very sable hue, it should be said — there was no cleansing process so inexpensive, simple, available, and efficient as running them vigorously into the earth a few times.

For lighting these huts the government furnished candles in limited quantities: at first long ones, which had to be cut for distribution; but later they provided short ones. I have said that they were furnished in limited quantities. I will modify that statement. Sometimes they were abundant, sometimes the contrary; but no one could account for a scarcity. It was customary to charge quartermasters with peculation in such cases, and it is true that many of them were rascals; but I think they

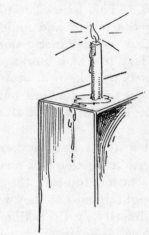

ARMY CANDLESTICKS.

were sometimes saddled with burdens that did not belong to them. Some men used more light than others. Indeed, some men were constitutionally out of everything. They seemed to have conscientious scruples against keeping rations of any description in stock for the limit of time for which they were drawn.

As to candlesticks, the government provided the troops with these by the thousands. They were of steel, and very durable, but were supplied only to the infantry, who had simply to unfix bayonets, stick the points of the same in the ground, and their candlesticks were ready for service. As a fact, the bayonet shank was *the* candlestick of the rank and file who used that implement. It was always available, and just "filled the bill" in other respects. Potatoes were too valuable to come into very general use for this purpose. Quite often the candle was set up on a box in its own drippings.

Whenever candles failed, *slush lamps* were brought into use. These I have seen made by filling a sardine box with cook-house grease, and inserting a piece of rag in one corner for a wick. The whole was then suspended from the ridge-pole of the hut by a wire. This wire came to camp around bales of hay brought to the horses and mules.

The bunks were the most popular institutions in the huts. Soldiering is at times a lazy life, and bunks were then liberally patronized; for, as is well known, ottomans, lounges, and easy-chairs are not a part of a soldier's outfit. For that reason the bunks served as a substitute for all these luxuries in the line of furniture.

I will describe in greater detail how they were used. All soldiers were provided with a woollen and a rubber blanket. When they retired, after tattoo roll-call, they did not strip to the skin and put on night-dresses as they would at home. They were satisfied, ordinarily, with taking off coat and boots, and perhaps the vest. Some, however, stripped to their flannels, and, donning a smoking-cap, would turn in, and pass a very comfortable night. There were a few in each regiment who never took off anything, night or day, unless compelled to; and these turned in at night in full uniform, with all the covering they could muster. I shall speak of this class in another connection.

There was a special advantage in two men bunking together in winter-quarters, for then each got the benefit of the other's blankets — no mean advantage, either, in much of the weather. It was a common plan with the soldiers to make an under-sheet of the rubber blanket, the lining side up, just as when they camped out on the ground, for it excluded the cold air from below in the one case as it kept out dampness in the other. Moreover, it prevented the escape of animal heat.

I think I have said that the half-shelters were not impervious to a hard rain. But I was about to say that whenever such a storm came on it was often necessary for the occupants of the upper bunk to cover that part of the tent above them with their rubber blankets or ponchos; or, if they did not wish to venture out to adjust such a protection, they would pitch them on the inside. When they did not care to bestir themselves enough to do either, they would compromise by spreading a rubber blanket over themselves, and let the water run off on to the tent floor.

At intervals, whose length was governed somewhat by the movements of the army, an inspector of government property put in an appearance to examine into the condition of the belongings of the government in the possession of an organization, and when in his opinion any property was unfit for further service it was declared condemned, and marked with his official brand, I C, meaning, *Inspected Condemned*. This I C became a byword among the men, who made an amusing application of it on many occasions.

In the daytime the men lay in their bunks and slept, or read a great deal, or sat on them and wrote their letters. Unless otherwise forbidden, callers felt at liberty to perch on them; but there was such a wide difference in the habits of cleanliness of the soldiers that some proprietors of huts had, as they thought, sufficient reasons why no one else should occupy their berths but themselves, and so, if the three-legged stools or boxes did not furnish seating capacity enough for company, and the regular boarders, too, the r. b. would take to the bunks with a dispatch which betokened a deeper interest than that required of simple etiquette. This remark naturally leads me to say something of the insect life which seemed to have enlisted with the soldiers for " three years or during the war," and which required and received a large share of attention in quarters, much more, in fact, than during active campaigning. I refer now, especially, to the *Pediculus Vestimenti*, as the scientific men call him, but whose picture when it is well taken, and somewhat magnified, bears this familiar outline. Old soldiers will recognize the *picture* if the *name* is an odd one to them. This was the historic "grayback" which went in and out before Union and Confederate soldiers without ceasing. Like death, it was no respecter of persons. It preyed alike on the just and the unjust. It inserted its bill as confidingly into the body of the major-general as of the lowest private. I once heard the orderly of a company officer relate that he had picked *fifty-two graybacks* from the shirt of his chief at one sitting. Aristocrat or plebeian

PEDICULUS VES-
TIMENTI.

it mattered not. Every soldier seemed foreordained to encounter this pest at close quarters. Eternal vigilance was *not* the price of liberty. That failed the most scrupulously careful veteran in active campaigning. True, the neatest escaped the longest, but sooner or later the time came when it was simply impossible for even them *not to let the left hand know what the right hand was doing.*

The secretiveness which a man suddenly developed when he found himself *inhabited* for the first time was very entertaining. He would cuddle all knowledge of it as closely as the old Forty-Niners did the hiding-place of their bag of gold-dust. Perhaps he would find only *one* of the vermin. This he would secretly murder, keeping all knowledge of it from his tent-mates, while he nourished the hope that it was the Robinson Crusoe of its race cast away on a strange shore with none of its kind at hand to cheer its loneliness. Alas, vain delusion! In ninety-nine cases out of a hundred this solitary *pediculus* would prove to be the advance guard of generations yet to come, which, ere its capture, had been stealthily engaged in sowing its seed; and in a space of time all too brief, after the first discovery the same soldier would appoint himself an investigating committee of one to sit with closed doors, and hie away to the desired seclusion. There he would seat himself taking his garments across his knees in turn, conscientiously doing his (k)nitting work, inspecting every fibre with the scrutiny of a dealer in broadcloths.

The feeling of intense disgust aroused by the first contact with these creepers soon gave way to hardened indifference, as a soldier realized the utter impossibility of keeping free from them, and the privacy with which he carried on his first "skirmishing," as this "search for happiness" came to be called, was soon abandoned, and the warfare carried on more openly. In fact, it was the mark of a cleanly soldier to be seen engaged at it, for there was no disguising the fact that everybody needed to do it.

(K)NITTING WORK.

In cool weather "skirmishing" was carried on in quarters, but in warmer weather the men preferred to go outside of camp for this purpose; and the woods usually found near camps were full of them sprinkled about singly or in social parties of two or three slaying their victims by the thousands. Now and then a man could be seen just from the quartermaster with an entire new suit on his arm, bent on starting afresh. He would hang the suit on a bush, strip off every piece of the old, and set fire to the

same, and then don the new suit of blue. So far well; but
he was a lucky man if he did not share his new clothes with
other hungry *pediculi* inside of a week.

"Skirmishing," however, furnished only slight relief from
the oppressive attentions of the grayback, and furthermore
took much time. Hot water was the sovereign remedy, for

it penetrated every mesh and seam,
and cooked the millions yet un-
born, which Job himself could not
have exterminated by the thumb-
nail process unaided. So tenacious
of life were these creatures that
some veterans affirm they have
seen them still creeping on garments taken out of *boiling water*,
and that only by putting salt in
the water were they sure of accomplishing their destruction.

I think there was but one opinion
among the soldiers in regard to the
graybacks; *viz.*, that the country
was being ruined by *over-produc-
tion*. What the Colorado beetle is
to the potato crop they were to the
soldiers of both armies, and that
man has fame and fortune in his

"TURNING HIM OVER."

hand who, before the next great war in any country, shall
have invented an extirpator which shall do for the *pediculus*
what paris-green does for the potato-bug. From all this it
can readily be seen why no good soldier wanted his bunk to
be regarded as common property.

I may add in passing that no other variety of insect life
caused any material annoyance to the soldier. Now and
then a wood-tick would insert his head, on the sly, into
some part of the human integument; but these were not
common or unclean.

I have already related much that the soldier did to pass away time. I will add to that which I have already given two branches of domestic industry that occupied a considerable time in log huts with a few, and less — very much less indeed — with others. I refer to washing and mending. Some of the men were just as particular about changing their underclothing at least once a week as they would be at home; while others would do so only under the severest pressure. It is disgusting to remember, even at this late day, how little care hundreds of the men bestowed on bodily cleanliness.

BOILING THEM.

The story, quite familiar to old soldiers, about the man who was so negligent in this respect that when he finally took a bath he found a number of shirts and socks

A WOOD-TICK.

which he supposed he had lost, arose from the fact of there being a few men in every organization who were most unaccountably regardless of all rules of health, and of whom such a statement would seem, to those that knew the parties, only slightly exaggerated.

How was this washing done? Well, if the troops were camping near a brook, that simplified the matter somewhat; but even then the clothes *must be boiled*, and for this purpose there was but one resource — *the mess kettles*. There is a familiar anecdote related of Daniel

Webster: that while he was Secretary of State, the French Minister at Washington asked him whether the United States would recognize the new government of France — I think Louis Napoleon's. Assuming a very solemn tone and posture, Webster replied: "Why not? The United States has recognized the Bourbons, the French Republic,

CLEANING UP.

the Directory, the Council of Five Hundred, the First Consul, the Emperor, Louis XVIII., Charles X., Louis Philippe, the " — "Enough! enough!" cried the minister, fully satisfied with the extended array of precedents cited.

So, in regard to using our mess kettles to boil clothes in, it might be asked "Why not?" Were they not used to boil our meat and potatoes in, to make our bean, pea, and meat soups in, to boil our tea and coffee in, to make our apple and peach sauce in? Why not use them as wash-boilers? Well, "gentle reader," while it might at first interfere somewhat with your appetite to have your food cooked in the wash-boiler, you would soon get used to it; and so this complex use of the mess kettles soon ceased to affect the appetite, or to shock the sense of propriety of the average soldier as to the eternal fitness of things, for he was often compelled by circumstances to endure much greater improprieties. It would indeed have been a most admirable arrangement in many respects could each man have been provided with an excellent Magee Range with copper-boiler annex, and set tubs near by; but the line had to be drawn somewhere, and so everything in the line of *impedimenta* was done away with, unless it was absolutely essential to the service. For this reason we could not take along a well equipped laundry, but must make some articles do double or triple service.

It may be asked what kind of a figure the men cut as washerwomen. Well, some of them were awkward and imperfect enough at it; but necessity is a capital teacher, and, in this as in many other directions, men did perforce what they would not have attempted at home. It was not necessary, however, for every man to do his own washing, for in most companies there was at least one man who, for a reasonable recompense, was ready to do such work, and he usually found all he could attend to in the time he had off duty. There was no ironing to be done, for "boiled shirts," as white-bosomed shirts were called, were almost an unknown garment in the army except in hospitals. Flannels were the order of the day. If a man had the courage to face the ridicule of his comrades by wearing a white collar, it was of the paper variety, and white cuffs were unknown in camp.

In the department of mending garments each man did his own work, or left it undone, just as he thought best; but no one hired it done. Every man had a "housewife" or its equivalent, containing the necessary needles, yarn, thimble, etc., furnished him by some mother, sister, sweetheart, or Soldier's Aid Society, and from this came his materials to mend or darn with.

Now, the average soldier was not so susceptible to the charms and allurements of sock-darning as he should have been; for this reason he always put off the direful day until both heels looked boldly and with hardened visage out the back-door, while his ten toes ranged themselves *en échelon* in

front of their quarters. By such delay or neglect good
ventilation and the opportunity of drawing on the socks
from either end were secured. The task of once more
restricting the toes to quarters was not an easy one, and

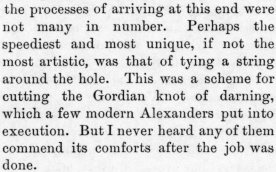

the processes of arriving at this end were
not many in number. Perhaps the
speediest and most unique, if not the
most artistic, was that of tying a string
around the hole. This was a scheme for
cutting the Gordian knot of darning,
which a few modern Alexanders put into
execution. But I never heard any of them
commend its comforts after the job was
done.

Then, there were other men who, having arranged a checker-board of stitches
over the holes, as they had seen their
mothers do, had not the time or patience
to fill in the squares, and the inevitable
consequence was that both heels and toes
would look through the bars only a few
hours before breaking jail again. But

A HOUSEWIFE.

there were a few of the boys
who were kept furnished with
home-made socks, knit, perhaps, by their good old grand-
mas, who seemed to inherit
the patience of the grandams
themselves; for, whenever

there was mending or darning to be done, they would sit by
the hour, and do the work as neatly and conscientiously as
any one could desire. I am not wide of the facts when I
say that the heels of the socks darned by these men remained firm when the rest of the fabric was well spent.

There was little attempt made to repair the socks drawn
from the government supplies, for they were generally of

the shoddiest description, and not worth it. In symmetry, they were like an elbow of stove-pipe; nor did the likeness end here, for, while the stove-pipe is open at both ends, so were the socks within forty-eight hours after putting them on.

Cooking was also an industry which occupied more or less of the time of individuals; but when the army was in settled camp company cooks usually took charge of the rations. Sometimes, where companies preferred it, the rations were served out to them in the raw state; but there was no invariable rule in this matter. I think the soldiers, as a whole, preferred to receive their coffee and sugar raw, for rough experience in campaigning soon made each man an expert in the preparation of this beverage. Moreover, he could make a more palatable cup for himself than the cooks made for him; for too often their handiwork betrayed some of the other uses of the mess kettles to which I have made reference. Then, again, some men liked their coffee strong, others weak; some liked it sweet, others wished little or no sweetening; and this latter class could and did save their sugar for other purposes. I shall give other particulars about this when I take up the subject of Army Rations.

It occurs to me to mention in this connection a circumstance which may seem somewhat strange to many, and that is that some parts of the army burned hundreds of cords of green pine-wood while lying in winter-quarters. It was very often their only resource for heat and warmth. People at the North would as soon think of attempting to burn water as green pine. But the explanation of the paradox is this — the pine of southern latitudes has more pitch in it than that of northern latitudes. Then, the heart-wood of all pines is comparatively dry. It seemed especially so South. The heart-wood was used to kindle with, and the pitchy sap-wood placed on top, and by the time the heart-wood had burned the sappy portion had also seasoned enough to blaze and make a good fire. These pines had

the advantage over the hard woods of being more easily
worked up — an advantage which the average soldier
appreciated.

Nearly every organization had its barber in established
camp. True, many men never used the razor in the ser-

THE CAMP BARBER.

vice, but allowed a shrubby,
straggling growth of hair
and beard to grow, as if
to conceal them from the enemy in time of battle. Many
more carried their own kit of tools and shaved themselves, frequently shedding innocent blood in the service
of their country while undergoing the operation. But
there was yet a large number left who, whether from
lack of skill in the use or care of the razor, or from want

of inclination, preferred to patronize the camp barber. This personage plied his vocation inside the tent in cold or stormy weather, but at other times took his post in rear of the tent, where he had improvised a chair for the comfort (?) of his victims. This chair was a product of home manufacture. Its framework was four stakes driven into the ground, two long ones for the back legs, and two shorter ones for the front. On this foundation a superstructure was raised which made a passable barber's chair. But not all the professors who presided at these chairs were finished tonsors, and the back of a soldier's head whose hair had been "shingled" by one of them was likely to show each course of the shingles with painful distinctness. The razors, too, were of the most barbarous sort, like the "trust razor" of the old song with which the Irishman got his "Love o' God Shave."

One other occupation of a few men in every camp, which I must not overlook, was that of studying the tactics. Some were doing it, perhaps, under the instructions of superior officers; some because of an ambition to deserve promotion. Some were looking to passing a competitive examination with a view of obtaining a furlough; and so these men, from various motives, were "booking" themselves. But the great mass of the rank and file had too much to do with the practice of war to take much interest in working out its theory, and freely gave themselves up, when off duty, to every available variety of physical or mental recreation, doing their uttermost to pass away the time rapidly; and even those troops having nearly *three years* to serve would exclaim, with a cheerfulness more feigned than real, as each day dragged to its close, "*It's only two years and a but.*"

CHAPTER VI.

JONAHS AND BEATS.

"Good people, I'll sing you a ditty,
   So bear with me all ye who can;
I make an appeal to your pity,
   For I'm a most unlucky man.
'Twas under an unlucky planet
   That I a poor mortal was born;
My existence since first I began it
   Has been very sad and forlorn.
Then do not make sport of my troubles,
   But pity me all ye who can,
For I'm an uncomfortable, horrible, terrible, inconsolable, unlucky man."
                                                    OLD SONG.

 N a former chapter I made the statement that Sibley tents furnished quarters capacious enough for twelve men. That statement is to be taken with some qualifications. If those men were all lying down asleep, there did not seem much of a crowd. But if one man of the twelve happened to be on guard at night, and, furthermore, was on what we used to know as the Third Relief guard, which in my company was posted at 12, midnight, and came off post at 2 A.M., when all were soundly sleeping, and, moreover, if this man chanced to quarter in that part of the tent opposite the entrance, and if, in seeking his blanket and board in the darkness, it was his luck to step on the stockinged foot of a recumbent form having a large voice, a large temper, but a small though forcible selection of English defiled, straightway that selection was hurled at the head of the offending even though well-meaning guard. And if,

90

under the excitement of his mishap, the luckless guard makes a spring thinking to clear all other intervening slumberers and score a home run, but alights instead amidships of the comrade who sleeps next him, expelling from him a groan that by all known comparisons should have been his last, the poor guard has only involved himself the more inextricably in trouble; for as soon as his latest victim recovers consciousness sufficiently to know that it was *not* a twelve-pound cannon ball that has doubled him up, and that stretcher bearers are *not* needed to take him to the rear, he strikes up in the same strain and pitch and force as that of the first victim, and together they make the midnight air vocal with choice invective against their representative of the Third Relief. By this time the rest of the tent's crew have been waked up, cross enough, too, at being thus rudely disturbed, and they all come in heavily on the chorus. As the wordy assault continues the inmates of adjoining tents who have also been aroused take a hand in it, and "Shut up!" — "Sergeant of the Guard!" — "Go lie down!" — "Shoot him on the spot!" — "Put him in the guard-house!" are a few of the many impromptu orders issued within and without the tent in question.

At last the tempest in a teapot expends itself and by the time that the sergeant of the guard has arrived to seek out the cause of the tumult and enforce the instructions of the officer of the day by putting the offenders against the rules and discipline of camp under arrest, for talking and disturbance after Taps, all are quiet, for no one would make a complaint against the culprits. Their temporary excitement has cooled, and the discreet sergeant is even in doubt as to which tent contains the offenders.

Now, accidents will happen to the most careful and the best of men, but the soldier whom I have been describing could be found in every squad in camp — that is, a man of his kind. Such men were called "Jonahs" on account of their ill luck. Perhaps this particular Jonah after getting

his tin plate level full of hot pea-soup was sure, on entering
the tent, to spill a part of it down somebody's back. The
higher he could hold it the better it seemed to please him as
he made his way to his accustomed place in the tent, and in
bringing it down into a latitude where he proposed to eat it

THE JONAH SPILLING PEA-SOUP.

he usually managed to dispose of much of the remainder,
either on his own or somebody else's blankets. When pea-
soup failed him for a diversion, he was a dead shot on kicking over his neighbor's pot of coffee, which the owner had
put down for a moment while he adjusted his lap-table to
receive his supper. The profuseness of the Jonah's apolo-
gies — and they always were profuse, and undoubtedly
sincere — was utterly inadequate as a balm for the wounds
he made. Anybody else in the tent might have kicked the
coffee to the remotest bounds of camp with malice afore-
thought, and it would not have produced a tithe of the
aggravation which it did to have this constitutional blunderer do it by accident. It may be that he wished to borrow

your ink. Of course you could not refuse him. It may have been made by you with some ink powders sent from home — perhaps the last you had and which you should want yourself that very day. It mattered not. He took it with complacency and fair promises, put it on a box by his side and tipped the box over five minutes afterward by the watch.

Cooking was the forte of this Jonah. He could be found most any time of day — or night, if he was a guardsman — around the camp-fire with his little mess of something in his tomato can or tin dipper, which he would throw an air of

THE CAMP-FIRE BEFORE THE JONAH APPEARS.

mystery around every now and then by drawing a small package from the depths of his pocket or haversack and scattering some of its contents into the brew. But there was a time in the history of his culinary pursuits when he rose to a supreme height as a blunderer. It was when he appeared at the camp-fire which, by the way, he never kindled himself, ready to occupy the choice places with his dishes; and after the two rails, between which fires were usually built, had been well burdened by the coffee-pots of his comrades it presented an opportunity which his evil genius was likely to take advantage of; for then he was suddenly seized with a thought of something else that he had forgotten to borrow. Turning in his haste to go to the

tent for this purpose he was sure to stumble over the end of
one or both of the rails, when the downfall of the coffee-
pots and the quenching of the fire followed as a matter of
course. At just this point in his career it would be to the
credit of his associates to drop the curtain on the picture;
but the sequel must be told. The average soldier was not
an especially devout man, and while in times of imminent
danger he had serious thoughts, yet at other times his many
trials, his privations, and the rigors of a necessary discipline

THE CAMP-FIRE AFTER THE JONAH APPEARS.

all conduced to make him a highly explosive creature on
demand. Moreover, coffee and sugar were staple articles
with the soldier, and the least waste of them was not to
be tolerated under ordinary circumstances; but to have a
whole line of coffee-pots with their precious contents upset
by the Jonah of the tent in his recklessness was the last
ounce of pressure removed from the safety valve of his
tent-mates' wrath; and such a discharge of hard names and
oaths, "long, loud, and deep," as many of these sufferers
would deliver themselves of, if it could have been utilized
against the enemy, might have demolished a regiment. And
the others who did not give vent to their passions by blows

or the use of strong language seemed to sympathize very keenly with those who did. Two chaplains apiece to some of the men would have been none too many to hold them in check.

I remember one man who seemed always to have hard luck in spite of himself. He was a good soldier and meant well,

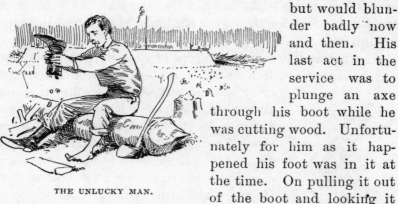

THE UNLUCKY MAN.

but would blunder badly now and then. His last act in the service was to plunge an axe through his boot while he was cutting wood. Unfortunately for him as it happened his foot was in it at the time. On pulling it out of the boot and looking it over he found that several of his toes had "got left"; so he took up his boot, turned it upside down, and shook out a shower of toes as complacently as if that was what he enlisted for. This casualty closed his career in active service.

There were divers other directions in which the Jonah distinguished himself; but I must leave him for the present to direct attention to the other class of men of whom I wish to say something. These were the *beats* of the service — a name given them by their comrades-in-arms. There were all grades of beats. The original idea of beat was that of a lazy man or a shirk, who would by hook or by crook get rid of all military or fatigue duty that he could; but the term grew to have a broader significance.

One of the milder forms of beat was the man who sat over the fire in the tent piling on wood all the time, and roasting out the rest of the tent's crew, who seemed to have no rights that this fireman felt bound to respect. He

was always cold. He wore overcoat, dress-coat, blouse, and
flannels the full government allowance all at once, but never
complained of being too warm. He never took off any of
these garments night or day unless compelled to on inspection. He was most at home on fatigue duty, for he seemed
fatigued from the start and moved like real estate. A
sprinkling of this class seemed necessary to the success of
the Union arms, for they were certainly to be found in every
organization.

Another and more positive type of beat were the men who
never had any water in their canteens. Even when the

GOING AFTER WATER.

army was in settled camp, water was not
always to be had without going some
distance for it ; but these men were never
known to go after any. They always
managed to hang their canteen on some
one else who was bound for the spring.
If, when the army was on the move, a
rush was made during a temporary halt,
for a spring or stream some distance away,
these men never rushed. They were satisfied to lie down and drink a supply which
they took their chances of begging, from
some recruit, perhaps, who did not know
their propensities. If it happened to any man to be so
straitened in his cooking operations as to be under the
necessity of borrowing from one of these, he was sure of
being called upon to requite the favor fully as many times
as his temper would endure it.

Then, as to rations, their hardtack never held out, and
they were ever on the alert to borrow. It mattered not
how great the scarcity, real or anticipated, they could not
provide for a contingency, and their neighbors in the same
squad were mean and avaricious — so the beats said — if
they would not give of their husbanded resources to these
profligate, improvident comrades. But this class did not

stop at borrowing hardtack. They were not all of them particular, and when hardtack could not be spared they would get along with coffee or sugar or salt pork ; or, if they could borrow a *dollar*, " just for a day or two," they would then repay it surely, because several letters from their friends at home, each one containing money, were already overdue. People in civil life think they know all about the imperfections of the United States postal service, and tell of their letters and papers lost, miscarried, or in some way delayed, with much pedantry ; but they have yet to learn the A B C of its imperfections, and no one that I know of is so competent to teach them as certain of the Union soldiers. I could have produced men in 1862-5, yes — I can now — who lost more letters in one year, three out of every four of which contained considerable sums of money, than any postmaster-general yet appointed is willing to admit have been lost since the establishment of a mail service. This, remember, the loss of one man ; and when it is multiplied by the number of men just like him that were to be found, not in one army alone but in all the armies of the Union, a special reason is obvious why the government should be liberal in its dealings with the old soldier.

In this connection I am reminded of another interesting feature of army experience, which is of some historical value. It was this : whenever the troops were paid off a very large majority of them wished to send the most of their pay home to their families or their friends for safe keeping. Of course there was some risk attending the sending of it in the mails. To obviate this risk an " allotment " plan was adopted by means of which when the troops were visited by the pay-master, on signing a roll prepared for that purpose, so much of their pay as they wished was allotted or assigned by the soldiers to whomsoever they designated at the North. To illustrate : John Smith had four months' pay due him at the rate of $13 a month. He decided to allot $10 per month of this to his wife at Plymouth, Mass.; so the paymaster pays him $12, and the remaining $40 is paid to his wife by check in Plymouth, without any further action on the part of John.

This plan was a great convenience to both the soldiers and their families. In this division of his income the calculation of the soldier was to save out enough for himself to pay all incidental expenses of camp life, such as washing, tobacco, newspapers, pies and biscuits, bought of "Aunty," and cheese and cakes of the sutler. But in spite of his nice calculations the rule was that the larger part of the money allotted home was returned, by request of the sender, in small amounts of a dollar or the fraction of a dollar. I have previously stated that at that time silver had gone out of use, it being only to be had by paying the premium on it, just as on gold, and so to take its place the government issued what was generally known as scrip, being paper currency of the denominations of fifty, twenty-five, ten, five, and, later, fifteen and three-cent pieces, some of which are still in circulation. They were a great convenience to the soldiers and their friends. But to resume: —

If the statements made by these beats as to the amount of money they had sent for and were expecting were to be believed they must not only have sent for their full allotment, but have drawn liberally on their home credit or the charity of their friends besides. In truth, however, the genuine beat never intended to return borrowed money. It is currently believed by outsiders that the soldiers who stood shoulder to shoulder battling for the Union, sharing the same exposures, the same shelter, the same mess would ever afterwards be likely to stand steadfastly by one another. The organization of the Grand Army of the Republic seems to strengthen such an opinion, yet human nature remains pretty much the same in all situations. If a man was a shirk or a thief or a beat or a coward or a worthless scoundrel generally in the army, it was because he had been educated to it before he enlisted. The leopard cannot change his spots nor the Ethiopian his skin. It will therefore create no great surprise when I remark that a large amount of money borrowed by one soldier of another has never been repaid; and such is the lack of honesty and manliness on the part of these men that they can meet the old comrades of whom in those trying war days they borrowed one, two, five, or ten dollars, and in some cases more, without so much as a blush or betraying in any manner the slightest recognition of their long standing obligation. Some are so worthless and brazen-faced even as to ask the same victims for more at this late day.

One favorite dodge of the beat was to have the corporal arouse him twice or three times before he would finally get out of his bunk; and then he would prepare to go out at a snail's pace. Once on his beat, his next dodge was to manœuvre so as to have the corporal of his relief do the most of his duty for him; for hardly would he have been posted before the corporal must be summoned, the beat having been seized with a desire to go to the company sink. That is good for half an hour out of the corporal at least. At last the dodger reappears moving at a slow pace, and wearing the appearance of a man suffering for his discharge from service. He retails his woes to the corporal, as he resumes his equipments, in a most doleful strain. But the corporal is in no mood to listen after his long wait, and hastily directs his steps towards the guard-tent.

He is not allowed to remain there long, however, ere a summons reaches him from the same post, to which he responds with excusable ill-humor and mutterings at the duplicity of the guardsman in question. This time the patient has happened to think of some medicine at his tent which will be of benefit to him. Of course the corporal is anxious enough to have him healed, and so he again assumes the duties of the post for the shirk, who does not reappear until his last hour of duty is well on its second quarter, feigning in excuse that he could not find his own panacea and so was obliged to go elsewhere. Thus in one way and another, by using the kind offices of his messmates together with those of the corporal, he would manage to get out of at least two-thirds of his guard duty.

After the battle of Fredericksburg a soldier belonging to a gallant regiment in Burnside's corps, whose courage had

THE RHEUMATIC DODGER.

evidently been put to a sore test in the above engagement, resorted to the *rheumatic dodge* to secure his discharge. He responded daily to sick call, pitifully warped out of shape, was prescribed for, but all to no avail. One leg was drawn up so that, apparently, he could not use it, and groans indicative of excruciating agony escaped him at studied intervals and on suitable occasions. So his case went on for six weeks, till at last the surgeon recommended his discharge. It was approved at regimental, brigade, and division headquarters, and had reached corps headquarters when the corps was ordered to Kentucky. At Covington the party having the supposed invalid in charge gained access in some manner to a barrel of whiskey. Not being a temperance man, the dodger was thrown off his guard by this *spirit*ual bonanza, and, taking his turn at the straw, for which entry had been made into the barrel, he was soon as sprightly on both legs as ever. In this condition his colonel found him. Of course his discharge was recalled from corps headquarters, and the way of this transgressor was made hard for months afterwards.

There was another field in which the beat played an interesting part. I use *played* with a double significance, for he never *worked* if he could avoid it. It was when a detail of men was made to do some line of *fatigue duty*, by which is meant all the labors of the service distinct from strict military duty, such as the "policing" or clearing up of camp, procuring wood and water for the company, digging and fitting up of sinks (the water-closets of the army), and, in addition to these duties, in cavalry and artillery, procuring grain and forage for the horses. It was a sad fate to befall

WATER FOR THE COOK-HOUSE.

a good duty soldier to get on to a detail to procure wood where every second or third man was a shirk or beat; for while they must needs bear the appearance of doing something, they were really in the way of those who could work and were willing to. Many of these shirkers would waste a great deal of time and breath maligning the government or their officers for requiring them to do such work, indignantly declaring that "they enlisted to fight and not to chop wood or dig sinks." But it was noticeable that when the fight came on, if any of these heroes got into it, they then appeared just as willing to bind themselves by contract to cut all the wood in Virginia, if they could only be let go just that once. These were the men who were "invincible in peace and invisible in war," as the late Senator Hill, of Georgia, once said. I may add here that, coming as the soldiers did from all avocations and stations in life, these details for fatigue often brought together men few of whom had any practical knowledge of the work in hand ; so that aside from the shirks, who *could* work but *would* not, there were others who *would* but *could* not, at least intelligently. Still, the army was a great educator in many ways to men who cared to learn, and some of the most ignorant became by force of circumstances quite expert, in time, in channels hitherto untraversed by them.

But there was one detail upon which our shirks, beats, and men unskilled in manual labor, such as the handling of the spade and pickaxe, appeared in all the glory of their artful dodging and ignorance. If a man did not take hold of the work lively, whether because he preferred to shirk it or because he did not understand it, the worse for him. The detail in question was one made to administer the last rites to a batch of deceased horses. It happened to the artillery and cavalry to lose a large number of these animals in winter, which, owing to the freezing of the ground, could not be buried until the disappearance of the frost in spring ; but by that time, through the action of rain and sun and the frequent depredations of dogs, buzzards, and crows, the remains were not always in the most inviting condition for the administrations of the sexton. Then, again, during the summer season, when the army made a halt for rest and recruiting, another sacrifice of glanders-infected and generally used-up horses was made to the god of war. But as they were not always promptly committed to mother earth, either from a desire to show a decent respect for the memory of the deceased or for some other reason best known to the red-tape of military rule, the odors that were wafted from them on the breezes were wont to become far more "spicy" than agreeable, so that a speedy interment was generally ordered by the military Board of Health.

As soon as the nature of the business for which such a detail was ordered became generally known, the fun began, for a lively protest was wont to go up from the men against being selected to participate in the impending equine obsequies. Perhaps the first objection heard from a victim who has drawn a prize in the business is that "he was on guard the day before, and is not yet physically competent for such a detail." The sergeant is charged with unfairness, and with having pets that he gives all the "soft jobs" to, etc. But the warrior of the triple *chevron* is inexorable, and his muttering, much injured subordinate finally reports to the corporal in charge of the detail in front of the camp, betraying in his every word and movement a heart-felt desire for his term of service or this cruel war to be over.

Another one whom his sergeant has booked for the enterprise has got wind of what is to be done, so that when found he is tucked up in his bunk. He stoutly insists that he is an invalid, and is only waiting for the next sounding of "Sick call" to respond to it. But his attack is so sudden, and his language and lungs so strong for a sick man, that he finds it difficult to establish his claim. He calls on his tent-mates to swear that he is telling the truth, but finds them strangely devout and totally ignorant of his ailments, for they are chuckling internally at their own good fortune in not being selected, which, if he proves his case, one of them *may* be; so, unless his plea is a pitiful and deserving one, they keep mum.

A third victim does not claim to have been selected out of turn, but nevertheless alleges that "the deal is unfair, because he was on the last detail but one made for this horse-burying business, and he does not think that he ought to be the chief mourner for his detachment, for a paltry thirteen dollars a month. Besides, there may be others who would *like* to go on this detail." But as he is unable to name or find the man or men having this highly refined ambition he finally goes off grumbling and joins the squad.

A fourth victim is the constitutionally high-tempered and profane man. He finds no fault with the justice of the sergeant in assigning to him a participation in the ceremonies of the hour; but he had got comfortably seated to write a letter when the summons came, and, pausing only long enough

THE HIGH-TEMPERED MAN.

to inquire the nature of the detail, he pitches his half-written letter and materials in one direction, his lap-board in another, gets up, kicks over the box or stool on which he was sitting, pulls on his cap with a vehement jerk, and then opens his battery. He directs none of his unmilitary English at the sergeant — that would hardly do; but he lays his furious lash upon the poor innocent back of the government, though just what *branch* of it is responsible he does not pause between his oaths long enough to state. He pursues it with the most terrible of curses uphill, and then with like violent language follows it down. He blank blanks the whole blank blank war, and hopes that the South may win. He wishes that all the blank horses were in blank, and adds by way of self-reproach that it serves any one, who is such a blank blank fool as to enlist, *right* to have this blank, filthy, disgusting work to do. And he leaves the stockade shutting the door behind him "with a wooden damn," as Holmes says, and goes off to report, making the air blue with his cursing. Let me say for this man, before leaving him, that he is not so hardened and bad at heart as he makes himself appear; and in the shock of battle he will be found standing manfully at his post minus his temper and profanity.

There is one more man whom I will describe here, representing another class than either mentioned, whose unlucky star has fated *him* to take a part in these obsequies; but he is not a shirk nor a beat. He is the *paper-collar young man*, just from the recruiting station, with enamelled long-legged boots and custom-made clothes, who yet looks with some measure of disdain on government clothing, and yet eats in a most gingerly way of the stern, unpoetical government rations. He is an only son, and was a dry-goods clerk in the city at home, where no reasonable want went ungratified; and now, when he is summoned forth to join the burial party, he responds at once. True, his heart and stomach both revolt at the work ahead, but he wants to be — not an angel — but a veteran among veterans, and his pride prevents his entering any re-

THE PAPER-COLLAR YOUNG MAN.

monstrance in the presence of the older soldiers. As he clutches the spade pointed out to him with one hand he shoves the other vacantly to the bottom of his breeches pocket, his mouth drawn down codfish-like at the corners. He attempts to appear indifferent as he approaches the detail, and as they congratulate him on his good-fortune a sickly smile plays over his countenance; but it is Mark Tapley feigning a jollity which he does not feel and which soon subsides into a pale melancholy. His fellow-victims feel their ill-luck made more endurable by seeing him also drafted for the loathsome task; but their glow of satisfaction is only superficial and speedily wanes as the officer of the day, who is to superintend the job, appears and orders them forward.

And now the fitness of the selection becomes apparent as the squad moves off, for a more genuine body of mourners, to the eye, could not have been chosen. Their faces, with, it may be, a hardened or indifferent exception, wear the most solemn of expressions, and their step is as slow as if they were following a muffled drum beating the requiem of a deceased comrade.

Having arrived at the place of sepulture, the first business is to dig a grave close to each body, so that it may be easily rolled in. But if there has been no fun before, it commences when the rolling in begins. The Hardened Exception, who

THE MOURNERS.

has occupied much of his time while digging in sketching distasteful pictures for the Profane Man to swear at, now makes a change of base, and calls upon the Paper-Collar Young Man to "take hold and help roll in," which the young man reluctantly and gingerly does; but when the noxious gases begin to make their presence manifest, and the Hardened Wretch hands him an axe to break the legs that would otherwise protrude from the grave, it is the last straw to an already overburdened sentimental soul; his emotions overpower him, and, turning his back on the deceased, he utters something which sounds like "hurrah! without the h," as Mark Twain puts it, repeating it with increasing emphasis. But he is not to express his enthusiasm on this question alone a great while. There are more sympathizers in the party than he had anticipated, and not recruits either; and in less time than I have taken to relate it more than half the detail, gallantly led off by the officer of the day, are standing about, leaning over at various angles like the tomb-stones in an old cemetery, disposing of their hardtack and coffee, and looking as if ready to throw up even the con-

"HURRAH WITHOUT THE H."

tract. The profane man is among them, and just as often as he can catch his breath long enough he blank blanks the government and then dives again. The rest of the detail stand not far away holding on to their sides and roaring with laughter. But I must drop the curtain on this picture. It has been said that one touch of nature makes the whole world kin. Be that as it may, certain it is that the officer, the good duty soldier, the recruit, and the beat, after an occasion of this kind, had a common bond of sympathy, which went far towards levelling military distinctions be-tween them.

CHAPTER VII.

ARMY RATIONS: WHAT THEY WERE. — HOW THEY WERE DISTRIBUTED. — HOW THEY WERE COOKED.

"Here's a pretty mess!"
THE MIKADO.

"God bless the pudding,
God bless the meat,
God bless us all;
Sit down and eat."
A HARVARD STUDENT'S BLESSING, 1796.

ALL in for your rations, Company A!" My theme is Army Rations. And while what I have to say on this subject may be applicable to all of the armies of the Union in large measure, yet, as they did not fare just alike, I will say, once for all, that my descriptions of army life pertain, when not otherwise specified, especially to that life as it was lived in the Army of the Potomac.

In beginning, I wish to say that a false impression has obtained more or less currency both with regard to the quantity and quality of the food furnished the soldiers. I have been asked a great many times whether I always got enough to eat in the army, and have surprised inquirers by answering in the affirmative. Now, some old soldier may say who sees my reply, "Well, you were lucky. *I* didn't." But I should at once ask him to tell me for how long a time his regiment was ever without food of some kind. Of course,

I am not now referring to our prisoners of war, who starved
by the thousands. And I should be very much surprised
if he should say more than twenty-four or thirty hours, at
the outside. I would grant that he himself might, perhaps,
have been so situated as to be deprived of food a longer
time, possibly when he was on an exposed picket post, or
serving as rear-guard to the army, or doing something which
separated him temporarily from his company; but his case

THE "COOPER SHOP," PHILADELPHIA.

would be the exception and not the rule. Sometimes, when
active operations were in progress, the army was compelled
to wait a few hours for its trains to come up, but no general
hardship to the men ever ensued on this account. Such a
contingency was usually known some time in advance, and
the men would husband their last issue of rations, or, perhaps, if the country admitted, would make additions to their
bill of fare in the shape of poultry or pork; — usually it was
the latter, for the Southerners do not pen up their swine as
do the Northerners, but let them go wandering about, getting their living much of the time as best they can. This

led some one to say jocosely, with no disrespect intended to the people however, "that every other person one meets on a Southern street is a hog." They certainly were quite abundant, and are to-day, in some form, the chief meat food of that section. But on the point of scarcity of rations I believe my statement will be generally agreed to by old soldiers.

Now, as to the *quality* the case is not quite so clear, but still the picture has been often overdrawn. There were, it is true, large quantities of stale beef or salt horse — as the men were wont to call it — served out, and also rusty, unwholesome pork; and I presume the word "hardtack" suggests to the uninitiated a piece of petrified bread honeycombed with bugs and maggots, so much has this article of army diet been reviled by soldier and civilian. Indeed, it is a rare occurrence for a soldier to allude to it, even at this late day, without some reference to its hardness, the date of its manufacture, or its propensity for travel. But in spite of these unwholesome rations, whose existence no one calls in question, of which I have seen — I must not say *eaten* — large quantities, I think the government did well, under the circumstances, to furnish the soldiers with so good a quality of food as they averaged to receive. Unwholesome rations were not the rule, they were the exception, and it was not the fault of the government that these were furnished, but very often the intent of the rascally, thieving contractors who supplied them, for which they received the price of good rations; or, perhaps, of the inspectors, who were in league with the contractors, and who therefore did not always do their duty. No language can be too strong to express the contempt every patriotic man, woman, and child must feel for such small-souled creatures, many of whom are to-day rolling in the riches acquired in this way and other ways equally disreputable and dishonorable.

I will now give a complete list of the rations served out to the rank and file, as I remember them. They were salt pork, fresh beef, salt beef, rarely ham or bacon, hard bread, soft bread, potatoes, an occasional onion, flour, beans, split pease, rice, dried apples, dried peaches, desiccated vegetables, coffee, tea, sugar, molasses, vinegar, candles, soap, pepper, and salt.

It is scarcely necessary to state that these were not all served out at one time. There was but one kind of meat served at once, and this, to use a Hibernianism, was usually

THE UNION VOLUNTEER SALOON, PHILADELPHIA.

pork. When it was hard bread, it wasn't *soft* bread or flour, and when it was pease or beans it wasn't rice.

Here is just what a single ration comprised, that is, what a soldier was entitled to have in one day. He should have had twelve ounces of pork or bacon, *or* one pound four ounces of salt or fresh beef; one pound six ounces of soft bread or flour, *or* one pound of hard bread, *or* one pound four ounces of corn meal. With every hundred such rations there should have been distributed one peck of beans or pease; ten pounds of rice or hominy; ten pounds of green coffee, *or* eight pounds of roasted and ground, *or* one pound eight ounces of tea; fifteen pounds of sugar; one pound four ounces of candles; four pounds of soap; two quarts of salt; four quarts of vinegar; four ounces of pepper; a half bushel of potatoes when practicable, and one quart of molasses. Desiccated potatoes or desiccated compressed vegetables might be substituted for the beans, pease, rice, hominy, or fresh potatoes. Vegetables, the dried fruits, pickles, and pickled cabbage were occasionally issued to prevent scurvy, but in small quantities.

But the ration thus indicated was a camp ration. Here is the *marching* ration: one pound of hard bread; three-fourths of a pound of salt pork, or one and one-fourth pounds of fresh meat; sugar, coffee, and salt. The beans, rice, soap, candles, etc., were not issued to the soldier when on the march, as he could not carry them; but, singularly enough, as it seems to me, unless the troops went into camp before the end of the month, where a regular depot of supplies might be established from which the other parts of the rations could be issued, they were *forfeited*, and *reverted to the government* — an injustice to the rank and file, who, through no fault of their own, were thus cut off from a part of their allowance at the time when they were giving most liberally of their strength and perhaps of their very heart's blood. It was possible for company commanders and *for no one else* to receive the equivalent of these missing parts of the ration *in cash* from the brigade commissary, with the expectation that when thus received it would be distributed among the rank and file to whom it belonged. Many officers did not care to trouble themselves with it, but many others did, and — forgot to pay it out afterwards. I have yet to learn of the first company whose members ever received any revenue from such a source, although the name of *Company Fund* is a familiar one to every veteran.

The commissioned officers fared better in camp than the enlisted men. Instead of drawing rations after the manner of the latter, they had a certain cash allowance, according to rank, with which to purchase supplies from the Brigade Commissary, an official whose province was to keep stores cn sale for their convenience. The monthly allowance of officers in infantry, including servants, was as follows: Colonel, six rations worth $56, and two servants; Lieuten-

A BRIGADE COMMISSARY AT
BRANDY STATION, VA.

ant-Colonel, five rations worth $45, and two servants; Major, four rations worth $36, and two servants; Captain, four rations worth $36, and one servant; First and Second Lieutenants, jointly, the same as Captains. In addition to the above, the field officers had an allowance of horses and forage proportioned to their rank.

I will speak of the rations more in detail, beginning with the hard bread, or, to use the name by which it was known in the Army of the Potomac, *Hardtack.* What was hardtack? It was a plain flour-and-water biscuit. Two which I have in my possession as mementos measure three and one-eighth by two and seven-eighths inches, and are nearly half an inch thick. Although these biscuits were furnished to organizations by weight, they were dealt out to the men by number, nine constituting a ration in some regiments, and ten in others; but there were usually enough for those who wanted more, as some men would not draw them. While hardtack was nutritious, yet a hungry man could eat his ten in a short time and still be hungry. When they were poor and fit objects for the soldiers' wrath, it was due to one of three conditions: First, they may have been so hard that they could not be bitten; it then required a very strong blow of the fist to break them. The cause of this hardness it would be difficult for one not an expert to determine.

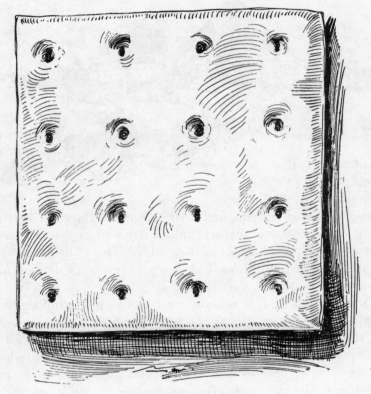

A HARD-TACK — FULL SIZE.

This variety certainly well deserved their name. They could not be *soaked* soft, but after a time took on the elasticity of gutta-percha.

The second condition was when they were mouldy or wet, as sometimes happened, and should not have been given to the soldiers. I think this condition was often due to their having been boxed up too soon after baking. It certainly was frequently due to exposure to the weather. It was no uncommon sight to see thousands of boxes of hard bread piled up at some railway station or other place used as a base of supplies, where they were only imperfectly sheltered from the weather, and too often not sheltered at all. The failure of inspectors to do their full duty was one reason that so many of this sort reached the rank and file of the service.

The third condition was when from storage they had become infested with maggots and weevils. These weevils were, in my experience, more abundant than the maggots. They were a little, slim, brown bug an eighth of an inch in length, and were great *bores* on a small scale, having the ability to completely riddle the hardtack. I believe they never interfered with the hardest variety.

When the bread was mouldy or moist, it was thrown away and made good at the next drawing, so that the men were not the losers ; but in the case of its being infested with the weevils, they had to stand it as a rule ; for the biscuits had to be pretty thoroughly alive, and well covered with the webs which these creatures left, to insure condemnation. An exception occurs to me. Two cargoes of hard bread came to City Point, and on being examined by an inspector were found to be infested with weevils. This fact was brought to Grant's attention, who would not allow it landed, greatly to the discomfiture of the contractor, who had been attempting to bulldoze the inspector to pass it.

The quartermasters did not always take as active an interest in righting such matters as they should have done ; and when the men growled at them, of course they were virtuously indignant and prompt to shift the responsibility to the next higher power, and so it passed on until the real culprit could not be found.

But hardtack was not so bad an article of food, even when traversed by insects, as may be supposed. Eaten in the dark, no one could tell the difference between it and hardtack that

was untenanted.   It was no uncommon occurrence for a man
to find the surface of his pot of coffee swimming with weevils,
after breaking up hardtack in it, which had come out of the
fragments only to drown; but they were easily skimmed off,
and left no distinctive flavor behind.   If a soldier cared to do

A BOX OF HARDTACK.

so, he could expel the weevils by heating the bread at the fire.
The maggots did not budge in that way.   The most of the
hard bread was made in Baltimore, and put up in boxes of
sixty pounds gross, fifty pounds net; and it is said that some
of the storehouses in which it was kept would swarm with
weevils in an incredibly short time after the first box was
infested with them, so rapidly did these pests multiply.

Having gone so far, I know the reader will be interested
to learn of the styles in which this particular article was
served up by the soldiers.   I say *styles* because I think there
must have been at least a score of ways adopted to make
this simple *flour tile* more edible.   Of course, many of them
were eaten just as they were received — hardtack *plain;*
then I have already spoken of their being crumbed in coffee,
giving the " hardtack and coffee."   Probably more were eaten
in this way than in any other, for they thus frequently furnished the soldier his breakfast and supper.   But there were

other and more appetizing ways of preparing them. Many of the soldiers, partly through a slight taste for the business but more from force of circumstances, became in their way and opinion experts in the art of cooking the greatest variety of dishes with the smallest amount of capital.

Some of these crumbed them in soups for want of other thickening. For this purpose they served very well. Some

FRYING HARDTACK.

crumbed them in cold water, then fried the crumbs in the juice and fat of meat. A dish akin to this one, which was said to "make the hair curl," and certainly was indigestible enough to satisfy the cravings of the most ambitious dyspeptic, was prepared by soaking hardtack in cold water, then frying them brown in pork fat, salting to taste. Another name for this dish was "skillygalee." Some liked them toasted, either to crumb in coffee, or, if a sutler was at hand whom they could patronize, to butter. The toasting generally took place from the end of a split stick, and if perchance they dropped out of it into the camp-fire, and were not recovered quickly enough to prevent them from getting pretty well charred, they were not thrown away on that account, being then thought good for weak bowels.

Then they worked into milk-toast made of condensed milk at seventy-five cents a can; but only a recruit with a big bounty, or an old vet the child of wealthy parents, or a re-enlisted man did much in that way. A few who succeeded by hook or by crook in saving up a portion of their sugar ration spread *it* upon hardtack. The hodge-podge of lobscouse also contained this edible among its divers other ingredients; and so in various ways the ingenuity of the men was taxed to make this plainest and commonest yet most serviceable of army food to do duty in every conceivable combination. There is an old song, entitled "Hard Times," which some one in the army parodied. I do not remember the verses, but the men used to sing the following chorus: —

> 'Tis the song of the soldier, weary, hungry, and faint,
>   Hardtack, hardtack, come again no more;
> Many days have I chewed you and uttered no complaint,
>   O Greenbacks, come again once more!

It is possible at least that this song, sung by the soldiers of the Army of the Potomac, was an outgrowth of the following circumstance and song. I am quite sure, however, that the verses were different.

For some weeks before the battle of Wilson's Creek, Mo., where the lamented Lyon fell, the First Iowa Regiment had been supplied with a very poor quality of hard bread (they were not then (1861) called hard*tack*). During this period of hardship to the regiment, so the story goes, one of its members was inspired to produce the following touching lamentation: —

> Let us close our game of poker,
> Take our tin cups in our hand,
> While we gather round the cook's tent door,
> Where dry mummies of hard crackers
> Are given to each man;
> O hard crackers, come again no more!

CHORUS: —'Tis the song and sigh of the hungry,
　"Hard crackers, hard crackers, come again no more!
　Many days have you lingered upon our stomachs sore,
　O hard crackers, come again no more!"

There's a hungry, thirsty soldier
Who wears his life away,
With torn clothes, whose better days are o'er ;
He is sighing now for whiskey,
And, with throat as dry as hay,
Sings, "Hard crackers, come again no more!"—CHORUS.

'Tis the song that is uttered
In camp by night and day,
'Tis the wail that is mingled with each snore,
'Tis the sighing of the soul
For spring chickens far away,
"O hard crackers, come again no more!" — CHORUS.

When General Lyon heard the men singing these stanzas in their tents, he is said to have been moved by them to the extent of ordering the cook to serve up corn-meal mush, for a change, when the song received the following alteration : —

But to groans and to murmurs
There has come a sudden hush,
Our frail forms are fainting at the door ;
We are starving now on horse-feed
That the cooks call mush,
O hard crackers, come again once more!

CHORUS: — It is the dying wail of the starving,
　Hard crackers, hard crackers, come again once more ;
　You were old and very wormy, but we pass your failings
　　o'er.
　O hard crackers, come again once more!

The name hardtack seems not to have been in general use among the men in the Western armies.

But I now pass to consider the other bread ration — the *loaf* or *soft bread*. Early in the war the ration of flour was served out to the men uncooked ; but as the eighteen ounces allowed by the government more than met the needs of the troops, who at that time obtained much of their living from outside sources (to be spoken of hereafter), it was allowed, as they innocently supposed, to be sold for the benefit of the Company Fund, already referred to. Some organizations

drew, on requisition, ovens, semi-cylindrical in form, which were properly set in stone, and in these regimental cooks or bakers baked bread for the regiment. But all of this was in the tentative period of the war. As rapidly as the needs

AN ARMY OVEN.

of the troops pressed home to the government, they were met with such despatch and efficiency as circumstances would permit. For a time, in 1861, the vaults under the broad terrace on the western front of the Capitol were converted into bakeries, where sixteen thousand loaves of bread were baked daily. The chimneys from the ovens pierced the terrace where now the freestone pavement joins the grassy slope, and for months smoke poured out of these in dense black volumes. The greater part of the loaves supplied to the Army of the Potomac up to the summer of 1864 were baked in Washington, Alexandria, and at Fort Monroe, Virginia. The ovens at the latter place had a capacity of thirty thousand loaves a day. But even with all these sources worked to their uttermost, brigade commissaries were obliged to set up ovens near their respective depots, to eke out enough bread to fill orders. These were erected on the sheltered side of a hill or woods, then enclosed in a stockade, and the whole covered with old canvas.

When the army reached the vicinity of Petersburg, the supply of fresh loaves became a matter of greater difficulty and delay, which Grant immediately obviated by ordering ovens built at City Point. A large number of citizen bakers were employed to run them night and day, and as a result *one hundred and twenty-three thousand fresh loaves* were furnished the army daily from this single source; and so closely did the delivery of these follow upon the manipulations of the bakers that the soldiers quite frequently

SOFT BREAD.

Commissary Department, Headquarters Army of the Potomac, Captain J. R. Coxe.

received them while yet warm from the oven. Soft bread was always a very welcome change from hard bread; yet, on the other hand, I think the soldiers tired sooner of the former than of the latter. Men who had followed the sea preferred the hard bread. Jeffersonville, in Southern Indiana, was the headquarters from which bread was largely supplied to the Western armies.

I began my description of the rations with the bread as being the most important one to the soldier. Some old veterans may be disposed to question the judgment which gives it this rank, and claim that *coffee*, of which I shall speak next, should take first place in importance; in reply to which I will simply say that he is wrong, because coffee, being a stimulant, serves only a temporary purpose, while the bread has nearly or quite all the elements of nutrition necessary to build up the wasted tissues of the body, thus conferring a permanent benefit. Whatever words of condemnation or criticism may have been bestowed on other government rations, there was but one opinion of the coffee which was served out, and that was of unqualified approval.

The rations may have been small, the commissary or quartermaster may have given us a short allowance, but what we

APPORTIONING COFFEE AND SUGAR.

got was good. And what a perfect Godsend it seemed to us at times! How often, after being completely jaded by a night march, — and this is an experience common to thousands, — have I had a wash, if there was water to be had, made and drunk my pint or so of coffee, and felt as fresh and invigorated as if just arisen from a night's sound sleep! At such times it could seem to have had no substitute.

It would have interested a civilian to observe the manner in which this ration was served out when the army was in active service. It was usually brought to camp in an oatsack, a regimental quartermaster receiving and apportioning his among the ten companies, and the quartermaster-sergeant of a battery apportioning his to the four or six detachments. Then the orderly-sergeant of a company or the sergeant of a detachment must devote himself to dividing it. One method of accomplishing this purpose was to spread a rubber blanket on the ground, — more than one if the company was large, — and upon it were put as many piles of the coffee as there were men to receive rations; and the care taken to make the piles of the same size to the eye, to keep the men from growling, would remind one of a country physician making his powders, taking a little from one pile and adding to another. The sugar which always accompanied the coffee was spooned out at the same time on another blanket. When both were ready, they were given out, each man taking a pile, or, in some companies, to prevent any charge of unfairness or injustice, the sergeant would turn his back on the rations, and take out his roll of the company. Then, by request, some one else would point to a pile and ask, "Who shall have this?" and the sergeant, without turning, would call a name from his list of the company or detachment, and the person thus called would appropriate the pile specified. This process would be continued until the last pile was disposed of. There were other plans for distributing the rations; but I have described this one because of its being quite common.

The manner in which each man disposed of his coffee and sugar ration after receiving it is worth noting. Every soldier of a month's experience in campaigning was provided with some sort of bag into which he spooned his coffee; but the *kind* of bag he used indicated pretty accurately, in a general way, the length of time he had been in the service. For example, a raw recruit just arrived would take it up in a paper, and stow it away in that well known receptacle for all eatables, the soldier's haversack, only to find it a part of a general mixture of hardtack, salt pork, pepper, salt, knife, fork, spoon, sugar, and coffee by the time the next halt was made.

A recruit of longer standing, who had been through this experience and had begun to feel his wisdom-teeth coming, would take his up in a bag made of a scrap of rubber blanket or a *poncho ;* but after a few days carrying the rubber would peel off or the paint of the *poncho* would rub off from contact with the greasy pork or boiled meat ration which was its travelling companion, and make a black, dirty mess, besides leaving the coffee-bag unfit for further use. Now and then some young soldier, a little starchier than his fellows, would bring out an oil-silk bag lined with cloth, which his mother had made and sent him ; but even oil-silk couldn't stand everything, certainly not the peculiar inside furnishings of the average soldier's haversack, so it too was not long in yielding. But your plain, straightforward old veteran, who had shed all his poetry and romance, if he had ever possessed any, who had roughed it up and down " Old Virginny," man and boy, for many months, and who had tried all plans under all circumstances, took out an oblong plain cloth bag, which looked as immaculate as the every-day shirt of a coal-heaver, and into it scooped without ceremony both his sugar and coffee, and stirred them thoroughly together.

There was method in this plan. He had learned from a hard experience that his sugar was a better investment thus disposed of than in any other way ; for on several occasions he had eaten it with his hardtack a little at a time, had got it wet and melted in a rain, or, what happened fully as often, had sweetened his coffee to his taste when the sugar was kept separate, and in consequence had several messes of coffee to drink *without* sweetening, which was *not* to his taste. There was now and then a man who could keep the two separate, sometimes in different ends of the same bag, and serve them up proportionally. The reader already knows that milk was a luxury in the army. It was a new experience for all soldiers to drink coffee without milk. But they soon learned to make a virtue of a necessity, and

I doubt whether one man in ten, before the war closed, would have used the lactic fluid in his coffee from choice. Condensed milk of two brands, the *Lewis* and *Borden*, was to be had at the sutler's when sutlers were handy, and occasionally milk was brought in from the udders of stray cows, the men milking them into their canteens; but this was early in the war. Later, war-swept Virginia afforded very few of these brutes, for they were regarded by the armies as more valuable for beef than for milking purposes, and only those survived that were kept apart from lines of march.

THE MILK RATION.

In many instances they were the chief reliance of Southern families, whose able-bodied men were in the Rebel army, serving both as a source of nourishment and as beasts of burden.

When the army was in settled camp, company cooks generally prepared the rations. These cooks were men selected from the company, who had a taste or an ambition for the business. If there were none such, turns were taken at it; but this did not often happen, as the office excused men from all other duty.

When company cooks prepared the food, the soldiers, at

the bugle signal, formed single file at the cook-house door, in winter, or the cook's open fire, in summer, where, with a long-handled dipper, he filled each man's tin with coffee from the mess kettles, and dispensed to him such other food as was to be given out at that meal.

For various reasons, some of which I have previously hinted at, the coffee made by these cooks was of a very in-

THE COMPANY COOK.

ferior quality and unpleasant to taste at times. It was not to be compared in excellence with what the men made for themselves. I think that when the soldiers were first thrown upon their own resources to prepare their food, they almost invariably cooked their coffee in the tin dipper with which all were provided, holding from a pint to a quart, perhaps. But it was an unfortunate dish for the purpose, forever tipping over and spilling the coffee into the fire, either because the coals burned away beneath, or because the Jonah upset it. Then if the fire was new and blazing, it sometimes needed a hand that could stand heat like a steam safe to get it when it was wanted, with the chance in favor of more than half of the coffee boiling out before it was rescued, all of which was conducive to ill-temper, so that

GOING INTO CAMP.

such utensils would soon disappear, and a recruit would afterwards be seen with his pint or quart preserve can, its improvised wire bail held on the end of a stick, boiling his coffee at the camp-fire, happy in the security of his ration from Jonahs and other casualties. His can soon became as black as the blackest, inside and out. This was the typical coffee-boiler of the private soldier, and had the advantage of being easily replaced when lost, as canned goods were in very general use by commissioned officers and hospitals. Besides this, each man was generally supplied with a small tin cup as a drinking-cup for his coffee and water.

The coffee ration was most heartily appreciated by the soldier. When tired and foot-sore, he would drop out of the marching column, build his little camp-fire, cook his mess of coffee, take a nap behind the nearest shelter, and, when he woke, hurry on to overtake his company. Such men were sometimes called stragglers; but it could, obviously, have no offensive meaning when applied to them. Tea was served so rarely that it does not merit any particular description. In the latter part of the war, it was rarely seen outside of hospitals.

One of the most interesting scenes presented in army life took place at night when the army was on the point of bivouacking. As soon as this fact became known along the column, each man would seize a rail from the nearest fence, and with this additional arm on the shoulder would enter the proposed camping-ground. In no more time than it takes to tell the story, the little camp-fires, rapidly increasing to hundreds in number, would shoot up along the hills and plains, and as if by magic acres of territory would be luminous with them. Soon they would be surrounded by the soldiers, who made it an almost invariable rule to cook their coffee first, after which a large number, tired out with the toils of the day, would make their supper of hardtack and coffee, and roll up in their blankets for the night. If a march was ordered at midnight, unless a surprise was intended, it must be preceded by a pot of coffee ; if a halt was ordered in mid-forenoon or afternoon, the same dish was inevitable, with hardtack accompaniment usually. It was coffee *at* meals and *between* meals ; and men going on guard or coming off guard drank it at all hours of the night, and to-day the old soldiers who can stand it are the hardest coffee-drinkers in the community, through the schooling which they received in the service.

At a certain period in the war, speculators bought up all the coffee there was in the market, with a view of compelling the government to pay them a very high price for the army supply ; but on learning of their action the agents of the United States in England were ordered to purchase several ship-loads then anchored in the English Channel. The purchase was effected, and the coffee " corner " tumbled in ruins.

At one time, when the government had advertised for bids to furnish the armies with a certain amount of coffee, one Sawyer, a member of a prominent New York importing firm, met the government official having the matter in charge — I think it was General Joseph H. Eaton — on the street, and anxiously asked him if it was too late to enter another bid, saying that he had been figuring the matter over carefully, and found that he could make a bid so much a pound lower than his first proposal. General Eaton replied that while the bids had all been opened, yet they had not been made public, and the successful bidder had not been notified, so that no injustice could accrue to any one on that account ; he would therefore assume the responsibility of taking his new bid. Having done so, the General informed Sawyer that he was the lowest bidder, and that the government would take not only the amount asked for but all his firm had at its disposal at the same rate. But when General Eaton informed him that his *first* bid was also lower than any other offered, Sawyer's rage at Eaton and disgust at his own undue ambition to bid a second time can be imagined.

The result was the saving of many thousands of dollars to the government.

I have stated that by Army Regulations the soldiers were entitled to either three-quarters of a pound of pork or bacon or one and one-fourth pounds of fresh or salt beef. I have also stated, in substance, that when the army was settled down for a probable long stop company cooks did the cooking. But there was no uniformity about it, each company commander regulating the matter for his own command. It is safe to remark, however, that in the early history of each regiment the rations were cooked for its members by persons especially selected for the duty, unless the regiment was sent at once into active service, in which case each man was immediately confronted with the problem of preparing his own food. In making this statement I ignore the experience which troops had before leaving their native State, for in the different State rendezvous I think the practice was general for cooks to prepare the rations; but their culinary skill — or lack of it — was little appreciated by men within easy reach of home, friends, and cooky shops, who displayed as yet no undue anxiety to anticipate the unromantic living provided for Uncle Sam's patriot defenders.

Having injected so much, by way of further explanation I come now to speak of the manner in which, first, the fresh-meat ration was cooked. If it fell into the hands of the company cooks, it was fated to be boiled twenty-four times out of twenty-five. There are rare occasions on record when these cooks attempted to broil *steak* enough for a whole company, and they would have succeeded tolerably if this particular tid-bit could be found all the way through a steer, from the tip of his nose to the end of his tail, but as it is only local and limited the amount of nice or even tolerable steak that fell to the lot of one company in its allowance was not very large. For this reason among others the cooks did not always receive the credit which they deserved for their efforts to change the diet or extend the variety on the bill of fare.   Then, on occasions equally rare, when the beef ration drawn was of such a nature as to admit of it, *roast beef* was prepared in ovens such as I have already described, and served " rare," " middling," or " well done."   More frequently, yet not very often, a *soup* was made for a change, but it was usually boiled meat; and when this accumulated, the men sometimes fried it in pork fat for a change.

When the meat ration was served out raw to the men, to prepare after their own taste, although the variety of its cooking may not perhaps have been much greater, yet it gave more general satisfaction.   The growls most commonly heard were that the cooks kept the largest or choicest portions for themselves, or else that they sent them to the company officers, who were not entitled to them.   Sometimes there was foundation for these complaints.

In drawing his ration of meat from the commissary the quartermaster had to be governed by his last selection.   If it was a hindquarter then, he must take a forequarter the next time, so that it will at once be seen, by those who know anything about beef, that it would not always cut up and distribute with the same acceptance.   One man would get a good solid piece, the next a flabby one.   When a ration of the latter description fell into the hands of a passionate man, such as I have described in another connection, he would instantly hurl it across the camp, and break out with such remarks as " something not being fit for hogs," " always his blank luck," etc.   There was likely to be a little something gained by this dramatic exhibition, for the distributor would give the actor a good piece for several times afterwards, to restrain his temper.

The kind of piece drawn naturally determined its disposition in the soldier's *cuisine*.   If it was a stringy, flabby piece, straightway it was doomed to a dish of lobscouse, made with such other materials as were at hand.   If onions were not in the larder, and they seldom were, the little garlic found in some places growing wild furnished a very acceptable substitute. If the meat was pretty solid, even though it *had* done duty when in active service well down on the shank or shin, it was quite likely to be served as beefsteak, and prepared for the palate in one of two ways ; — either fried in pork fat, if pork was to be had, otherwise tallow fat, or impaled on a ramrod or forked stick ; it was then salted and peppered and broiled in the flames ; or it may have been thrown on the coals. This broiling was, I think, the favorite

BROILING STEAKS.

style with the oldest campaigners. It certainly was more healthful and palatable cooked in this wise, and was the most convenient in active service, for any of the men could prepare it thus at short notice.

The meat generally came to us quivering from the butcher's knife, and was often eaten in less than two hours after slaughtering. To fry it necessitated the taking along of a frying-pan with which not many of the men cared to burden themselves. These fry-pans — Marbleheadmen called them *Creepers* — were yet comparatively light, being made of thin wrought iron. They were of different sizes, and were kept on sale by sutlers. It was a common sight on the march to see them borne aloft on a musket, to which they were lashed, or tucked beneath the straps of a knapsack. But there was another fry-pan which distanced these both in respect of lightness and space. The soldier called in his own ingenuity to aid him here as in so many other directions, and consequently the men could be seen by scores frying the food in their tin plate, held in the jaws of a split stick, or fully as often an old canteen was unsoldered and its concave sides mustered into active duty as fry-pans. The fresh-meat ration was thoroughly appreciated by the men, even though they rarely if ever got the full allowance stipulated in Army Regulations, for it was a relief from the salt pork, salt beef, or boiled fresh meat ration of settled camp. I remember one occasion in the Mine Run Campaign, during the last days of November, 1863, when the army was put on short beef rations, that the men cut and scraped off the little rain-bleached shreds of meat that remained on the head of a steer which lay near our line of battle at Robertson's Tavern. The animal had been slaughtered the day before, and what was left of its skeleton had been soaking in the rain, but not one ounce of muscular tissue could have been gleaned from the bones when our men left it.

The liver, heart, and tongue were perquisites of the butcher. For the liver, the usual price asked was a dollar, and for the heart or tongue fifty cents.

The "salt horse" or salt beef, of fragrant memory, was rarely furnished to the army except when in settled camp, as it would obviously have been a poor dish to serve on the march, when water was often so scarce. But even in camp the men quite generally rejected it. Without doubt, it was the vilest ration distributed to the soldiers.

It was thoroughly penetrated with saltpetre, was often yellow-green with rust from having lain out of brine, and, when boiled, was four times out of five if not nine times out of ten a stench in the nostrils, which no delicate palate cared to encounter at shorter range. It sometimes happened that the men would extract a good deal of amusement out of this ration, when an extremely unsavory lot was served out, by arranging a funeral, making the appointments as complete as possible, with bearers, a bier improvised of boards or a hardtack box, on which was the beef accompanied by scraps of old harness to indicate the original of the remains, and then, attended by solemn music and a mournful procession, it would be carried to the company sink and dumped, after a solemn mummery of words had been spoken, and a volley fired over its unhallowed grave.

So salt was this ration that it was impossible to freshen it too much, and it was not an unusual occurrence for troops encamped by a running brook to tie a piece of this beef to the end of a cord, and throw it into the brook at night, to remain freshening until the following morning as a necessary preparative to cooking.

Salt pork was the principal meat ration — the main stay as it were. Company cooks boiled it. There was little else they could do with it, but it was an extremely useful ration to the men when served out raw. They almost never boiled it, but, as I have already shown, much of it was used for frying purposes. On the march it was broiled and eaten with hard bread, while much of it was eaten raw, sandwiched between hardtack. Of course it was used with stewed as well as baked beans, and was an ingredient of soups and lobscouse. Many of us have since learned to call it an indigestible ration, but we ignored the existence of such a thing as a stomach in the army, and then regarded pork as an indispensable one. Much of it was musty and rancid, like the salt horse, and much more was flabby, stringy, "sow-belly," as the men called it, which, at this remove in distance, does not seem appetizing, however it may have seemed at the time. The government had a pork-packing factory of its own in Chicago, from which tons of this ration were furnished.

Once in a while a ration of ham or bacon was dealt out to the soldiers, but of such quality that I do not retain very grateful remembrances of it. It was usually black, rusty, and strong, and decidedly unpopular. Once only do I recall a lot of smoked shoulders as being supplied to my company, which were very good. They were never duplicated. For that reason, I presume, they stand out prominently in memory.

The bean ration was an important factor in the sustenance of the army, and no edible, I think, was so thoroughly appreciated. Company cooks stewed them with pork, and

MESS KETTLES AND A MESS PAN.

when the pork was good and the stew or soup was well done and not burned, — a rare combination of circumstances, — they were quite palatable in this way. Sometimes ovens were built of stones, on the top of the ground, and the beans were baked in these, in mess pans or kettles. But I think the most popular method was to bake them in the ground. This was the almost invariable course pursued by the soldiers when the beans were distributed for them to cook. It was done in the following way: A hole was dug large enough to set a mess pan or kettle in, and have ample space around it besides. Mess kettles, let me explain here, are cylinders in shape, and made of heavy sheet iron. They are from thirteen to fifteen inches high, and vary in diameter from seven inches to a foot. A mess pan stands about six inches high, and is a foot in diameter at the top. I think one will hold nearly six quarts. To resume; — in the bottom of the hole dug a flat stone was put, if it could be obtained, then a fire was built in the hole and kept burning some hours, the beans being prepared for baking meanwhile. When all was ready, the coals were shovelled out, the kettle of beans and pork set in, with a board over the top, while the coals were shovelled back around the kettle; some poles or boards were then laid across the hole, a piece of sacking or other material spread over the poles to exclude dirt, and a mound of earth piled above all; the net result of which, when the hole was opened the next morning, was the most enjoyable dish that fell to the lot of the common soldier. Baked beans at the homestead seemed at a discount in comparison. As it was hardly practicable to bake a single ration of beans in this way, or, indeed, in any way, a tent's crew either saved their allowance until enough accumulated for a good baking, or a half-dozen men would form a joint stock company, and cook in a mess kettle; and when the treasure was unearthed in early morning not a stockholder would be absent from the roll-call, but all were promptly on hand with plate or coffee dipper to receive their dividends.

Here is a post-bellum jingle sung to the music of "The Sweet By and By," in which some old veteran conveys the affection he still feels for this edible of precious memory: —

THE ARMY BEAN.

There's a spot that the soldiers all love,
    The mess-tent's the place that we mean,
And the dish we best like to see there
    Is the old-fashioned, white Army Bean.

CHORUS. — 'Tis the bean that we mean,
        And we'll eat as we ne'er ate before;
    The Army Bean, nice and clean,
        We'll stick to our beans evermore.

Now the bean, in its primitive state,
    Is a plant we have all often met;
And when cooked in the old army style
    It has charms we can never forget. — CHORUS.

> The German is fond of sauer-kraut,
>   The potato is loved by the Mick,
> But the soldiers have long since found out
>   That through life to our beans we should stick.— CHORUS.

Boiled potatoes were furnished us occasionally in settled camp. On the march we varied the programme by frying them. Onions, in my own company at least, were a great rarity, but highly appreciated when they did appear, even in homœopathic quantities. They were pretty sure to appear on the army table, fried.

Split peas were also drawn by the quartermaster now and then, and stewed with pork by the cooks for supper, making pea-soup, or "Peas on a Trencher"; but if my memory serves me right, they were a dish in no great favor, even when they were not burned in cooking, which was usually their fate.

The dried-apple ration was supplied by the government, "to swell the ranks of the army," as some one wittily said. There seemed but one practicable way in which this could be prepared, and that was to stew it; thus cooked it made a sauce for hardtack. Sometimes dried peaches were furnished instead, but of such a poor quality that the apples, with the fifty per cent of skins and hulls which they contained, were considered far preferable.

At remote intervals the cooks gave for supper a dish of boiled rice (burned, of course), a sergeant spooning out a scanty allowance of molasses to bear it company.

Occasionally, a ration of what was known as desiccated vegetables was dealt out. This consisted of a small piece per man, an ounce in weight and two or three inches cube of a sheet or block of vegetables, which had been prepared, and apparently *kiln-dried*, as sanitary *fodder* for the soldiers. In composition it looked not unlike the large cheeses of beef-scraps that are seen in the markets. When put in soak for a time, so perfectly had it been dried and so firmly pressed that it swelled to an amazing extent, attaining to several times its dried proportions. In this pulpy state a favorable opportunity was afforded to analyze its composition. It seemed to show, and I think really *did* show, layers of cabbage leaves and turnip tops stratified with layers of sliced carrots, turnips, parsnips, a bare suggestion of onions,— they were too valuable to waste in this compound,— and some other among known vegetable quantities, with a large residuum of insoluble and in*solvable* material which appeared to play the part of warp to the fabric, but which defied the powers of the analyst to give it a name. An inspector found in one lot which he examined *powdered glass* thickly sprinkled through it, apparently the work of a Confederate emissary ; but if not it showed how little care was exercised in preparing this diet for the soldier. In brief, this coarse vegetable compound could with much more propriety have been put before Southern swine than Northern soldiers. "*Desecrated* vegetables" was the more appropriate name which the men quite generally applied to this preparation of husks.

I believe it was the Thirty-Second Massachusetts Infantry which once had a special ration of three hundred boxes of *strawberries* dealt out to it. But if there was another organization in the army anywhere which had such a delicious experience, I have yet to hear of it.

I presume that no discussion of army rations would be considered complete that did not at least make mention of the whiskey ration so called. This was not a ration, properly speaking. The government supplied it to the army only on rare occasions, and then by order of the medical department. I think it was never served out to my company more than three or four times, and then during a cold rainstorm or after unusually hard service. Captain N. D. Preston of the Tenth New York Cavalry, in describing Sheridan's raid to Richmond in the spring of 1864, recently, speaks of being instructed by his brigade commander to make a light issue of whiskey to the men of the brigade, and adds, " the first and only regular issue of whiskey I ever made or know of being made to an enlisted man." But although he belonged to the arm of the service called " the eyes and ears of the army," and was no doubt a gallant soldier, he is not well posted ; for men who belonged to other organizations in the Army of the Potomac assure me that it was served out to them much more frequently than I have related as coming under my observation. I think there can be no doubt on this point.

The size of the whiskey allowance was declared, by those whose experience had made them competent judges, as trifling and insignificant, sometimes not more than a `table-spoonful; but the quantity differed greatly in different organizations. The opinion was very prevalent, and undoubtedly correct, that the liquor was quite liberally sampled by the various headquarters, or the agents through whom it was transmitted to the rank and file. While there was considerable whiskey drank by the men " unofficially," that is, which was obtained otherwise than on the order of the medical department, yet, man for man, the private soldiers were as abstemious as the officers. The officers who did not drink more or less were too scarce in the service. They had only to send to the commissary to obtain as much as they pleased, *whenever* they pleased, by paying for it; but the private soldier could only obtain it of this official on an order signed by a commissioned officer, — usually the captain of his company. In fact, there was nothing but his sense of honor, his self-respect, or his fear of exposure and punishment, to restrain a captain, a colonel, or a general, of whatever command, from being intoxicated at a moment when he should have been in the full possession of his senses leading his command on to battle; and I regret to relate that these motives, strong as they are to impel to right and restrain from wrong-doing, were no barrier to many an officer whose appetite in a crisis thus imperilled the cause and disgraced himself. Doesn't it seem strange that the enforcement of the rules of war was so lax as to allow the lives of a hundred, a thousand, or perhaps fifty or a hundred thousand sober men to be jeopardized, as they so often were, by holding them rigidly obedient to the orders of a man whose head at a critical moment might be crazed with commissary whiskey? Hundreds if not thousands of lives were sacrificed by such leadership. I may state here that drunkenness was equally as common with the Rebels as with the Federals.

The devices resorted to by those members of the rank and file who hungered and thirsted for *commissary* to obtain it, are numerous and entertaining enough to occupy a chapter; but these I must leave for some one of broader experience and observation. I could name two or three men in my own company whose experience qualified them to fill the bill completely. They were always on the scent for something to drink. Such men were to be found in all organizations.

It has always struck me that the government should have increased the size of the marching ration. If the soldier on the march had received one and one-half pounds of hard bread and one and one-half pounds of fresh beef daily with his sugar, coffee, and salt, it would have been no more than marching men require to keep up the requisite strength and resist disease.

By such an increase the men would have been compensated for the parts of rations not issued to them, or the increase might have been an equivalent for these parts, and the temptation to dishonesty or neglect on the part of company commanders thus removed. But, more than this, the men would not then have eaten up many days' rations in advance. It mattered not that the troops, at a certain date, were provided with three, four, or any number of days rations; if these rations were exhausted before the limit for which they were distributed was even half reached, more must be immediately issued. As a consequence, in every summer campaign *the troops had drawn ten or fifteen days marching rations ahead of time*, proving, season after season, the inadequacy of this ration. This deficiency of active service had to be made up by shortening the rations issued in camp when the men could live on a contracted diet without detriment to the service. But *they* knew nothing of this shortage at the time, — I mean now the rank and file, — else what a universal growl would have rolled through the camps of each army corps while the commissary was "catching up." "Where ignorance is bliss," etc.

CHAPTER VIII.

OFFENCES AND PUNISHMENTS.

They braced my aunt against a board,
  To make her straight and tall;
They laced her up, they starved her down,
  To make her light and small;
They pinched her feet, they singed her hair,
  They screwed it up with pins; —
Oh, never mortal suffered more
  In penance for her sins.

HOLMES.

BALL AND CHAIN.

NO popular history of the war has yet treated in detail of the various indiscretions of which soldiers were guilty, nor of the punishments which followed breaches of discipline. Perhaps such a record is wanting because there are many men yet alive who cannot think with equanimity of punishments to which they were at some period of their service subjected. Indeed, within a few months I have seen veterans who, if not breathing out threatenings and slaughter, like Saul of Tarsus, are still unreconciled to some of their old commanders, and are brooding over their old-time grievances, real or imaginary, or both, when they ought to be engaged in more entertaining and profitable business. I shall not, because I cannot, name all the offences of soldiering to which punishments were affixed, as no two commanding officers had just the same violations of military discipline to deal with, — but I shall

143

endeavor in this chapter to include all those which appeal to a common experience.

The most common offences were drunkenness, absence from camp without leave, insubordination, disrespect to superior officers, absence from roll-call without leave, turbulence after taps, sitting while on guard, gambling, and leaving the beat without relief. To explain these offences a little more in detail — no soldier was supposed to leave camp without a pass or permit from the commander of the regiment or battery to which he belonged. A great many *did* leave for a few hours at a time, however, and took their chances of being missed and reported for it. In some companies, when it was thought that several were absent without a permit, a roll-call was ordered simply to catch the culprits. Disrespect to a superior officer was shown in many ways. Some of the more common ways were to " talk back," in strong unmilitary language, and to refuse to salute him or recognize him on duty, which military etiquette requires to be done. The other offences named explain themselves.

CARRYING A LOG.

The methods of punishment were as diverse as the dispositions of the officers who sat in judgment on the cases of the offenders. In the early history of a regiment there was a guard-house or guard-tent where the daily guard were wont to assemble, and which was their rendezvous when off post during their twenty-four hours of duty. But when the ranks of the regiment had become very much depleted, and the men pretty well seasoned in military duty, the guard-tent was likely to be dispensed with. In this guard-tent offenders were put for different periods of time. Such confinement was a common punishment for drunkenness. This may not be thought a very severe penalty; still, the men did not enjoy it, as it imposed quite a restriction on their freedom to be thus pent up and cut off from the rest of their associates.

Absence from camp or roll-call without leave was punished in various ways. There was no special penalty for it. I think every organization had what was known as a Black List, on which the names of all offenders against the ordinary rules of camp were kept for frequent reference, and when there was any particularly disagreeable task about camp to be done the black list furnished a quota for the work. The galling part of membership in the ranks of the black list was that all of the work done as one of its victims was a gratuity, as the member must stand his regular turn in his squad for whatever other fatigue duty was required.

Among the tasks that were thought quite interesting and profitable pastimes for the black-listed to engage in, were policing the camp and digging and fitting up new company sinks or filling abandoned ones. A favorite treat meted out to the unfortunates in the artillery and cavalry was the burying of dead horses or cleaning up around the picket rope where the animals were tied. In brief, the men who kept *off* the black list in a company were spared many a hard and disagreeable job by the existence of a good long list of offenders against camp discipline.

This placing of men on the black list was not as a rule resorted to by officers who cherished petty spites or personal malice, but by it they designed rather to enforce a salutary discipline. Such officers had no desire to torture the erring, but aimed to combine a reasonable form of punishment with utility to the camp and to the better behaved class of soldiers, and in this I think they were successful. But there was a class of officers who felt that every violation of camp rules should be visited with the infliction of bodily pain in some form. As a consequence, the sentences imposed by

BUCKED AND GAGGED.

these military judges all looked towards that end. Some would *buck and gag* their victims; some would *stand them on a barrel* for a half-day or a day at a time; a favorite punishment with some was to knock out both heads of a barrel, then make the victim stand on the ends of the staves; some would compel them to wear an inverted barrel for several hours, by having a hole cut in the bottom, through which the head passed, making a kind of wooden overcoat; some culprits were compelled to stand a long time with their arms, extending horizontally at the side, lashed to a heavy stick of wood that ran across their backs; others were lashed to a tall wooden horse which stood perhaps eight or nine feet high; some underwent the knapsack drill, that is, they walked a beat with a guardsman two hours on and two or four hours off, wearing a knapsack filled with bricks or stones. Here is an incident related by a veteran who served in the Gulf Department: One day a captain in General Phelps' Brigade put a man on knapsack drill; in other words, he filled his knapsack with bricks, and made him march with it up and down the company street. The General had the habit of going through the camps of his brigade quite fre-

quently, and that day he happened around just in time to
see the performance, but returned to his quarters apparently
without noticing it. Soon, however, he sent his Orderly to
the Captain with a request to come to his tent. The Captain was soon on his way, dressed in his best uniform,
probably expecting, at least, a commendation for his efficiency, or perhaps a promotion. On
reaching the General's tent, he was
admitted, when, after the usual
salute, the following dialogue took
place : —

General P. — " Good-morning,
Captain."

Captain. — " Good-morning, General."

General P. — " I sent for you,
Captain, to inquire of you what
knapsacks were made for."

Captain. — " Knapsacks! — why,
I suppose they were made for soldiers to carry their spare clothing in."

General P. — " Well, Captain, I
passed your camp a short time ago
and saw one of your men carrying
bricks in his knapsack up and down
the company street. Now, go back
to your company, send that man to
his quarters, and don't let me know

POSTED.

of your ordering any such punishment again while you are
in my brigade."

One regiment that I know of had a platform erected, between twenty-five and thirty feet high, on which the offender was isolated from the camp, and left to broil in the sun
or soak in the rain while a guard paced his beat below, to
keep away any who might like to communicate with him.

Some were tied up by the thumbs, with arms extended full
length, and compelled to stand in that position for hours;

A LOADED KNAPSACK.

some were put into what was known as
the sweat-box. This was a box eighteen inches square, and of the full
height of a man, into which the culprit was placed to stand until re-
leased. Some had their full offence
written out on a board with chalk,
and, with this board strapped to their
backs, were marched up and down
through camp the entire day, without
rest or refreshment.

In the artillery, the favorite punishment was to lash the guilty party to
the spare wheel — the extra wheel
carried on the rear portion of every

caisson in a battery. In
the cavalry, men were sometimes punished by being
compelled to carry their
packed saddle a prescribed
time — no small or insig-
nificant burden to men un-
used to a knapsack. Some-
times the guilty parties
were required to carry a
heavy stick of wood on the
shoulder. I knew one such
man, who, because of this
punishment, took a solemn
oath that he would never
do another day's duty in
his company; and he never

ISOLATED ON A PLATFORM.

did. From that day forward he reported at sick-call, but
the surgeon could find no traces of disease about him, and

so returned him for duty. Still the man persistently refused to do duty, claiming that he was not able, and continued to report at sick-call. By refusing to eat anything, he reduced himself to such a condition that he really appeared diseased, and at last was discharged, went home, and boasted of his achievement.

Sometimes double guard-duty was ordered for a man on account of an omission or act of his while on guard. This

ON THE SPARE WHEEL.

punishment gave him four hours on and two off his post or beat instead of the reverse. His offence may have been failing or refusing to salute his superior officer. It may have been that he was not properly equipped. It may have been for being found off his beat, or for leaving it without having been properly relieved; or he may have failed in his duty when the "Grand Rounds" appeared.

When non-commissioned officers sinned, which they did sometimes, they were punished by being reduced to the ranks.

In some organizations gambling was not allowed, in others

it was carried on by both officers and privates. In one command, at least, where this vice was interdicted, culprits in the ranks were punished by having one-half of the head shaved — a most humiliating and effective punishment.

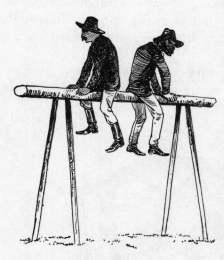

ON A WOODEN HORSE.

Then "back talk," as it was commonly called, which, interpreted, means answering a superior officer insolently, was a prolific cause of punishments. It did not matter in some organizations who the officer was, from colonel or captain to the last corporal, to hear was to obey, and under such discipline the men became the merest puppets. In theory, such a regiment was the perfect military machine, where every man was in complete subordination to one master mind. But the value of such a machine, after all, depended largely upon the kind of a man the ruling spirit was, and whether he associated his inflexibility of steel with the justice of Aristides. If he did that, then was it indeed a model organization; but such bodies were rare, for the conditions were wanting to make them abundant. The master mind was too often tyrannical and abusive, either by nature, or from having been suddenly clothed with a little brief authority over men. And often when nature, if left to herself, would have made him a good commander, an excessive use of "commissary" interfered to prevent, and the subordinates of such a leader, many of them appointed by his influence, would naturally partake of his characteristics; so that such regiments, instead of standing solidly on all occasions, were weakened as a fighting body by a lack of confidence in and personal respect for their leaders, and by a hatred begotten of unjust treatment. Hundreds of officers were put in commission through influence at court, wealth or personal influence deciding appointments that should have been made solely on the basis of merit. At the beginning of the war it was inevitable that the officers should have been inexperienced and uninstructed in the details of warfare, but later this condition changed, and the service would have been strengthened and materially improved by promoting men who had done honorable service and shown good conduct in action, to commissions in new regiments. It is true that such was the intent and partial practice in some States, but the governors, more or less from necessity, took the advice of some one who was a warm personal friend of the applicant, so that shoulder-straps, instead of being always conferred for gallant conduct in the front rank, were sometimes a

IN THE SWEAT-BOX.

mark of distinguished prowess in the mule-train or the cookhouse, which seemed to maintain readier and more influential communication with the appointing power at the rear than was had by the men who stood nearest to the enemy.

To bow in meek submission to the uneducated authority of the civilian, or to the soldier whose record was such as not to command the respect of his fellows, was the lot of thousands of intelligent and brave soldiers, the superiors in all respects, save that of military rank alone, of these self-same officers; and to be commanded not to answer back, when they felt that they must utter a protest against injustice, was a humiliation that the average volunteer did not fully realize when he put his name to the roll, — a humiliation which grew bitterer with every new indignity. Punishments or rebukes administered by social inferiors were galling even when deserved.

ON THE CHINES.

It seems ludicrous to me when I recall the threats I used to hear made against officers for some of their misdeeds. Many a wearer of shoulder-straps was to be shot by his own men in the first engagement. But, somehow or other, when the engagement came along there seemed to be Rebels enough to shoot without throwing away ammunition on Union men ; and about that time too the men, who in more peaceful retreats were so anxious to shoot their own officers, could not always be found, when wanted, to shoot more legitimate game. In these days, when private soldiers are so scarce and officers so exceedingly abundant, the question might very naturally arise how the abundance came about if the officers were so often between two fires ; but what I have said will furnish a solution to the mystery.

Then, there were hundreds of officers that were to be settled with when they reached *home*, and were on an equality with the private soldier so far as military rank was concerned. But while there were, as I have previously intimated, a few who took their resentments out of the service with them, they were *only* few in number, and it is

doubtful whether any of them ever executed their threatened deeds of violence. Poor underpaid non-commissioned
officers, who occupied the perplexing and uncomfortable
position of go-betweens, were frequently invited by privates
to strip off their chevrons and be handsomely whipped for
some act annoying to said privates; but I never heard of
any n. c. o. sacrificing his chevrons to any such ambition —
for various reasons, of which the fear of a thrashing was
not necessarily one.

There were regiments each of which, when off duty,
seemed to contain at least two or three hundred colonels
and captains, so much social free-
dom obtained between officers and
rank and file, yet at the proper
time there was just one commander of such a regiment to
whom the men looked ready to
do his bidding, even to follow him
into the jaws of death. These
officers were not always devout
men; at an earlier period in their
lives some of them may have
learned to be profane ; some drank
commissary whiskey occasionally,
it may be ; but in all their dealings with subordinates, while they
made rigid exactions of them as
soldiers, they never forgot that
they were *men*, and hence, endeavoring to be just in the settlement of camp troubles, protecting their command in the full
enjoyment of all its rights
among similar organizations,

A WOODEN OVERCOAT.

never saying "go!" but "come !" in the hour of danger,
they welded their regiment into a military engine as

solid and reliable as the old Grecian Phalanx. Punishments in such regiments were rare, for manliness and self-respect were never crushed out by tyrants in miniature. The character of the officers had so much to do with determining the nature and amount of the punishments in the army that I consider what I have thrown in here as germane to the subject of this chapter.

STRAPPED TO A STICK.

It should be said, in justice to both officers and privates, that the first two years of the war, when the exactions of the service were new, saw three times the number of punishments administered in the two subsequent years; but, aside from the getting accustomed to the restraints of the service, campaigning was more continuous in the later years, and this kept both mind and body occupied. It is inactivity which makes the growler's paradise. Then, in the last years of the war the rigors of military discipline, the sharing of common dangers and hardships, and promotions from the ranks, had narrowed the gap between officers and privates so that the chords of mutual sympathy were stronger than before, and trivial offences were slightly rebuked or passed unnoticed.

At the beginning of the war many generals were very fearful lest some of the acts of the common soldier should give offence to the Southern people. This encouraged the latter to report every chicken lost, every bee-hive borrowed, every rail burnt, to headquarters, and subordinates were required to institute the most thorough search for evidence that should lead to the detection and punishment of the culprits, besides requiring them to make full restitution of the value of the property taken. Our government and its leading officers, military and civil, seemed at that time to stand hat in hand apologizing to the South for invading its sacred territory, and almost appearing to want only a proper pretext to retire honorably from the conflict. But by the time that the Peninsular Campaign was brought to a close this kid-glove handling of the enemy had come to an end, and the wandering shote, the hen-roosts, the Virginia fence and the straw stack came to be regarded in a sense as perquisites of the Union army. Punishments for appropriating them after this time were much rarer, and the difficulty of finding the culprits increased, as the officers were becoming judiciously near-sighted.

Drumming out of camp was a punishment administered for cowardice. Whenever a man's courage gave out in the face

DRUMMING OUT OF CAMP.

of the enemy, at the earliest opportunity after the battle, he was stripped of his equipments and uniform, marched through the camp with a guard on either side and four soldiers following behind him at " charge bayonets," while a fife and drum corps brought up the rear, droning out the "Rogue's March." He was sure of being hooted and jeered at throughout the whole camp. There were no restraints put upon the language of his recent associates, and their vocabularies were worked up to their full capacity in reviling him. After he had been thoroughly shown off to the entire command, he was marched outside the lines and set free. This whole performance may seem at first thought a very light punishment for so grave an offence, and an easy escape from the service for such men. But it was considered a most disgraceful punishment. No man liked to be called a *coward*, much less to be turned out of the army in that disreputable way, and the facts recorded on his regimental roll side by side with the honorable record of his fellows. He was liable to the death penalty if found in camp afterwards. Many more men deserved this punishment than ever received it. There were very few soldiers put out of the service by this method.

TIED UP BY THE THUMBS.

Sometimes an officer was assaulted by a private soldier or threatened by him. For all such offences soldiers were tried by court-martial, and sentenced to the guard-house or to hard labor at the Rip Raps or the Dry Tortugas, with loss of pay; or to wear a ball and chain attached to their ankles for a stated period. These offences were often committed under the influence of liquor, but frequently through temper or exasperation at continued and unreasonable exactions, as the victim believed.

The penalty for sleeping at one's post, that is, when it was a post of danger, was death; but whether this penalty was ever enforced in our army I am unable to state. There is a very touching story of a young soldier who was pardoned by President Lincoln for this offence, through the pitiful intercession of the young man's mother. Whether it was a chapter from real life, I am in doubt. I certainly never heard of a sentinel being visited with this extreme penalty for this offence.

The penalty attaching to desertion is death by shooting, and this was no uncommon sight in the army; but it did not seem to stay the tide of desertion in the least. I have seen it stated that there was no time in the history of the Army of the Potomac, after its organization by McClellan, when it reported less than one-fourth its full membership as absent without leave. The general reader will perhaps be interested in the description of the first execution of a deserter that I ever witnessed. It took place about the middle of October, 1863. I was then a member of Sickles' Third Corps, and my company was attached for the time being to General Birney's First Division, then covering Fairfax Station, on the extreme left of the army. The guilty party was a member of a Pennsylvania regiment. He had deserted more than once, and was also charged with giving information, to the enemy whereby a wagon-train had been captured. The whole division was ordered out to witness the execution. The troops were drawn up around three sides of a rectangle in two double ranks, the outer facing inward and the inner facing outward. Between these ranks, throughout their entire extent, the criminal was obliged to march, which he did with lowered head. The order of the solemn procession was as shown in the accompanying diagram, the arrows indicating its direction.

First came the provost-marshal, — the sheriff of the army,

—mounted; next, the band playing (what to me from its associations has now come to be the saddest of all tunes)

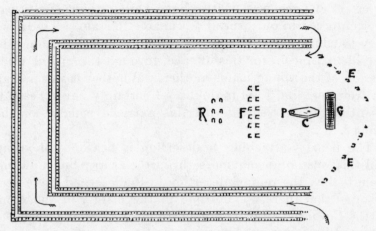

P, prisoner; *C*, coffin; *G*, grave; *F*, firing party; *R*, reserve firing party; *E*, twelve guards.

Pleyel's Hymn, even sadder than the Dead March in "Saul," which I heard less frequently; then followed twelve armed men, who were deployed diagonally across the open end of the space, after the procession had completed its round, to guard against any attempt the prisoner might make to escape; fourth in order came four men bearing the coffin, followed by the prisoner, attended by a chaplain, and a single guard on either side; next, a shooting detachment of twelve men. Eleven of these had muskets loaded with ball, while the twelfth had a blank cartridge in his musket; but as the muskets had been loaded beforehand by an officer, and mixed up afterwards, no one knew who had possession of the musket with the blank cartridge, so that each man, if he wanted it, had the benefit of a faint hope, at least, that his was the musket loaded without ball. After these marched an additional shooting force of six, to act in case the twelve should fail in the execution of their duty.

When the slow and solemn round had been completed, the

prisoner was seated on an end of his coffin, which had been placed in the centre of the open end of the rectangle, near his grave. The chaplain then made a prayer, and addressed a few words to the condemned man, which were not audible to any one else, and followed them by another brief prayer. The provost-marshal next advanced, bound the prisoner's eyes with a handkerchief, and read the general order for the execution. He then gave the signal for the shooting party to execute their orders. They did so, and a soul passed into

DEATH OF A DESERTER.

eternity. Throwing his arms convulsively into the air, he fell back upon his coffin but made no further movement, and a surgeon who stood near, upon examination, found life to be extinct. The division was then marched past the corpse, off the field, and the sad scene was ended.

I afterwards saw a deserter from the First Division of the Second Corps meet his end in the same way, down before Petersburg, in the summer of 1864. These were the only exhibitions of this sort that I ever witnessed, although there were others that took place not far from my camp. The artillery was brigaded by itself in 1864 and 1865, and artillerymen were not then compelled to attend executions which took place in the infantry.

Here is a story of another deserter and spy, who was shot in or near Indianapolis in 1863. He had enlisted in the Seventy-First Indiana Infantry. Not long afterwards he deserted and went over to the enemy, but soon reappeared in the Union lines as a Rebel spy. While in this capacity he was captured and taken to the headquarters of General Henry B. Carrington, who was then in command of this military district. He indignantly protested his innocence of the charge, but a thorough search for evidence of his treachery was begun. His coat was first taken and cut into narrow strips and carefully scrutinized, to assure that it contained nothing suspicious. One by one, the rest of his garments were examined and thrown aside, until at last he stood naked before his captors with no evidence of his guilt having been discovered. He was then requested to don a suit of clothes that was brought in. This he did, and then triumphantly demanded his release. But the General told him to keep cool, as the search was not yet completed; that full justice should be done him whether guilty or innocent. Taking up the trousers again, the General noticed that one of the spring-bottoms was a little stiffer than the other, and on further investigation with his scissors, sure enough, carefully sewed in under the buckram, found a pass from the Rebel General Kirby Smith.

At this discovery the culprit dropped on his knees, and begged for his life. He was tried by court-martial, and sentenced to be hanged — hanging is the penalty for treason, shooting being considered too honorable a death for traitors. But General Carrington, wishing the influence of the execution to be exerted as a check against desertion, which was very common, decided that he should be shot. It is customary to detail the shooting squad from the company to which the deserter belongs. But so enraged were the members of this man's company at his offence that they sent a *unanimous* request that the entire company might act as firing party. This request was refused, however, and a detail of fifteen men made for that purpose. But whereas it is usual for the sergeant in charge of such a detail to load the muskets himself, putting blank cartridges into one, two, or three of the muskets, on this occasion the men were allowed to load for themselves, and when the surgeon examined the lifeless body he found *fifteen bullets* in it, showing that each one of the fifteen men had felt it to be his duty to shoot his former comrade, and that he had conscientiously acted up to that duty.

Shocking and solemn as such scenes were, I do not believe that the shooting of a deserter had any great deterring influence on the rank and file; for the opportunities to get away safely were most abundant. Indeed, any man who was base enough to desert his flag could almost choose his time for doing it. The wife of a man in my own company brought him a suit of citizen's clothing to desert in, which he availed himself of later; but citizen's clothes, even, were not always necessary to ensure safety for deserters. When a man's honor failed to hold him in the ranks, his exit from military life in the South was easy enough.

I have been asked if all deserters captured were shot. No; far from it. There were times in the war when the death penalty for this offence was entirely ignored, and then it would be revived again with the hope of diminishing the rapid rate at which desertions took place. Desertion was the most prevalent in 1864, when the town and city governments hired so many foreigners, who enlisted solely to get the large bounties paid, and then deserted, many of them before getting to the field, or immediately afterwards. They had no interest in the cause, and could not be expected to have. These men were called bounty-jumpers, and, having deserted, went to some other State and enlisted again, to secure another bounty. In this manner many of them obtained hundreds of dollars without being detected; but many more were apprehended, and suffered for it. I knew of three such being shot at one time, each having taken three bounties before they were finally captured. The greater part of these bounty-jumpers came from Canada. A large number of reliable troops were necessary to take these men from the recruiting rendezvous to the various regiments which they were to join.

The mass of recaptured deserters were put to hard labor on government works. Others were confined in some penitentiary, to work out their unexpired term of service. I believe the penitentiary at Albany was used for this purpose, as was also the Old Capitol Prison in Washington. Many more were sent to the Rip Raps, near Fort Monroe. On the 11th of March, 1865, President Lincoln issued a proclamation offering full pardon to all deserters who should return to their respective commands within sixty days, that is, before May 10, 1865, with the understanding that they should serve out the full time of their respective organizations, and make up all time lost as well. A large number whose consciences had given them no peace since their lapse, availed themselves of this proclamation to make amends as far as possible, and leave the service with a good name. This act was characteristic of the Emancipator's matchless magnanimity and forgiving spirit, but scarcely deserved by the parties having most at stake.

I have already intimated that death by hanging was a punishment meted out to certain offences against military law. One of these offences was desertion to the enemy, that is, going from our army over to the enemy, and enlisting in his ranks to fight on that side. In the autumn of 1864 — near Fort Welch, I think it was — I saw three military criminals hanged at the same moment, from the same gallows, for this crime against the government. They were members of the Sixth Corps. There was less ceremony about this execution than that of the deserter, whose end I more fully described. The condemned men were all foreigners, and rode to the gallows in an ambulance attended by a chaplain. The ambulance was well guarded in front, in rear, and on the flanks. The gallows also was strongly guarded. If I recollect aright, the troops were not ordered out to witness the spectacle. Nevertheless, thousands of them from adjoining camps lined the route, and, standing around the gallows, saw the prisoners meet their fate. No loyal heart gave them any sympathy.

In April, 1864, I saw a man hanged for a different offence, on the plains of Stevensburg. He belonged to the second division of my own corps. Most of the corps, which was then twenty-seven thousand strong, must have witnessed the scene, from near or afar. In hanging the culprit the provost-marshal made a dreadful botch of the job, for the rope was too long, and when the drop fell the man's feet touched the ground. This obliged the provost-marshal to seize the rope, and by main strength to hold him clear of the ground till death ensued. It is quite probable that strangulation instead of a broken neck ended his life. His body was so light and emaciated that it is doubtful if, even under more favorable circumstances, his fall could have broken his neck.

The report of the Adjutant-General, made in 1870, shows that there were one hundred and twenty-one men executed during the war — a very insignificant fraction of those who, by military law, were liable to the death penalty.

CHAPTER IX.

A DAY IN CAMP.

"I hear the bugle sound the calls
  For *Réveillé* and *Drill*,
  For *Water, Stable*, and *Tattoo*,
  For *Taps* — and all was still.
  I hear it sound the *Sick-Call* grim,
  And see the men in line,
  With faces wry as they drink down
  Their whiskey and quinine."

 PARTIAL description of the daily programme of the rank and file of the army in the monotony of camp life, more especially as it was lived during the years 1861, '62, and '63, covers the subject-matter treated in this chapter. I do not expect it to be all new to the outside public even, who have attended the musters of the State militia, and have witnessed something of the routine that is followed there. This routine was the same in the Union armies in many respects, only with the latter there was a reality about the business, which nothing but stern war can impart, and which therefore makes soldiering comparatively uninteresting in State camp — such, at least, is the opinion of old campaigners.

The private soldiers in every arm of the service had many experiences in common in camp life, so that it will not be profitable to describe each in detail, but where the routine differs I shall be more entertaining and exact by adhering to the branch with which I am the most familiar, *viz.:* the light

164

artillery; and this I shall do, and, in so doing, shall narrate not the routine of my own company alone, but essentially of that branch of the service throughout the army as artillery-men saw and lived it.

Beginning the army day, then, the first bugle-call blown was one known in artillery tactics as the *Assembly of Buglers,* to sound which the corporal or sergeant of the guard would call up the bugler.

ASSEMBLY OF BUGLERS (*artillery*).

ASSEMBLY OF BUGLERS (*infantry*).

It was sounded in summer about five o'clock, and in winter at six. It was the signal to the men to get out of their blankets and prepare for the morning roll-call, known as *Réveillé.* At this signal, the hum of life could be heard within the tents. "Put the bugler in the guard-house!" — "Turn out!" — "All up!" — and other similar expressions, mingled with yawns, groans, and exclamations of deep disgust, formed a part of the response to this always unwelcome summons. But as only the short space of fifteen minutes was to intervene before the next call, the *Assembly,* would be blown, the men had to bestir themselves. Most of them would arise at once, do the little dressing that was required, and perform or omit their toilet, according to the inclination or habit or time of the individual.

A common mode of washing was for one man to pour water from a canteen into the hands of his messmate, and

A CANTEEN WASH.

thus take turns; but this method was practised most on the march. In settled camp, some men had a short log scooped out for a wash-basin. Some were not so particular about being washed every day, and in the morning would put the time required for the toilet into another "turn over" and nap. As such men always slept with their full uniform on, they were equivalent to a kind of Minute Men, ready to take the field for roll-call, or any other call, at a minute's notice.

ASSEMBLY (*artillery*).

ASSEMBLY (*infantry*).

As soon as the Assembly sounded, the sight presented was quite an interesting one. The men could be seen emerging from their tents or huts, their toilet in various stages of completion. Here was a man with one boot on, and the other in his hand; here, one with his clothes buttoned in skips and blouse in hand, which he was putting on as he went to the line; here was one with a blouse on; there, one with his jacket or overcoat (unless uniformity of dress on line was required — it was not always at the morning roll-calls, and in some companies never, only on inspections). Here and there was a man just about half awake,

FALL IN FOR ROLL-CALL.

having a fist at each eye, and looking as disconsolate and forsaken as men usually do when they get from the bed before the public at short notice.

Then, this roll-call was always a powerful cathartic on a large number, who must go at once to the sinks, and let the Rebel army wait, if it wanted to fight, until their return. The exodus in that direction at the sounding of the assembly was really quite a feature. All enlisted men in a company, except the guard and sick, must be present at this roll-call, unless excused for good reasons. But as the shirks always took pride in dodging it, their notice of intention to be absent from it for any reason was looked at askance by the sergeants of detachments. The studied agony that these men would work not only into their features but their voice and even their gait would have been ludicrous in the extreme, if frequent repetitions had not rendered it disgusting; and the humorous aspect of these dodgers was not a little enhanced by the appearance which they usually had of having been dressed much as is a statue about to be dedicated, which, at the signal, by the pulling of a single cord, is instantly stripped of all its drapery and displayed in its full glory.

Other touches, which old soldiers *not* artillerymen would readily recognize as familiar, might be added to the scene presented in camp, when the bugle or the drum called the men into line for the first time in the day. When at last the line was formed, it was dressed by the orderly, — now called, I believe, first sergeant, — and while at "Parade Rest" the bugles blew.

RÉVEILLÉ.

There were words improvised to many of these calls, which I wish I could accurately remember. Those adapted to Réveillé, in some regiments, ran as follows: —

I can't get 'em up, I can't get 'em up,
I can't get 'em up, I tell you.
I can't get 'em up, I can't get 'em up,
I can't get 'em up at all.
The corporal's worse than the private,
The sergeant's worse than the corporal,

The lieutenant's worse than the sergeant,
But the captain's worst of all.

I can't get 'em up, I can't get 'em up,
I can't get 'em up this morning;
I can't get 'em up, I can't get 'em up,
I can't get 'em up to-day.

These are more appropriate when applied to the **infantry**, where the call was blown before the men came into line.

When the bugle ceased to sound, the orderly-sergeant of a battery said, "Pay attention to Roll-call"; and the roll was called by the six line or duty sergeants, each of whom had charge of twenty-five men, more or less. These sergeants then made their report of "all present or accounted for," or whatever the report was, to the orderly-sergeant, who, in turn, reported to the officer of the day in charge. If there were no special orders to be issued for fatigue duty, or no checks or rebukes or instructions to be given "for the good of the order," the line was dismissed. Any men who were absent without leave were quite likely to be put on the Black List for their temerity.

Shortly after Réveillé, the buglers sounded forth the shrill notes of

STABLE CALL.

Here are the words sung to this call:—

Go to the stable, as quick as you're able,
And groom off your horses, and give them some corn;
For if you don't do it the captain will know it,
And then you will rue it, as sure as you're born.

This call summoned all the drivers in the company to assemble at the grain pile with their pair of canvas nose-bags, where the stable sergeant, so called (his rank was that of a private, though he sometimes put on the airs of a brigadier-general), furnished each with the usual ration of grain, either oats or corn.   With this forage, and a curry-comb and

AT THE GRAIN PILE.

brush, they at once proceeded to the picket rope, where, under the inspection of the six sergeants, supervised also by the officer of the day and orderly, the horses were thoroughly groomed.   At a given signal, the grooming ceased, and the nose-bags were strapped on.   Sometimes the feed was given while the grooming was in progress.

The only amusing phase of this duty that I now recall, occurred when some luckless cannoneer, who would insist that he did not know the difference between a curry-comb and a curry of mutton, was detailed to minister to the sanitary needs of some poor, unsavory, glanders-infected, or greasy-heeled, or sore-backed, or hoof-rotten brute, that could not be entirely neglected until he was condemned by governmental authority.   Now the cannoneers of a battery, who constituted what was known as the Gun Detachment, were an aristocracy.   It is worthy of notice that when artillery companies received their first outfit of horses, there were always at least three men who wished to be drivers to one who cared to serve as a cannoneer, the prevailing idea among the uninitiated being that a driver's position was a safer place in battle than that of a cannoneer. I will only say, in passing this point, that they were much disappointed at its exposures when they came to the reality; but the cannoneers, taking the recognized post of danger from choice, a post whose duties when well executed were the most showy on parade, as well as the most effective in action, upon whose coolness and courage depended the safety not only of their own company but often that of regiments, were nursed by these facts into the belief that they rightfully outranked the rest of the rank and file. The posturings and facial contortions of a cannoneer, therefore, who cherished these opinions, when called upon to perform such a task as I have specified, can readily be imagined; if they cannot, I will only say that they would have excited the risibilities of the most sympathetic heart. The four-footed patients alluded to were usually assigned to the charge of "Spare Men," that is, men who were neither drivers nor members of the gun detachments, who, by use, had come to fill the situation meekly and gracefully. There was one service that a cannoneer *would* occasionally condescend to do a driver. When the army was on the march, a driver would sometimes get weary of riding and ask a cannoneer to spell him while he stretched his legs; and just to oblige him, you know, the cannoneer would get into the saddle and ride two or three miles, but beyond that he kept to his own sphere.

Following close upon the completion of stable duties came Breakfast Call, when the men prepared and ate their breakfast, or received their dipper of coffee and other rations from the company cook-house. I can add nothing in this connection to what I have already related in the chapter on Rations.

BREAKFAST CALL (*in artillery*).

BREAKFAST CALL (*in infantry*).

At eight o'clock the bugler blew

SICK CALL (*in artillery*).

SICK CALL (*in infantry*).

Here are the words improvised to this call: —

Dr. Jones says, Dr. Jones says:
Come and get your quin, quin, quin, quinine,
Come and get your quinine,
Q–u–i–n–i–n–e !!!

In response to this call, some who were whole and needed not a physician, as well as those who were sick, reported at the surgeon's tent for prescriptions. Much used to be said by the soldiers in regard to the competency or incompetency of army surgeons. It was well understood in war time that, even though an examination of fitness was required of surgeons to secure an appointment in the army, — at least in some States, — many charlatans, by some means, received commissions. Such an examination had as much value as those the medicine men made of recruits in '64 and '65, for those who have occasion to remember will agree that a sufficient number of men too old or diseased came to the front in those years — no, they did not all get as far as the front — to fairly stock all the hospitals in the country. A part of this showing must be charged to incompetent physicians, and a part to the strait the government was in for recruits. The appointment of incompetent surgeons, on the other hand, is to be condoned in a government sorely pressed for medical assistance, and all too indifferent, in its strait, to the qualifications of candidates.

Nothing in this line of remark is to be construed as reflecting on the great mass of army surgeons, who were most assiduous workers, and whose record makes a most creditable chapter in the history of the Rebellion. There are incompetents in every class.

Every soldier who tried to do his duty, and only responded to sick-call when in the direst need, should have received the most skilful treatment to be had ; but a strict regard for the facts compels the statement that a large number of those who waited upon the doctor deserved no better treatment than the most ignorant of these men of medicine were likely to administer. Yes, there were a few individuals to be found, I believe, in every company in the service, who, to escape guard or fatigue duty, would feign illness, and, if possible, delude the surgeon into believing them proper subjects for his tenderest care. Too often they succeeded,

and threw upon their own intimate associates the labors of
camp, which they themselves were able to perform, and
degraded their bodies by swallowing drugs, for the ailments
to which they laid claim. I can see to-day, after a lapse of
more than twenty years, these "beats on the government"
emerging from their tents at sick-call in the traditional army
overcoat, with one hand tucked
into the breast, the collar up,
cap drawn down, one trousers-

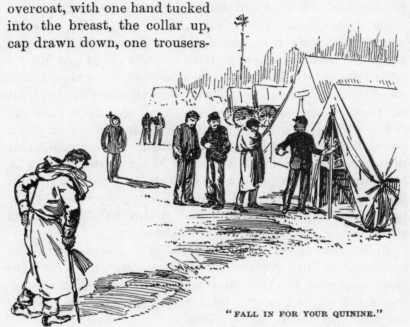

"FALL IN FOR YOUR QUININE."

leg hung up on the strap of a government boot, and a
pace slow and measured, appearing to bear as many of
the woes and ills of mankind as Landseer has depicted
in his "Scapegoat."

Sometimes the surgeons were shrewd enough to read
the frauds among the patients, in which case they often
gave them an unpalatable but harmless dose, and reported
them back for duty, or, perhaps, reported them back for
duty *without* prescription, at the same time sending an
advisory note to the captain of the company to be on the
lookout for them. It was, of course, a great disappointment

to these would-be shirkers to fail in their plans, but some of the more persistent would stick to their programme, and, by refusing food and taking but little exercise, would in a short time make invalids of themselves in reality. There were undoubtedly many men in the service who secured admission to the hospitals, and finally their discharge, by this method; and some of these men, by such a course of action, planted the seeds of real diseases, to which they long since succumbed, or from which they are now sufferers.

I must hasten to say that this is not a burlesque on *all* the soldiers who answered to sick-call. God forbid! The genuine cases went with a different air from the shams. I can see some of my old comrades now, God bless them! sterling fellows, soldiers to the core, stalwart men when they entered the army, but, overtaken by disease, they would report to sick-call, day after day, hoping for a favorable change; yet, in spite of medicine and the nursing of their messmates, pining away until at last they disappeared — went to the hospitals, and there died. Oh, if such men could only have been sent to their homes before it was too late, where the surroundings were more congenial and comfortable, the nursing tender, and more skilful, because administered by warmer hearts and the more loving hands of mother, wife, or sister, thousands of these noble souls could have been saved to the government and to their families. But it was not to be, and so they wasted away, manfully battling for life against odds, dying with the names of dear ones on their lips, dear ones whose presence at the death-bed was in so many cases impossible, but dying as honorable deaths as if they had gone down

" With their back to the field and their feet to the foe."

This is one of the saddest pictures that memory brings me from Rebellion days.

The proverbial prescription of the average army surgeon was quinine, whether for stomach or bowels, headache or toothache, for a cough or for lameness, rheumatism or fever and ague. Quinine was always and everywhere prescribed with a confidence and freedom which left all other medicines far in the rear. Making all due allowances for exaggerations, that drug was unquestionably the popular dose with the doctors.

After Sick-Call came *Water-Call*, or

WATERING CALL,

at which the drivers in artillery and the full rank and file of the cavalry repaired to the picket-rope, and, taking their horses, set out to water them. This was a very simple and

THE PICKET ROPE.

expeditious matter when the army was encamped near a river, as it frequently was; but when it was not, the horses were ridden from one-half a mile to two miles before a stream or pond was found adequate to the purpose. It was no small matter to provide the animals of the Army of the Potomac with water, as can be judged from the following figures: After Antietam McClellan had about thirty-eight thousand eight hundred horses and mules. When the army crossed the Rapidan into the Wilderness, in 1864, there were fifty-six thousand four hundred and ninety-nine horses and mules in it. Either of these is a large number to provide with water. But of course they were not all watered at the same pond or stream, since the army stretched across many miles of territory. In the summer of 1864, the problem of water-getting before Petersburg was quite a serious one for man and beast. No rain had fallen for several weeks, and the animals belonging to that part of the army which was at quite a remove from the James and Appomattox Rivers had to be ridden nearly two miles (such was the case in my own company, at least; perhaps others went further) for water, and then got only a warm, muddy, and stagnant fluid that had accumulated in some hollow. The soldiers were sorely pressed to get enough to supply their own needs. They would scoop out small holes in old water courses, and patiently await a dipperfull of a warm, milky-colored fluid to ooze from the clay, drop by drop. Hundreds wandered through the woods and valleys with their empty canteens, barely finding water enough to quench thirst. Even places usually dank and marshy became dry and baked under the continuous drought. But such a state of affairs was not to be endured a great while by live, energetic Union soldiers; and as the heavens continued to withhold the much needed supply of water, shovels and pickaxes were forthwith diverted from the warlike occupation of intrenching to the more peaceful pursuit of well-digging, it soon being ascertained that an abundance of excellent water was to be had ten or twelve feet below the surface of the ground. These wells were most of them dug broadest at the top and with shelving sides, to prevent them from caving, stoning a well being obviously out of the question. Old-fashioned well-curbs and sweeps were then erected over them, and man and beast were provided with excellent water in camp.

Fatigue call was the next in regular order.

FATIGUE CALL.

FATIGUE CALL (*infantry*).

The artillery were almost never detailed for fatigue duty outside of their own company. The only exception now occurring to me was when an artillery brigade headquarters was established near by, and an occasional detail was made and sent there for temporary service; but that was all. Our camp fatigue duty consisted in policing or cleaning camp, building stables, or perhaps I should more accurately designate them if I called them shelters, for the horses and mules, burying horses, getting wood and water, and washing gun-carriages and caissons for inspections.

This building of horse-shelters was at times no mean or trivial enterprise, and sometimes employed a great many men a great many days. When the army was on the march, with no danger impending, the horses were unharnessed and tied to the picket-rope. This was a rope about two hundred feet long and two inches in diameter, which, when the battery was drawn up in park, was hitched to the outer hind wheel of a caisson on one flank of the battery, and then carried through the hind wheels and over the ammunition-chests of the intervening caissons and made fast to a hind wheel of the caisson on the other flank.

In camp, a different plan was adopted. If it was in the open, a line of posts was set at intervals, such as would keep the rope from sagging low, and to them it was secured. The earth for ten feet on either side was then thrown up beneath like a well graded street, so as to drain off readily. Sometimes the picket was established in the edge of woods, in which case the rope ran from tree to tree. In summer camp a shelter of boughs was constructed over the picket. In winter, a wall of pine-boughs was set up around, to fend off bleak winds. Now and then, one was roofed with a thatch of confiscated straw; and I remember of seeing one nearly covered with long clapboard-like shingles, which were rifted out **of** pine-logs.

The character and stability of all such structures depended largely upon the skill displayed by regimental and company commanders in devising means to keep men employed, and on the tenure of a company's stay in a place. But at this late day I fail to recall a single instance where the men called a meeting and gave public expression to their gratitude and appreciation in a vote of thanks for the kind thoughtfulness displayed by said commanders. In fact, not this alone but *all* varieties of fatigue were accompanied in their doing with no end of growling.

It *was* aggravating after several days of exhausting labor, of cutting and carting and digging and paving, — for some of the " high-toned " commanders had the picket paved with cobble-stones, — to have boot-and-saddle call blown, summoning the company away, never to return to that camp, but to go elsewhere and repeat their building operations. It was the cheapest kind of balm to a company's feelings, where so much of love's — or rather *unwilling* — labor had been lost, to see another company appear, just as the first was leaving, and literally enter into the labors of the former, taking quiet and full possession of everything left behind. Yet such was one of the inevitable concomitants of war, and so used did the men become to such upsettings of their calculations that twenty-four hours sufficed, as a rule, to wipe out all yearnings for what so recently had been.

I will add a few words in this connection in regard to the mortality of horses. Those who have not looked into the matter have the idea that actual combat was the chief source of the destruction of horseflesh. But, as a matter of fact, that source is probably not to be credited with *one-tenth* of the full losses of the army in this respect. It is to be remembered that the exigencies of the service required much of the brutes in the line of hard pulling, exposure, and hunger, which conspired to use them up very rapidly; but the various diseases to which horses are subject largely swelled the death list. Every few weeks a veterinary surgeon would look over the sick-list of animals, and prescribe for such as seemed worth saving or within the reach of treatment, while others would be condemned, led off, and shot. To bury these, and those dying without the aid of the bullet, I have shown, was a part of the fatigue duty of artillerymen and cavalrymen.

The procuring of wood was often a task involving no little labor for all arms of the military service. At Brandy Station, Virginia, before the army left there on the 3d of May, 1864, some commands were obliged to go four or five miles for it. The inexperienced can have little idea of how rapidly a forest containing many acres of heavy growth would disappear before an army of seventy-five or a hundred thousand men camped in and about it. The scarcity of wood was generally made apparent by this fact, that when an army first went into camp trees were cut with the scarf two or three feet above the ground, but as the scarcity increased these stumps would get chipped down often below a level with the ground.

After fatigue call the next business, as indicated by the drum or army bugle, was to respond to

DRILL CALL (*artillery*).

DRILL CALL (*infantry*).

I will anticipate a little by saying that the last drill of any kind in which my own company engaged took place among the hills of Stevensburg, but a day or two before the army started into the Wilderness in '64. From that time until the close of the war batteries were kept in constant motion, or placed in the intrenchments on siege duty, thus putting battery drill out of the question; such at least was the fact with light batteries attached to the various army corps. The Artillery Reserve, belonging to the Army of the Potomac, may have been an exception to this. I have no information in regard to it.

The artillery, like the infantry, had its squad drill, but, as the marchings and facings were of only trifling importance, there was an insignificant amount of time spent on them. The drivers were usually exempted from drill of this kind, the cannoneers of the gun detachments doing enough of it to enable them, while drilling the standing-gun drill, so called, — a drill without horses, — to get from line into their respective stations about the gun and limber, and *vice versa*. But long after this drill became obsolete and almost forgotten, the men seemed never to be at a loss to find their proper posts whenever there was need of it.

So far as I know, artillerymen never piqued themselves on their skill in marchings by platoons, keeping correct alignment meanwhile, whether to the front, the rear, obliquely, or in wheelings. Indeed, I remember this part of their schooling as rather irksome to them, regarding it as they did, whether rightfully or wrongfully, as ornamental and not essential. It undoubtedly *did* contribute to a more correct military bearing and soldierly carriage of the body, and, in a general way, improved military discipline: but these advantages did not always appear to the average member of the rank and file, and, when they did, were not always appreciated at their worth.

The drill of light-artillerymen in the school of the piece occupied a considerable time in the early history of each company. Before field movements could be undertaken, and carried out either with much variety or success, it was indispensable for the cannoneers and drivers to be fully acquainted with their respective duties; and not only was each man drilled in the duties of his *own* post, but in those of every other man as well. The cannoneers must know how to be drivers, and the drivers must have some knowledge of the duties of cannoneers. This qualified a man to fill not only any other place than his own when a vacancy occurred, but another place *with* his own if need came. This education included a knowledge of the ordinary routine of loading and firing, the ability to estimate distances with tolerable accuracy, cut fuses, take any part in the dismounting and mounting of the piece and carriage, the transfer of limber-chests, the mounting of a spare wheel or insertion of a spare pole, the slinging of the gun under the limber in case a piece-wheel should be disabled; even all the parts of the harness must be known by cannoneer as well as driver, so that by the time a man had graduated from this school he was possessed of quite a liberal military education.

Doing this sort of business over and over again, day after day, got to be quite tedious, but it all helped to pass away the three years. One part of this instruction was quite interesting, particularly if the exercise was a match against time, or if there was competition between detachments or sections; this was the dismounting and remounting the piece and carriage. In this operation each man must know his precise place, and fit into it as accurately as if he were a part of a machine. This was absolutely necessary, in order to secure facility and despatch. In just the measure that he realized and lived up to this duty, did his gun detachment succeed in reducing the time of the exercise. One gun's crew in my company worked with such speed, strength, unanimity, and precision, that they reduced the time for performing this manœuvre, including loading and firing, to forty-nine seconds. Other batteries may have done even better. The guns we then used were the steel Rodmans, weighing something over eight hundred pounds, and four of us could toss them about pretty much at will. I say four of us, because just four were concerned in the lifting of the gun. We could not have handled the brass Napoleons with equal readiness, for they are somewhat heavier.

After cannoneers and drivers came to be tolerably familiar with the school of the piece, field manœuvres with the battery began. The signal which announced this bit of "entertainment for man and beast" is known to Army Regulations as

BOOTS AND SADDLES,

a call whose tones at a later period sent the blood of artillerymen and cavalrymen coursing more rapidly through the veins when it denoted that danger was nigh, and seeking encounter.

Battery drill was an enterprise requiring ample territory. When the vicinity of the camp would not furnish it, the battery was driven to some place that would. If cannoneers as a class were more devout than the other members of a light-artillery company, it must have been because they were stimulated early in their military career to pray — to pray that the limits of the drill-ground should be so contracted that the battery could not be cantered up and down a plain more than half a mile in extent, with cannoneers dismounted and strung along in the rear at intervals varying with their running capacity or the humor of the commanding officer ; or, if mounted, clutching at the handles or edge of the limber-chest, momently expecting to be hurled headlong as the carriages plunged into an old sink or tent ditch or the gutter of an old company street, or struck against a stump or stone with such force as to shake the ammunition in the chests out of its packing, making it liable to explode from the next concussion — at least so feared the more timid of the cannoneers, when their fears of being thrown off were quieted so that they could think of anything else. On such occasions they appreciated the re-enforced trousers peculiar to artillerymen, and wished government had been even more liberal in that direction. But this mental state of timidity soon wore off, and the men came to feel more at home while mounted on these noisiest and hardest-riding of vehicles ; or else sulked in the rear, with less indifference to consequences.

Notwithstanding the monotony that came of necessity to be inseparable from them, battery drills were often exhilarating occasions. It was in the nature of things for them to be so, as when the artillery in action moved at all it must needs move promptly. A full six-gun battery going across a plain at a trot is an animated spectacle. To see it quietly halted, then, at the command, " Fire to the rear. — Caissons pass your pieces-trot-march. — In Battery," break into moving masses, is a still more animated and apparently confused scene, for horses and men seem to fly in all directions. But the apparent confusion is only brief, for in a moment the guns are seen unlimbered in line, the cannoneers at their posts, and the piece-limbers and caissons aligned at their respective distances in the rear.

There was an excitement about this turmoil and despatch which I think did not obtain in any other branch of the service. The rattle and roar was more like that which is heard in a cotton-factory or machine-shop than anything else with which I can compare it. The drill of a light battery possessed much interest to outsiders, when well done. It was not unusual, when the drill-ground was in proximity to an infantry camp, for the men to look on by hundreds. To see six cannons, with their accompanying six caissons, sped by seventy-two horses across the plain at a lively pace, the cannoneers either mounted or in hot pursuit, suddenly halt at the bugle signal, and in a moment after appear " In Battery" belching forth mimic thunder in blank cartridge at a rapid rate, and in the next minute "limbered up" and away again to another part of the field, was a sight full of interest and spirit to the unaccustomed beholder; and if, as sometimes happened, there was a company of cavalry out on drill, to engage in a sham fight with the battery, a thrilling and exciting scene ensued, which later actual combats never superseded in memory; for while the cavalry swept down on the guns at a gallop, with sabres flashing in the air, the cannoneers with guns loaded with blank cartridges, of course, stand rigid as death awaiting the onset, until they are within a few rods of the battery. Then the lanyards are pulled, and the smoke, belched suddenly forth, completely envelops both parties to the bloodless fray.

As the drilling of a battery was done for the most part by sounding the commands upon a bugle, it became necessary for cannoneers and drivers to learn the calls; and this they did after a short experience. Even the horses became perfectly familiar with some of these calls, and would proceed to execute them without the intervention of a driver. Cavalry horses, too, exhibited great sagacity in interpreting bugle signals.

Sometimes the lieutenants who were chiefs of sections were sent out with their commands for special drill. A section comprised two guns with their caissons. There was little enthusiasm in this piecemeal kind of practice, especially after familiarity and experience in the drill of the full battery; but it performed a part in making the men self-possessed and expert in their special arm of the service. Beyond that, it gave men and horses exercise, and appetite for government food, which, without the exercise, would have been wanting, to a degree at least, and occupied time that would otherwise have been devoted to the soldier's pastime of grumbling.

At twelve o'clock the *Dinner Call* was sounded.

DINNER CALL.

DINNER CALL (*infantry*).

I can add nothing of interest here beyond what I have already presented in my talk on rations.

There was nothing in the regular line of duty in light artillery for afternoons which could be called routine, although there was more or less standing-gun drill for cannoneers early in the service. In the infantry, battalion drill often occupied the time. The next regular call for a battery was *Water Call*, sounded at four o'clock, or perhaps a little later. On the return of the horses *Stable Call* was again blown, and the duties of the morning, under this call, repeated.

At about 5.45 P. M., *Attention* was blown, soon to be followed by the *Assembly*, when the men fell in again for *Retreat* roll-call.

RETREAT.

The music for this was arranged in three parts, and when there were three bugles to blow it the effect was quite pleasing. The name *Retreat* was probably given this call because

GOING TO WATER.

it came when there was a general retiring from the duties of the day. This roll-call corresponded with the *Dress Parade* of the infantry. Uniformity of dress was a necessity at this time with the latter, and quite generally too in the artillery; but the commanders of batteries differed widely in taste and military discipline. A company of soldiers was what its captain made it. Some were particular, others were not, but all should have been in this matter of dress for at least one roll-call in the day. At this parade all general orders were read, with charges, specifications, and findings of courts-martial, etc., so that the name of E. D. Townsend, Assistant Adjutant-General, became a household word. At this time, too, lectures on the shortcomings of the company were in order. The lecturer employed by the government to do this was usually the officer of the day, though now and then the captain would spell him. A lecturer of this kind had two great advantages over a lecturer in civil life; first, he was always sure of an audience, and, second, he could hold their attention to the very close. None of them left while the lecture was in progress. Now and then an orderly-sergeant would try his hand in the lecture field, but unless he was protected by the presence of a pair of shoulder-straps he was quite likely to be coughed or groaned down, or in some other way discouraged from repeating the effort.

The shortcomings alluded to were of a varied character. I think I mentioned some of them in the chapter on punishments. Sometimes the text was the general delinquency of the men in getting into line; sometimes it was a rebuke for being lax in phases of discipline; the men were not sufficiently respectful to superior officers, did not pay the requisite attention to *saluting*, had too much *back talk*, were *too boisterous in camp, too untidy in line*. These, and twenty other allied topics, all having a bearing on the characteristics essential in the make-up of a good soldier, were preached upon with greater or less unction and frequency, as circumstances seemed to require, or the standard in a given company demanded.

After the dismission of the line, guard-mounting took place; but this in the artillery was a very simple matter. The guard at once formed on the parade line were assigned to their reliefs, and dismissed till wanted. Sometimes the guard-mounting took place in the morning, as did that of the infantry. The neatest and most soldierly appearing guardsman was selected as captain's orderly. But guard-mounting in light artillery was not always thus simple. Camp Barry, near Washington, was used as a school of instruction for light batteries, for a period of at least three years. During the greater part of this time there were ten or a dozen batteries there on an average. Under one of its commandants, at least, a brigade guard-mounting was held at eight o'clock A. M., and here members of my company responded to the bugle-call known as the "Assembly of Guard," for the first and last time.

ASSEMBLY OF GUARD.

The infantry bugle-call for the same purpose was more familiar, as it was heard daily for months. It ran as follows : —

This call was immediately followed by other music, either a brass band or a fife-and-drum corps, to which the details from the various companies marched out on to the color-line, where the usual formalities ensued, such in substance as may be seen at a muster to-day. The guard necessary in a single company of artillery was so small that the call with the bugle was rarely if ever sounded, at least in volunteer companies. A detail of cannoneers stood guard over the guns night and day, and over the cook-house and quarter-master's stores at night, and sometimes there was one posted in front of company headquarters. A detail of drivers, also, went on duty at night at the picket-rope, to assure that the horses were kept tied and not stolen by marauding cavalry-men.

In the safe rear, where, as the men used to say, the officers were wont to sit up late at night burning out government candles, while they devised ways and means to keep the men exercised as well as ex*or*cised, a guard tent was pitched in front of the camp, in which the guard were compelled to stay when off post, much to their disgust sometimes; but when the company or regiment was in line along the glorious front, that unpopular lodging-house was abandoned, and each guardsmen slept in his own quarters, on his own army feather-bed, whither the corporal of the guard must come for his victim in the silent hours when that victim was wanted to go on post.

With the infantry, guard-mounting took place in the morning at eight o'clock. The guard was divided into three equal portions, called reliefs, first, second, and third. each relief being on post two hours and off four, thus serving eight hours out of the twenty-four. With all the irksomeness of the detail, the guardsman enjoyed a temporary triumph as such, for on that day, at least, he could snap his fingers at roll-calls and all calls for fatigue duty — in short, was an independent gentleman within certain limits.

I have stated it to have been the duty of the corporal of the guard to seek out the members of the various reliefs in their quarters, when the time came for them to go on post. There was more or less of lively incident attending these explorations — not, however, with the sanction of the corporal, to whom the liveliness was anything but amusing. Your corporal of the guard was up to the average of ordinary officers in intelligence, and, as he was just started on the ladder of promotions, fully intended to do his whole duty at least; and so he was wont to prepare himself for his nightly rounds by obtaining such a knowledge of the local geography of the camp as would enable him to arouse and assemble his guard with the least inconvenience to himself and the least commotion to the camp. But the best laid plans of corporals of the guard would frequently "gang agley," even though they used every precaution, and so it was the rule rather than the exception for him to get into the wrong tent, and, after waking up all the inmates and getting the profane to swearing, and all to abusing him for his stupid intrusion, to retreat in as good order as possible and try again. The next time perhaps he would get into the right one, and, after scrutinizing his list of the guard once more, call out the name of *Smith*, for example.   No answer.

STOCKADED SIBLEY TENTS.

There was a kind of deafness generated in the service, which was almost epidemic among guardsmen, especially night guard; at least, such seemed to be the case, for the man that was wanted to go out and take his post was invariably the last one in the tent to be awakened by the summons of the corporal; and long before that waking moment came, the corporal had as aids on his staff all these self-same inmates who had been victims to the assumed deafness of the man sought, and whose voices now furnished no mean chorus to the corporal's refrain.

Sometimes, when the knight of the double chevron was a man of retiring and quiet demeanor, he would save his lungs and make an effort to find his man by stepping inside the tent, and flashing the light of his army candle from the open side of his tin lantern upon the features of each of the slumberers until he came to his victim, when he would shake him by the shoulder and arouse him. The only drawback to this method occurred when the reflections of the corporal woke up the wrong man, who, if he happened to be one of those explosive creatures whom I have before mentioned, was not always complimentary to the intruder in his use of language.

Once in a while, in making his midnight rounds, when calling the name of one of his guard through the door of the stockade, the corporal would be politely directed by some one from within, perhaps the very man he wanted, to "Next tent below"; and many a time this officer succeeded in getting such an innocent and unsuspecting household completely by the ears before being convinced of the joke which had been played on him, when he would return to the first tent in no enviable humor; for meanwhile the men to be relieved were chafing and sputtering away at the non-appearance of the corporal and the relief. I think there was no one minor circumstance which vexed soldiers more than tardy relief from their posts, for every minute that they waited after the expiration of their allotted time seemed to them at least ten; so that the reception which the corporal and relief received when they *did* arrive was likely to be far from fraternal.

Speaking of the corporal of the guard reminds me of a snatch of a song which used to be sung in camp to the tune of "When Johnny comes marching home." Here is the fragment: —

> My Johnny he now a Corporal is!
> Hurrah! Hurrah!
> My Johnny he now a Corporal is,
> You bet he knows his regular biz,
> And we'll all feel gay, etc.

At 8.30 P. M., the bugle again sounded "Attention," followed by the "Assembly," about five minutes afterwards, and the tumbling-out of the company from their evening sociables, to form in line for the final roll-call of the day, known as *Tattoo*.

TATTOO.

But this was Tattoo in the artillery. A somewhat more inspiriting call was that of the infantry, which gave the bugler quite full scope as a soloist. Here it is : —

Ere the last tone had died away, we could hear, when camped near enough to the infantry for the purpose, a very comical medley of names and responses coming from the several company streets of the various regiments within ear-shot. It was " Jones!"—" Brown!"— " Smith!"—" Joe Smith!"—" Green!"—" Gray!"—" O'Neil!"—" O'Reilly!" —" O'Brien!" and so on through the nationalities, only that the names were intermingled. Then, the responses were replete with character. I believe it to be among the abilities of a man of close observation to write out quite at length prominent characteristics of an entire company, by noting carefully the manner in which the men answer "Here!" at roll-call. Every degree of pitch in the gamut was represented. Every degree of force had its exponent. Some answered in a low voice, only to tease the sergeant, and *roar* out a second answer when called again. There were upward slides and downward slides, guttural tones and nasal tones. Occasionally, some one would answer for a messmate, who was absent without leave, and take his chances of being detected in the act. Darkness gave cover to much good-natured knavery.

Tattoo was blown in artillery with the company at " Parade Rest," as at Réveillé. The roll-call and reports followed just as before, and the company was then dismissed. Well do I recall, after the lapse of more than twenty years, the melodious tones of this little bit of army music coming to our ears so consecutively from various parts of the army as to make continuous vibrations for nearly fifteen minutes, softened and sweetened by varying distances, as more than a thousand bugles gave tongue to the still and clear evening air, telling us that in the time specified a hundred thousand men had come out of their rude temporary homes — possibly the last ones they would ever occupy — to respond to their names, and give token that, though Nature's pall had now overshadowed the earth, they were yet loyally at their posts awaiting further orders for their country's service.

After this roll-call was over, the men had half an hour in which to make their beds, put on their nightcaps, and adjust themselves for sleep, as at nine o'clock *Taps* was sounded, which in the artillery ran as follows : —

TAPS.

In the infantry, the bugle-call for Taps was identical with the Tattoo call in artillery. At its conclusion a drummer beat a few single, isolated taps, which closed the army day. At this signal all lights must be put out, all talking and other noises cease, and every man, except the guard, be inside his quarters. In a previous chapter I think I stated that the Black List caught the men who violated this regulation. Some officers enforced it with greater rigidity than others, but all must have a quiet camp. Yet here, as elsewhere, rank interposed to shield culprits from violations of military regulations, and, while the private soldier was punished for burning his candle or talking to his messmate after the bugle-signal, general, field, staff, or line officers could and did get together and carouse, and make the night turbulent with their revelry into the small hours, with no one to molest or call them to an account for it, although making tenfold the disturbance ever caused by the high private after hours.

Taps ended the army day for all branches of the service, and, unless an alarm broke in upon the stillness of the night, the soldiers were left to their slumbers ; or, what was oftener the case, to meditations on home ; the length of time in months and days they must serve before returning thither ; their prospects of surviving the vicissitudes of war ; of the boys who once answered roll-call with them, now camped over across the Dark River; or of plans for business, or social relations to be entered upon, if they should survive the war. All these, and a hundred other topics which furnished abundant field for air-castle-building, would chase one another through the mind of the soldier-dreamer, till his brain would grow weary, his eyes heavy, and balmy sleep would softly steal him away from a world of trouble into the realm of sweet repose and pleasant dreams.

TAPS

CHAPTER X.

RAW RECRUITS.

She asked for men, and up he spoke, my handsome and hearty Sam,
"*I'll* die for the dear old Union, if she'll take me as I am ":
And if a better man than he there's mother that can show,
From Maine to Minnesota, then let the people know.

LUCY LARCOM.

 ANY facts bearing upon the subject of this sketch have been already presented in the opening chapter, but much more remains to be told, and the reader will pardon me, I trust, for now injecting a little bit of personal history to illustrate what thousands of young men were doing at that time, and had been doing for months, as it leads up directly to the theme about to be considered.

After I had obtained the reluctant consent of my father to enlist, — my mother never gave hers, — the next step necessary was to make selection of the organization with which to identify my fortunes. I well remember the to me eventful August evening when that decision to enlist was arrived at. The Union army, then under McClellan, had been driven from before Richmond in the disastrous Peninsular campaign, and now the Rebel army, under General Lee, was marching on Washington. President Lincoln had issued a call for three hundred thousand three-years' volunteers. One evening, shortly after this call was made, I met three of my former school-mates and neighbors in the chief village of the town I then called home, and, after a brief discussion of the outlook, one of the quartette challenged, or "stumped," the others to enlist. The challenge was promptly accepted all around, and hands were shaken to bind the agreement. I will add in passing, that three of the four stood by that agreement ; the fourth was induced by increased wages to remain with his employer, although he entered the service later in the war, and bears a shell scar on his face to attest his honorable service.

After the decision had been reached, not to be revoked on my part as I fully determined, I returned to my home, and either that night or the next morning informed my father of the resolution I had taken. Instead of interposing an emphatic objection, as he had done the previous year, he said, in substance, "Well, you know I do not want you to go, but it is very evident that a great many more must go, and if you have fully determined upon it I shall not object."

Having already determined upon the arm of the service which I should enter, accompanied by three other acquaintances of the same opinion. two of them the school-fellows mentioned, I started for Cambridge, with a view of seeing Captain Porter, who was then at home recruiting for the First Massachusetts Battery, which he commanded, and enlisting with him, as there were at least two men in his company who were fellow-townsmen. But we were much disappointed when the Captain informed us that his company was now recruited to the number required. However, we directed our steps back to Boston without delay, and there, in the second story of the Old State House, enlisted in a new organization then rapidly filling.

Here is a copy of a certificate, still in my possession, which I was to present on enlisting. It tells its own story.

VOLUNTEER ENLISTMENT.

STATE OF  TOWN OF

I,   born in
in the State of   aged   years,
and by occupation a   DO HEREBY ACKNOWLEDGE to have
volunteered this   day of   18 ,
to serve as a **Soldier** in the 𝔄rmy of t𝔥e 𝔘nited 𝔖tates of 𝔄merica, for
the period of *THREE YEARS*, unless sooner discharged by proper
authority: Do also agree to accept such bounty, pay, rations, and
clothing, as are, or may be, established by law for volunteers. And
I,   do solemnly swear, that I will bear
true faith and allegiance to the **United States of America,**
and that I will serve them honestly and faithfully against all their
enemies or opposers whomsoever; and that I will observe and
obey the orders of the President of the United States, and the
orders of the officers appointed over me, according to the Rules
and Articles of War.

Sworn and subscribed to, at
    this   day of   18 ,
BEFORE

I CERTIFY, ON HONOR, That I have carefully examined the above
named Volunteer, agreeably to the General Regulations of the Army, and
that in my opinion he is free from all bodily defects and mental infirmity,
which would, in any way, disqualify him from performing the duties of a
soldier.

                                        EXAMINING SURGEON.

I CERTIFY, ON HONOR, That I have minutely inspected the Volunteer,   previously to his enlistment, and that he was
entirely sober when enlisted; that, to the best of my judgment and
belief, he is of lawful age; and that, in accepting him as duly qualified to
perform the duties of an able-bodied soldier, I have strictly observed the
Regulations which govern the recruiting service. This soldier has
eyes,   *hair,*   *complexion, is*   *feet*   *inches high.*

            Regiment of   *Volunteers.*
                                    RECRUITING OFFICER.

DECLARATION OF RECRUIT.

ℑ, desiring
to VOLUNTEER as a Soldier in the **Army of the United States,** for the term of
THREE YEARS, Do Declare, That I am years and months
of age; That I have never been discharged from the United States service on account of
disability or by sentence of a court-martial, or by order before the expiration of a term
of enlistment; and I know of no impediment to my serving honestly and faithfully as a
soldier for three years.

GIVEN at

The day of

Witness:

No.————

Volunteered at ————

By ———— *18* ,

Regiment of ————

———— *enlistment; last served in Company* ( )

Reg't of ————

Discharged ———— *18* .

CONSENT IN CASE OF MINOR.

I, Do CERTIFY, That I am the father of
that the said is years of age; and I do hereby freely
give my CONSENT to his volunteering as a SOLDIER IN THE ARMY OF THE UNITED
STATES for the period of THREE YEARS.

GIVEN at the day of 186 .

Witness:

How often in later years did the disappointment I experienced at not obtaining membership in the company I at first decided upon recur to me, and how grateful I always felt for the fate which thus controlled my enlistment. For the lot of a recruit in an old company was, at the best, not an enviable one, and sometimes was made very disagreeable for him. He stood in much the same relation to the veterans of his company that the Freshman in college does to the Sophomores, or did when hazing was the rule and not the exception. It is to be remembered that he was utterly devoid of experience in everything which goes to make up the soldier, the details of camping, cooking, drilling, marching, fighting, etc., which put him at a disadvantage on all occasions. For this reason he easily became the butt of a large number of his company — not all, for there were some men who were ever ready to extend sympathy and furnish information to him, when they saw it was needed, and did what they could to raise him to the same general plane occupied by the old members. But many of the veterans seemed to forget how they themselves obtained their army education little by little, and so ofttimes bore down on recruits with great severity.

In the later years of the war, when large bounties were being paid by town, city, and State governments, to encourage enlistments, these recruits were often addressed as "bounty-jumpers" by the evil disposed among the old members. But that term was a misnomer, unless these men proved later that they were deserving of it, for a bounty-jumper was a man — I hate to call him one — who enlisted *only* to get the bounty, and deserted at the earliest opportunity.

Recruits, it should be said, as a class, stood the abuse which was heaped upon them with much greater serenity of temper than they should have done, and, indeed, so anxious were they to win favor with the veterans, and to earn the right to be called and pass for old soldiers, that they generally bore indignities without turning upon their assailants. The term "recruit" in the mouth of a veteran was a very reproachful one, but after one good brush with the enemy it was dropped, if the new men behaved well under fire. In fact, those who abused the recruits most were themselves, as a rule, the most unreliable in action and the greatest shirks when on camp duty.

A WOOD DETAIL.

When a detail made up of recruits and veterans was sent with the wagons for wood, the recruits would be patted on the back by their wily associates, and cajoled into doing most of the chopping, and then challenged to lift the heaviest end of the logs into the wagons, which they seldom refused to do. In the artillery, it usually fell to their lot to care for the spare and used-up horses, not from any intention of imposing upon them, but because cannoneers and drivers had their regular tasks to perform, and all recruits entering the artillery began as spare men, and worked up from the position of private to that of the highest private — a cannoneer.

They always came to camp "flush" with money, and
received every encouragement from the bummers of the
company to spend it freely; if they did not do this, they
were in a degree ostracised, and their lot made much
harder. When their boxes of goodies arrived from home,
the lion's share went to the old hands. If the recruit did
not give it to them, the meanest of them would steal it
when he was away on detail.

Then, all sorts of games were played on recruits by men
who liked nothing so well as a practical joke. I recall the
case of a young man in my own company who had just
arrived, and, having been to the quartermaster for his outfit
of clothing and equipments, was asked by one of the practical jokers why he did not get his umbrella.

"Do they furnish an umbrella?" he asked.

"Why, certainly," said his persecutor, unblushingly. "It's
just like that fraud of a quartermaster to jew a recruit out
of a part of his outfit, to sell for his own benefit. Go back
and *demand* your umbrella of him, and a good one too!"

And the poor beguiled recruit returned to the quartermaster in high dudgeon at the imagined attempt to swindle
him, only to find, after a little breeze, that he had been
victimized by one of the practical jokers of the camp.

There were at least two kinds of recruits to be found in
every squad that arrived in camp. One of these classes
was made up of modest, straightforward men, who accepted
their new situation with its deprivations gracefully, and
brought no sugar-plums to camp with which to ease their
entrance into stern life on government fare and the hardships of government service. They wore the government
clothing as it was furnished them, from the unshapely, un-
comely forage cap to the shoddy, inelastic sock. It mattered naught to them that the limited stock of the quartermaster furnished nothing that fitted them. They accepted
what he tendered cheerfully, believing it to be all right, and
seemed as happy and as much at ease in a wilderness of

overcoat and breeches as others did who had been artisti-
cally renovated by the company tailor. But they were
none the less ludicrous and unsoldierly sights to look upon

RECRUITS IN UNIFORM.

in such rigs, and after a while would see themselves as
others saw them, and "spruce up" somewhat.

These men drew their army rations to the full, not slight-
ing the "salt horse," which I have intimated was rarely
taken by old soldiers. They found no fault when detailed
for fatigue duty, were always ready to learn, and in every
way seemed anxious only to do the proper thing to be done,
hoping by such a course to win a speedy and easy ascent to
the plane of importance occupied by the veterans ; and this
course undoubtedly did much to give them caste in the eyes
of the latter.

Unlike these men in many particulars was the other class
of recruits. This latter class was not modest or retiring in
demeanor. Its members came to camp in a uniform calculated to provoke impertinent remarks from the old vets.
Their caps were from the store of a professional hatter, and
the numbers and emblem on the crown were of silver and
gilt instead of homely brass. Their clothing was generally

custom-made. The pantaloons in particular were not only made to fit well, but were of the finest material obtainable, much unlike the government shoddy which covered the old veteran, and through whose meshes peas of ordinary calibre would almost rattle.

Then, their boots! such masterpieces of elegance and extravagance! Of the cavalry pattern, reaching above the knee, almost doing away with the necessity for pantaloons, sometimes of plain grained leather, sometimes of enamelled, elaborately stitched and stamped, but always seeming to mark their occupant as a man of note and distinction among his comrades. They seemed a sort of fortification about their owner, protecting him from too close contact with his vulgar surroundings. Alas! it never required more than one day's hard march in these dashing appendages to humble their possessor so much that he would evacuate in as good order as possible when camp was reached, if not compelled to before.

Their underwear was such as the common herd did not use in service. Their shirts were "boiled," that is, white ones, or, if woollen, were of some "loud" checkered pattern, only less conspicuous than the flag which they had sworn to defend. In brief, their general make-up would have stamped them as military "dudes," had such a class of creatures been then extant. Of course, it was their privilege to wear whatever did not conflict with Army Regulations, but I am giving the impressions they made on the minds of the old soldiers.

As for government rations, they scoffed at them so long as there was a dollar of bounty left, and a sutler within reach of camp to spend it with. But when the treasury was exhausted they were disconsolate indeed, and wished that the wicked war was over, with all their hearts. On fatigue duty they were useless at first, and the old soldiers made their lot an unhappy one; but by dint of bulldozing and an abundance of hard service, most of them got their fine sentimental notions pretty well knocked out before they had been many weeks in camp. The sergeants into whose hands they were put for instruction did not spare them, keeping them hard at work until the recall from drill.

It was fun in the artillery to see one of these dainty men, on his first arrival, put in charge of a pair of spare horses, — spare enough, too, usually. It was expected of him that he would groom, feed, and water them. As it often happened that such a man had had no experience in the care of horses, he would naturally approach the subject with a good deal of awe. When the *Watering Call* blew, therefore, and the bridles and horses were pointed out to him by the sergeant, the fun began. Taking the bridle, he would

A SPARE MAN AND SPARE HORSES.

look first at it, then at the horse, as if in doubt which end of him to put it on. In going to water, the drivers always bridled the horse which they rode, and led the other by the halter. But our unfledged soldier seemed innocent of all proper information. For the first day or two he would *lead* his charges; then, as his courage grew with acquaintance, he would finally mount the near one, and, with his legs crooked up like a V, cling for dear life until he got his lesson learned in this direction. But all the time that he was getting initiated he was a ridiculous object to observers.

The drilling of raw recruits of both the classes mentioned was no small part of the trials that fell to the lot of billeted officers, for they got hold of some of the crookedest sticks to make straight military men of that the country — or, rather, *countries* — produced. Not the least among the obstacles in the way of making good soldiers of them was the fact that the recruits of 1864–5, in particular, included many who could neither speak nor understand a word of English.   In referring to the disastrous battle of Reams Station, not long since, the late General Hancock told me that the Twentieth Massachusetts Regiment had received an accession of about two hundred German recruits only two or three days before the battle, not one of whom could understand the orders of their commanding officers.   It can

DRILLING THE AWKWARD SQUAD.

be easily imagined how much time and patience would be required to mould such subjects as those into intelligent, reliable soldiery.

But outside of this class there were scores of men that spoke English who would "hay-foot" every time when they should "straw-foot."   They were incorrigibles in almost every military respect.   Whenever they were out with a squad — usually the "awkward squad" — for drill, they made business lively enough for the sergeant in charge. When they stood in the rear rank their loftiest ambition seemed to be to walk up the backs of their file-leaders, and then they would insist that it was the file-leaders who were out of step.   Members of the much abused front rank often had occasion to wish that the regulation thirteen inches from breast to back might be extended to as many feet; but when the march was backward in line, these front rank men would get square with their persecutors in the rear.

To see such men attempt to change step while marching was no mean show. I can think of nothing more apt to compare it with than the game of Hop Scotch, in which the player hops first on one foot, then on both; or to the blue jay, which, in uttering one of its notes, jumps up and down on the limb; and if such a squad under full headway were surprised with a sudden command to halt, they went all to pieces. It was no easy task to align them, for each man had a line of his own, and they would crane their heads out to see the buttons on the breast of the second man, to such an extent that the sergeant might have exclaimed, with the Irish sergeant under like circumstances, "O be-gorra, what a bint row! Come out here, lads, and take a look at yoursels!"

The awkward squad excelled equally in the infantry manual-of-arms. Indeed, they displayed more real individuality here, I think, than in the marchings, probably because it was the more noticeable. At a "shoulder" their muskets pointed at all angles, from forty-five degrees to a vertical. In the attempt to change to a "carry," a part of them would drop their muskets. At an "order," no two of the butts reached the ground together, and if a man could not always drop his musket on his *own* toe he was a pretty correct shot with it on the toe of his neighbor. But, with all their awkwardness and slowness at becoming acquainted with a soldier's duties, the recruits of the earlier years in time of need behaved manfully. They made a poor exhibition on dress parade, but could generally be counted on when more serious work was in hand. Sometimes, when they made an unusually poor display on drill or parade, they were punished — unjustly it may have been, for what they could not help — by being subjected to the knapsack drill, of which I have already spoken.

It was a prudential circumstance that the war came to an end when it did, for the quality of the material that was sent to the army in 1864 and 1865 was for the most part of no credit or value to any arm of the service. The period of enlistments from promptings of patriotism had gone by, and the man who entered the army solely from mercenary motives was of little or no assistance to that army when it was in need of valiant men, so that the chief burden and responsibility of the closing wrestle for the mastery necessarily fell largely on the shoulders of the men who bared their breasts for the first time in 1861, '62, and '63.

I have thus far spoken of a recruit in the usual sense of a man enlisted to fill a vacancy in an organization already in the field. But this seems the proper connection in which to say something of the experiences of men who enlisted with original regiments, and went out with the same in '61 and '62. In many respects, their education was obtained under as great adversity as fell to the lot of recruits. In *some* respects, I think their lot was harder. They knew absolutely nothing of war. They were stirred by patriotic impulse to enlist and crush out treason, and hurl back at once in the teeth of the enemy the charge of cowardice and accept their challenge to the arbitrament of war. These patriots planned just two moves for the execution of this desire : first, to enlist — to join some company or regiment ; second, to have that regiment transferred at once to the immediate front of the Rebels, where they could · fight it out and settle the troubles without delay. Their intense fervor *to do something right away* to humble the haughty enemy, made them utterly unmindful that they must first go to school and learn the art of war from its very beginnings, and right at that point their sorrows began.

I think the greatest cross they bore consisted in being compelled to settle down in home camp, as some regiments did for months, waiting to be sent off. Here they were in sight of home in many cases, yet outside of its comforts to a large extent; soldiers, yet out of danger; bidding their friends a tender adieu to-day, because they are to leave them — perhaps forever — to-morrow. But the morrow comes, and finds them still in camp. Yes, there were soldiers who bade their friends a long good-by in the morning, and started for camp expecting that very noon or afternoon to leave for the tented field, but who at night returned again to spend a few hours more at the homestead, as the departure of the regiment had been unexpectedly deferred.

The soldiers underwent a great deal of wear and tear from false alarms of this kind, owing to various reasons. Sometimes the regiment failed to depart because it was not full ; sometimes it was awaiting its field officers ; sometimes complete equipments were not to be had ; sometimes it was delayed to join an expedition not yet ready ; and thus, in one way or other, the men and their friends were kept long on the tiptoe of expectation. Whenever a rumor became prevalent that the regiment was surely going to leave on a certain day near at hand, straightway there was an exodus from camp for home, some obtaining a furlough, but more going without one, to take another touching leave all around, for the dozenth time perhaps. Many of those who lived too far away to be sure of returning in time, remained in camp, and telegraphed friends to meet them at some large centre, as they passed through on the specified day, which of course the friends faithfully tried to do, and succeeded if the regiment set forth as rumored.

I said that many soldiers went home *without* furloughs. There was a camp guard hemming in every rendezvous for troops, with which I was familiar; but no sentinel could see a man cross his beat *if he did not look at him*, and this few of them did. Indeed, many of the sentinels themselves, as soon as they were posted and the relieving squad were out of sight, stuck their inverted muskets into the ground and decamped, either for their two hours or for the day, and took their chances of being brought to answer for it. The fact is, the men of '61 and '62 *wanted to go to war*, and, whether they left the camp with or without leave, they were sure to return to it. This fact was quite generally understood by their superiors.

This home camp life seems interesting to look back upon. Hundreds of men did not spend one day in six in camp. They came often enough to have it known that they had not deserted, and then flitted again, but other hundreds conscientiously remained. The company streets on every pleasant day were radiant with the costumes of "fair women, and brave men" — *to be*. On such a day a young man sauntering along the parade, or winding in and out of the various company streets, the willing prisoner of one or more interesting young women — his sisters, perhaps, or somebody else's — walked, the envy of the men who had no such friends to enliven their camp life, or whose friends were too far away to visit them. If these latter men secured an introduction to such a party, it tempered their loneliness somewhat. And if such a party entered a tent, and joined in the social round, it made a merry gathering while they tarried. But there were other promenaders whose passing aroused no emotions of envy. The husband and father attended by the loving wife and mother, whose brow had already begun to wear that sober aspect arising from a fore-casting of the future, seeing, possibly, in the contingencies of war, herself a widow, her children fatherless — dependent on her own unaided hands for all of this world's comforts, which must be provided for the helplessness of childhood and youth. The husband, too, leading his boy or girl by the hand as he walks, is not unmindful of the risks he has assumed or the comforts he must sacrifice. But his hand is on the plough, and he will not turn back.

Another interesting party often to be seen in the company street comprised a father, mother, and son, perhaps an only boy, who had volunteered for the war. Their reluctance at the step which he had taken was manifested by turns in their looks, words, and acts. But while he remained in the State, they must be with him as much as possible. See that carpet-bag which the mother opens, as they take a seat on the straw in the son's tent! Notice the solicitude which she betrays as she takes out one comfort or convenience after another — the socks for cold weather, the woollens to ward off fever and ague, the medicine to antidote foul water, the little roll of bandages which — may he never have occasion for ; the dozen other comforts that he ought to be provided with, including some goodies which he had better take along if the regiment should chance to go in a day or two. And so she loads him up — God bless her ! — utterly unmindful that the government has already provided him with more than he can carry very far with his unaided strength.

Then, the camps were full of pedlers of " Yankee notions," which soldiers were supposed to stand in need of. I shall refer to some of these in another connection.

The lesson of submission to higher military authority was a hard one for free, honest American citizens to learn, and, while learning it, they chafed tremendously. It was difficult for them to realize the difference between men *with* shoulder-straps and *without* them ; in fact, they *would not* realize it for a long time. When the straps crowned the shoulders of social inferiors, submission to such authority was at times degrading indeed. I have already touched upon this subject. But the most judicious code of military discipline, even if administered by an accomplished officer of estimable character, would have met with vigorous opposition, for a time, from these impetuous and hitherto untrammelled American citizens. Fortunately for them, perhaps, but unfortunately for the service, the line officers were men of their own selection, their neighbors and friends, who had met them as equals on all occasions. But now, if such an officer attempted to enforce the authority conferred by his rank, in the interest of better drill or discipline, he was at once charged by his late equals with "showing off his authority," "putting on airs," "feeling above his fellows"; and letters written home advertised him as a "miniature tyrant," etc., which made his position a very uncomfortable one to hold for a time. But this condition of affairs wore away soon after troops left the State, when the necessity for rigid discipline became apparent to every man. And when the private soldier saw that his captain was held responsible by the colonel for uncleanly quarters or arms, or unsoldierly and ill disciplined men, the colonel in turn being held to accountability by *his* next superior, the growls grew less frequent or were aimed at the government rather than the captain, and the growlers began to settle down and accept the inevitable, taking lessons in something new every day.

It will be readily seen, I think, that the men composing the earliest regiments and batteries had also their trials to endure, and they were many; for not only they but their superiors were learning by rough experience the art of war. They were, in a sense, "achieving greatness," while the recruits had "greatness thrust upon them," often at short notice. Furthermore, recruits from the latter part of 1862 forward went out with a knowledge of much which they must undergo in the line of hardship and privation, which the first rallies had to learn by actual experience. And while it may be said that it took more courage for men to go with the stern facts of actual war confronting them than when its realities were unknown to them, yet it is also true that many of these later enlistments were made under the advantage of pecuniary and other inducements, without which many would not have been made. For patriotism unstimulated by hope of reward saw high-water mark in 1861, and rapidly receded in succeeding years, so that whereas men enlisted in 1861 and early in '62 because they wanted to go, and without hope of reward, later in '62 towns and individuals began to offer bounties to stimulate lagging enlistments, varying in amount from $10 to $300; and increased in '63 and '64 until, by the addition of State bounties, a recruit, enlisting for a year, received in the fall of '64 from $700 to $1000 in some instances. It was this large bounty which led old veterans to haze recruits in many ways. Of course, there was no justification for their doing it, only as the recruits in some instances provoked it.

There was a song composed during the war, entitled the "Raw Recruit," sung to the tune of "Abraham's Daughter," which I am wholly unable to recall, but a snatch of the first verse, or its parody, ran about as follows: —

DRAFTED.

I'm a raw recruit, with a bran'-new suit,
  Nine hundred dollars bounty,
And I've come down from Darbytown
  To fight for Oxford County.

The name of the town and county were varied to suit the circumstances.

In 1863 a draft was ordered to fill the ranks of the army, as volunteers did not come forward rapidly enough to meet the exigencies of the service. Men of means, if drafted, hired a substitute, as allowed by law, to go in their stead, when patriotism failed to set them in motion. Many of these substitutes did good service, while others became deserters immediately after enlisting. Conscription was never more unpopular than when enforced upon American citizens at this time.

Here is a suggestive extract from a rhyme of that period, entitled

THE SUBSTITUTE.

A friend stepped up to me one day;
These are the words that he did say:
" A thousand dollars to you I'll owe,
If in my place to war you'll go."
" A thousand dollars ?   Done! " says I ;
" 'Twill help to keep my family."
I soon was clothed in a soldier's suit,
And off to war as a substitute.

To a conscript camp first I was sent
And to the barracks my steps I bent.
I saw many there who wore blue suits,
And learned they were all substitutes.
Then orders came for us to go,
Way down where blood like rivers flow.
When the soldiers saw me, they yelled, " Recruit!
Why did you come as a substitute ? "

CHAPTER XI.

SPECIAL RATIONS. — BOXES FROM HOME. — SUTLERS.

> Can we all forget the bills on Sutler's ledger haply yet,
> Which we feared he would remember, and we hoped he would forget?
> May we not recall the morning when the foe were threatening harm,
> And the trouble chiefly bruited was, "The coffee isn't warm"?
>
> PROF. S. B. SUMNER.

IF there was a red-letter day to be found anywhere in the army life of a soldier, it occurred when he was the recipient of a box sent to him by the dear ones and friends he left to enter the service. Whenever it became clear, or even tolerably clear, that the army was likely to make pause in one place for at least two or three weeks, straightway the average soldier mailed a letter home to mother, father, wife, sister, or brother, setting forth in careful detail what he should like to have sent in a box at the earliest possible moment, and stating with great precision the address that must be put on the cover, in order to have it reach its destination safely. Here is a specimen address: —

Sergeant JOHN J. SMITH,
Company A., 19th Mass. Regiment,
SECOND BRIGADE, SECOND DIVISION, SECOND CORPS,
ARMY OF THE POTOMAC,
STEVENSBURG, VA.
Care Capt. James Brown.

As a matter of fact much of this address was unnecessary, and the box would have arrived just as soon and safely if the address had only included the name, company, and regiment, with *Washington, D. C.,* added, for everything was forwarded from that city to army headquarters, and thence distributed through the army. But the average soldier wanted to make a sure thing of it, and so told the whole story.

The boxes sent were usually of good size, often either a shoe-case or a common soap-box, and were rarely if ever less than a peck in capacity. As to the contents, I find on the back of an old envelope a partial list of such articles ordered at some period in the service. I give them as they stand, to wit: "Round-headed nails" (for the heels of boots), "hatchet" (to cut kindlings, tent-poles, etc.), "pudding, turkey, pickles, onions, pepper, paper, envelopes, stockings, potatoes, chocolate, condensed milk, sugar, broma, butter, sauce, preservative" (for the boots). The *quantity* of the articles to be sent was left to the discretion of thoughtful and affectionate parents.

In addition to the above, such a list was likely to contain an order for woollen shirts, towels, a pair of boots made to order, some needles, thread, buttons, and yarn, in the line of dry goods, and a boiled ham, tea, cheese, cake, preserve, etc., for edibles. As would naturally be expected, articles for the repair and solace of the inner man received most consideration in making out such a list.

How often the wise calculations of the soldier were rudely dashed to earth by the army being ordered to move before the time when the box should arrive! And how his mouth watered as he read over the invoice, which had already reached him by mail, describing with great minuteness of detail all the delicacies he had ordered, and many more that kind and loving hearts and thoughtful minds had put in. For the neighborhood generally was interested when it became known that a box was making up to send to a soldier, and each one must contribute some token of kindly remembrance, for the enjoyment of the far-away boy in blue. But the thought that some of these good things might spoil before the army would again come to a standstill came upon the veteran now and then with crushing force. Still, he must needs endure, and take the situation as coolly as possible.

It was a little annoying to have every box opened and inspected at brigade or regimental headquarters, to assure that no intoxicating liquors were smuggled into camp in that way, especially if one was not addicted to their use. There was many a growl uttered by men who had lost their little pint or quart bottle of some choice stimulating beverage, which had been confiscated from a box as "contraband of war," although the sender had marked it with an innocent name, in the hope of passing it through unsuspected and uninspected. Yet the inspectors were often baffled. A favorite ruse was to have the bottle introduced into a well roasted turkey, a place that no one would for a moment suspect of containing such unique stuffing. In such a case the bottle was introduced into the bird empty, and filled after the cooking was completed, the utmost care being taken to cover up all marks of its presence. Some would conceal it in a tin can of small cakes; others inserted it in a loaf of cake, through a hole cut in the bottom. One member of my company had some whiskey sent for his enjoyment, sealed up in a tin can; but when the box was nailed up a nail was driven into the can, so that the owner found only an empty can and a generally diffused odor of "departed spirits" pervading the entire contents of food and raiment which the box contained.

It was really vexing to have one's knick-knacks and dainties overhauled by strangers under *any* circumstances, and all the more so when the box contained no proscribed commodity. Besides, the boxes were so nicely packed that it was next to impossible for the inspector to return all the contents, having once removed them; and he often made more or less of a jumble in attempting to do so. I think I must have had as many boxes sent as the average among the soldiers, and simple justice to those who had the handling of them requires me to state that I never missed a single article from them, and, barring the breakage of two or three bottles, which may or may not have been the fault of the opener, the contents were always undamaged. Sometimes the boxes were sent directly from brigade headquar-

A WAGON-LOAD OF BOXES.

ters to the headquarters of each company without inspection, and there only those were opened whose owners were known to imbibe freely on occasion.

The boxes came, when they came at all, by wagon-loads — mule teams of the company going after them. I have already intimated that none were sent to the army when it was on the move or when a campaign was imminent; and as these moves were generally foreshadowed with tolerable accuracy, the men were likely to send their orders home at about the same time, and so they would receive their boxes together. In this way it happened that they came to camp by wagon-loads, and a happier, lighter-hearted body of men than those who were gathered around the wagons could not have been found in the service. I mean now those who were the fortunate recipients of a box, for there was always a second party on hand who did not expect a box, but who were on the spot to offer congratulations to the lucky ones; perhaps these would receive an invitation to quarters to see the box unpacked. This may seem a very tantalizing invitation for them to accept; but, nevertheless, next to being the owner of the prize, it was most entertaining to observe what some one else was to enjoy.

I think the art of box-packing must have culminated during the war. It was simply wonderful, delightfully so, to see how each little corner and crevice was utilized. Not stuffed with paper by those who understood their business, thus wasting space, but filled with a potato, an apple, an onion, a pinch of dried apples, a handful of peanuts, or some other edible substance. These and other articles filled the crannies between carefully wrapped glass jars or bottles of toothsome preserves, or boxes of butter, or cans of condensed milk or well roasted chickens, and the turkey that each box was wont to contain. If there was a new pair of boots among the contents, the feet were filled with little notions of convenience. Then, there was likely to be, amid all the other merchandise already specified, a roll of bandages and lint, for the much-feared but unhoped-for contingency of battle. It added greatly to the pleasures of the investigator to come now and then upon a nicely wrapped package, labelled " From Mary," " From Cousin John," and perhaps a dozen other relatives, neighbors, school-mates or shop-mates, most of which contributions were delicious surprises, and many of them accompanied by notes of personal regard and good-wishes.

There were some men in every company who had no one at home to remember them in this tender and appreciative manner, and as they sat or stood by the hero of a box and saw one article after another taken out and unwrapped, each speaking so eloquently of the loving care and thoughtful remembrance of kindred or friends, they were moved by

mingled feelings of pleasure and sadness : pleasure at their
comrade's good-fortune and downright enjoyment of his
treasure, and sadness at their own lonely condition, with
no one to remember them in this pleasant manner, and often
would their eyes fill with tears by the contrast of their own
situation with the pleasant scene before them. But these
men were generally remembered by a liberal donation whenever a box came to camp.

Still, there were selfish men in every company, and, if
they were selfish by nature, the war, I think, had a tendency
to make them more so. Such men would keep their precious box and its precious contents away from sight, smell,
and taste of all outsiders. It was a little world to them,
and all their own. "Send for a box yourself, if you want
one," appeared in their every look, and often found expression in words. As a boy I have seen a school-mate munch-
ing an apple before now with two or three of his less favored
acquaintances wistfully watching and begging for the core.
But the men of whom I speak never had any core to their
apples ; they absorbed everything that was sent them.

I knew one man who, I think, came uncomfortably near
belonging to this class of soldiers. The first box he ever
received contained, among other delicacies, about a peck of
raw onions. Before these onions had been reached in this
man's consumption of the contents of his box a move was
ordered. What was to be done ? It was one of the trying
moments of his life. Nineteen out of every twenty men, if
not ninety-nine out of every hundred, would at this eleventh
hour have set them outside of the tent and said, "Here they
are, boys. Take hold and help yourselves !" But not he.
He was the hundredth man, the exception. So, packing
them up with some old clothes, he at once expressed them
back to his home. But, as I have intimated, such men
were few in number, and, while war made this class more
selfish, yet its community of hardship and danger and suffering developed sympathy and large-hearted generosity among

the rank and file generally, and they shared freely with their less fortunate but worthy comrades.

Nothing, to my mind, better illustrates the fraternity developed in the army than the following poem, composed by Private Miles O'Reilly:—

WE'VE DRANK FROM THE SAME CANTEEN.

There are bonds of all sorts in this world of ours,
Fetters of friendship and ties of flowers,
    And true lover's knots, I ween.
The girl and the boy are bound by a kiss,
But there's never a bond, old friend, like this —
    We have drank from the same canteen.

WE DRANK FROM THE SAME CANTEEN.

It was sometimes water, and sometimes milk,
And sometimes apple-jack fine as silk.
    But, whatever the tipple has been,
We shared it together, in bane or bliss,
And I warm to you friend, when I think of this·
    We have drank from the same canteen.

The rich and the great sit down to dine,
And they quaff to each other in sparkling wine,
    From glasses of crystal and green.

But I guess in their golden potations they miss
The warmth of regard to be found in this —
    We have drank from the same canteen.

We have shared our blankets and tents together,
And have marched and fought in all kinds of weather,
    And hungry and full we have been;
Had days of battle and days of rest;
But this memory I cling to, and love the best —
    We have drank from the same canteen.

For when wounded I lay on the outer slope,
With my blood flowing fast, and but little to hope
    Upon which my faint spirit could lean,
Oh, then I remember you crawled to my side,
And, bleeding so fast it seemed both must have died,
    We drank from the same canteen.

But I will now leave this — to me deeply interesting theme — and introduce

THE ARMY SUTLER.

This personage played a very important part as *quartermaster extraordinary* to the soldiers. He was not an enlisted man, only a civilian. By Army Regulations sutlers could be appointed "at the rate of one for every regiment, corps, or separate detachment, by the commanding officer of such regiment, corps, or detachment," subject to the approval of higher authority. These persons made a business of sutling, or supplying food and a various collection of other articles to the troops. Each regiment was supplied with one of these traders, who pitched his hospital tent near camp, and displayed his wares in a manner most enticing to the needs of the soldier. The sutler was of necessity both a dry-goods dealer and a grocer, and kept, besides, such other articles as were likely to be called for in the service. He made his chief reliance, however, a stock of goods that answered the demands of the stomach. He had a line of canned goods which he sold mostly for use in officers' messes. The canning of meats, fruits, and vegetables was then in its infancy, and the prices, which in time of peace were high, by the demands of war were so inflated that the highest of high privates could not aspire to sample them unless he was the child of wealthy parents who kept him supplied with a stock of scrip or greenbacks. It can readily be seen that his thirteen

A SUTLER'S TENT. FROM A WAR-TIME PHOTOGRAPH.

dollars a month (or even sixteen dollars, to which the pay was advanced June 20, 1864, through the efforts of Henry Wilson, who strove hard to make it twenty-one dollars) would not hold out a great while to patronize an army sutler, and hundreds of the soldiers when the paymaster came round had the pleasure of signing away the entire amount due them, whether two, three, or four months' pay, to settle claims of the sutler upon them. Here are a few of his prices as I remember them : —

Butter (warranted to be rancid), one dollar a pound; cheese, fifty cents a pound; condensed milk, seventy-five cents a can; navy tobacco, of the blackest sort, one dollar and a quarter a plug. Other than the milk I do not remember any of the prices of canned goods. The investment that seemed to pay the largest dividend to the purchaser was the *molasses cakes* or *cookies* which the sutlers vended at the rate of six for a quarter. They made a pleasant and not too rich or expensive dessert when hardtack got to be a burden. Then, one could buy sugar or molasses or flour of them, though at a higher price than the commissary charged for the same articles.

The commissary, I think I have explained, was an officer in charge of government rations. From him quartermasters obtained their supplies for the rank and file, on a written requisition given by the commander of a regiment or battery. He also sold supplies for officers' messes at cost price, and also to members of the rank and file, if they presented an order signed by a commissioned officer.

Towards the end of the war sutlers kept self-raising flour, which they sold in packages of a few pounds. This the men bought quite generally to make into fritters or pancakes. It would have pleased the celebrated four thousand dollar cook at the Parker House, in Boston, could he have seen the men cook these fritters. The mixing was a simple matter, as water was the only addition which the flour required, but the fun was in the turning. A little experience enabled a man to turn them without the aid of a knife, by first giving the fry-pan a little toss upward and forward. This threw the cake out and over, to be caught again the uncooked side down — all in a half-second. But the miscalculations and mishaps experienced in performing this piece of culinary detail were numerous and amusing, many a cake being dropped into the fire, or taken by a sudden puff of wind, just as it got edgewise in the air, and whisked into the dirt.

COOKING PANCAKES.

Then, the sutler's pies! Who can forget them? "Moist
and indigestible below, tough and indestructible above,
with untold horrors within." The most mysterious products that he kept, I have yet to see the soldier who can
furnish a correct analysis of what they were made from.
Fortunately for the dealer, it mattered very little as to that,
for the soldiers were used to mystery in all its forms, and
the pies went down by hundreds; price, twenty-five cents
each. Not very high, it is true, compared with other edibles, but they were small and thin, though for the matter of
thickness several times the amount of such stuffing could
have added but little to the cost.

I have said that these army merchants were dry-goods
dealers. The only articles which would come under this
head, that I now remember of seeing, were army regulation hats, cavalry boots, flannels, socks, and suspenders.
They were not allowed to keep liquors, and any one of them
found guilty of this act straightway lost his permit to suttle
for the troops, if nothing worse happened him.

I am of the opinion that the sutlers did not always receive
the consideration that they deserved. Owing to the high
prices which they asked the soldiers for their goods, the
belief found ready currency that they were little better than
extortioners; and I think that the name "sutler" to-day
calls up in the minds of the old soldiers a man who would
not enlist and shoulder his musket, but who was better satisfied to take his pack of goods and get his living out of the
soldiers who were doing his fighting for him. But there is
something to be said on the other side. In the first place,
he filled a need recognized, long before the Rebellion, by
Army Regulations. Such a personage was considered a
convenience if not a necessity at military posts and in campaigns, and certain privileges were accorded him.

In the second place, no soldier was compelled to patronize
him, and yet I question whether there was a man in the
service any great length of time, within easy reach of one

of these traders, who did not patronize him more or less. In the third place, when one carefully considers the expense of transporting his goods to the army, the wastage of the same from exposure to the weather, the cost of frequent removals, and the risk he carried of losing his stock

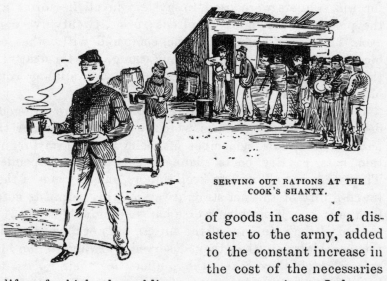

SERVING OUT RATIONS AT THE
COOK'S SHANTY.

of goods in case of a disaster to the army, added to the constant increase in the cost of the necessaries of life, of which the soldiers were not cognizant, I do not believe that sutlers as a class can be justly accused of overcharging. I have seen one of these merchants since the war, who seemed seized with the fullest appreciation of the worth of his own services to the country, and, with an innocent earnestness most refreshing, applied for membership in the Grand Army of the Republic, into which only men who have an honorable discharge from the government are admitted.

There undoubtedly were Shylocks among them, and they often had a hard time of it; and this leads me to speak of another risk that sutlers had to assume — the risk of being raided — or "cleaned out," to quote the language of the expressive army slang. This meant the secret organization of a party of men in a regiment to fall upon a sutler in the darkness of night, throw down his tent, help themselves liberally to whatever they wanted, and then get back speedily and quietly to quarters. It did not do to carry stolen goods to the tents, for the next day was likely to see a detachment of men, accompanied by the sutler, searching the quarters for the missing property. Sometimes this raiding was done in a spirit of mischief, by unprincipled men, sometimes to get satisfaction for what they considered his exorbitant charges. Sometimes the officers of a regiment sympathized in such a movement, if they thought the sutler's exactions deserved a rebuke. When this was the case, it was no easy task to find the criminals, for the officers were very blind and stupid, or, if the culprits were detected, they were quietly reminded that if they were foolish enough to get caught they must suffer the penalty. But sutlers, like other people, profited by the teachings of experience, and, if they had faults, soon mended them, so that late in the war they rarely found it necessary to beg deliverance from their friends.

The following incident came under my own knowledge in the winter of '64, while the Artillery Brigade of the Third Corps lay encamped in the edge of a pine woods near Brandy Station, Virginia. Just in rear of the Tenth Battery camp, near company headquarters, the brigade sutler had erected his tent, and every wagon-load of his supplies passed through this camp under the eyes of any one who cared to take note. A load of this description was thus inspected on a particular occasion, and while the wagon was standing in front of the tent waiting to be unloaded, and without special guarding, an always thirsty veteran stole up to it, seized upon a case of whiskey, said to have been destined for a battery commander, and was off in a jiffy. Less than three minutes elapsed before the case was missed. At once the captain of the company was notified, who immediately gave his instructions to the officer of the day. The bugler blew the *Assembly*, summoning every man into line; and

every man had to be there or be otherwise strictly accounted
for by his sergeant. What it all meant no one apparently
knew. Meanwhile, two lieutenants and the orderly were
carrying on a thorough search of the men's quarters. When
it was completed, the orderly returned to the line, and the
company was dismissed, in a curious frame of mind as to
the cause of all the stir. This soon leaked out, as did also
the fact that no trace of the missing property had been discovered. All was again quiet along the Potomac, except
when the culprit and his coterie waxed a little noisy over
imbibitions of *ardent* mysteriously obtained, and not until
after the close of the war was the mystery made clear.

It seems that as soon as he had seized his prize he passed
swiftly down through the camp to the picket rope, where
the horses were tied, and there, *in a pile of manure thrown
up behind them*, quickly concealed the case, and, at the bugle
signal, was prompt to fall into line. Under cover of darkness, the same night, the plunder was taken from the manure-
heap and carried to a hill in front of the camp, where it was
buried in a manner which would not disclose it to the casual
traveller, and yet leave it easily accessible to its unlawful
possessor, and here he resorted periodically for a fresh supply, until it was exhausted.

I have quoted a few of the prices charged by sutlers.
Here are a few of the prices paid by people in Richmond,
during the latter part of the war, in Confederate money : —

Potatoes $80 a bushel; a chicken $50; shad $50 per pair;
beef $15 a pound; bacon $20 a pound; butter $20 a pound;
flour $1500 a barrel; meal $140 a bushel; beans $65 a
bushel; cow-peas $80 a bushel; hard wood $50 a cord;
green pine $80 a cord; and a dollar in gold was worth $100
in Confederate money.

CHAPTER XII.

FORAGING.

Can we all forget the foraging the boys were prone to do,
As with problematic rations we were marching Dixie through;
And the dulcet screech of chanticleer or soothing squeal of swine,
When occurred the grateful halt or brief excursion from the line?
PROF. S. B. SUMNER.

THERE was one other source from which soldiers — at least, some soldiers — replenished their larder, or added to its variety. The means employed to accomplish this end was known as *Foraging*, which is generally understood to mean a seeking after food, whether for man or beast, and appropriating to one's own use whatsoever is found in this line, wheresoever it is found in an enemy's country. It took the army some time to adopt this mode of increasing its stores. This arose from the fact that early in the war many of the prominent government and military officers thought that a display of force with consideration shown the enemy's property would win the South back to her allegiance to the Union; but that if, on the other hand, they devastated property and appropriated personal effects, it would only embitter the enemy, unite them more solidly, and greatly prolong the war; so that for many months after war began, Northern troops were prohibited from seizing fence-rails, poultry, swine, straw, or any similar merchandise in which

231

they might under some circumstances feel a personal interest; and whenever straw-stacks and fences *were* appropriated by order of commanding officers, certificates to that effect were given the owners, who might expect at some time to be reimbursed. But the Rebellion waxed apace, and outgrew all possibility of certificating everybody whose property was entered upon or absorbed, and furthermore it came to be known that many who had received certificates were in collusion with the enemy, so that the issuance of these receipts gradually grew beautifully less.

Then, there was another obstacle in the way of a general adoption of foraging as an added means of support. It was the presence in the army of a large number of men who had learned the ten commandments, and could not, with their early training and education, look upon this taking to themselves the possessions of others without license as any different from stealing. These soldiers would neither forage nor share in the fruits of foraging. It can be readily imagined, then, that when one of this class commanded a regiment the diversion of foraging was not likely to be very general with his men. But as the war wore on, and it became more evident that such tender regard for Rebel property only strengthened the enemy and weakened the cause of the Union, conscientious scruples stepped to the rear, and the soldier who had them at the end of the war was a curiosity indeed.

There are some phases of this question of foraging which at this late day may be calmly considered, and the right and wrong of it carefully weighed. In the first place, international law declares that in a hostile section an army may save its rations and live off the country. To the large majority of the soldiers this would be sufficient warrant for them to appropriate from the enemy whatever they had a present liking for in the line of provisions. If all laws were based on absolute justice, the one quoted would settle the question finally, and leave nothing as an objection to forag-

ing.   But while the majority make the laws, the consciences
and convictions of the minority are not changed thereby.
Each man's conscience must be a final law unto himself.

It is well for it
to be so. I on-
ly enlarge upon
this for a mo-
ment to show
that on all moral
questions every
intelligent man
must in a meas-

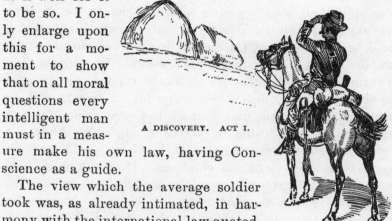

A DISCOVERY.   ACT I.

ure make his own law, having Conscience as a guide.

The view which the average soldier
took was, as already intimated, in harmony with the international law quoted.
This view was, in substance, that the
people of the South were in a state of rebellion against
the government, notwithstanding that they had been duly

ACT II.

warned to desist from war and return to their allegiance;
that they had therefore forfeited all claim to whatever
property the soldier chose to appropriate; that this was
one of the risks they assumed when they raised the banner of secession; that for this, and perhaps other reasons,

they should be treated just as a foreign nation waging war against the United States, all of which may seem plausible at first view, and indeed it may be said just here that if the soldiers had always despoiled the enemy to supply their own pressing personal needs, or if they had always taken or destroyed only those things which could be of service to the enemy in the prosecution of the war, the arguments against foraging would be considerably weakened; but the authority to forage carried with it also the exercise of the office of judge and jury, from whom there was no appeal. If the owner of a lot of corn or poultry was to protest against losing it, on the ground that he was a Unionist, unless the proof was at hand, he would lose his case — that is, his corn and chickens. However sincere he may have been, it was not possible for him to establish his Union sentiments at short notice. Indeed, so many who really were "secesh" claimed to be good Union men, it came latterly to be assumed that the victim was playing a false rôle on all such occasions, and so the soldiers went straight for the plunder, heeding no remonstrances. Without doubt, hundreds of Union men throughout the South suffered losses in this way, which, if their loyalty could have been clearly shown, they would have been spared.

A good deal of the foraging, while unauthorized and forbidden by commanding officers, was often connived at by them, and they were frequently sharers in the spoils; but I was about to say that it was not always of the most judicious kind. No one, better than the old soldiers, knows how destitute many, if not most, of the houses along the line of march were of provisions, clothing, and domestic animals, after the first few months of the war. I will amend that statement. There *was* one class who knew better than the soldiers, — the *tenants* of those houses knew that destitution better — sometimes feigned it, may be, but as a rule it was the ugly and distressing reality. I am dealing now with the Army of the Potomac, which travelled the same roads year after year, either before or behind the Rebel Army of Northern Virginia. In or near the routes of these bodies little was attempted by the people in the way of crop-raising, for their products were sure to feed one or the other of the two armies as they tramped up and down the state, so that destitution in some of the wayside cabins and farm-houses was often quite marked. No one with a heart less hard than flint could deprive such families of their last cow, shote, or ear of corn. Yet there were many unauthorized foragers who would not hesitate a moment to seize and carry off the last visible mouthful of food. So it has seemed to me that the cup of Rebellion was made unnecessarily bitter from the fact that such appeals too often fell on deaf ears. Granting it to be true that the Rebels had forfeited all right to whatever property their antagonists saw fit to appropriate, yet in the absence of those Rebels their families ought not to suffer want and distress; the innocent should not suffer for the guilty, and when nothing was known against them they should not have been deprived of their last morsel. But there were exceptions. There were some families who gave information to the Rebel army or detachments of it, by which fragments of ours were killed or captured, and when this was known the members of that family were likely sooner or later to suffer for it, as would naturally be expected.

Some of these families were so destitute that they were at times driven to appeal to the nearest army headquarters for rations to relieve their sufferings. To do this it was often necessary for them to walk many miles. Horses they had not. They could not keep them, for if the Union cavalry did not "borrow," the Rebel cavalry would impress them; so that they were not only without a beast of burden for farm work, but had none to use as a means of transportation. Now and then a sore-backed, emaciated, and generally used-up horse or mule, which had been abandoned and left in the track of the army to die, was taken charge of, when the coast was clear, and nursed back into vitality enough to stand on at least three of his legs, when, by means of bits of tattered rope, twisted corn-husks, and odds and ends of leather which had seen better days, the sorry-looking brute, still bearing the brand *U. S.* or *C. S.* on his rump, partly concealed perhaps by his rusty oufit, was tackled into a nondescript vehicle, possibly the skeleton remains of what had been, in years

GOING TO ARMY HEADQUARTERS.

gone by, the elegant and stylish family carriage, but fully as often into a two-wheeled cart, which now answered all the purposes of the family in its altered circumstances. One would hardly expect to find in such a brute a *Goldsmith Maid* or a *Jay Eye See* in locomotion, and so as a matter of fact such a beast was urged on from behind by lusty thwacks from a cudgel, propelling the family at a headlong *walk* — headlong, because he was likely to go headlong at any moment, from lack of strength, over the rough Virginia roads.

When such a brute got to be pretty lively once more, unless he was concealed, he would soon fall into service again in one of the armies, and possibly another gasping skeleton left in his place; but later in the war all animals abandoned by the Union army were shot if any life remained in them, so that even this resource was to that extent cut off from the inhabitants, and the family *cow*, while she was spared, was fitted out for such service.

But the soldiers did not always content themselves with taking eatables and forage. Destruction of the most wanton and inexcusable character was sometimes indulged in. It is charged upon them when the army entered Fredericksburg, in 1862, that they took especial delight in bayonetting mirrors, smashing piano-keys with musket-butts, pitching crockery out of windows, and destroying other such inoffensive material, which could be of no possible service to either party. If they had been imbibing commissary whiskey, they were all the more unreasonable and outrageous in their destruction. Whenever a man was detected in the enactment of such disgraceful and unsoldierly conduct, he was put under arrest, and sentenced by court-martial. But this class of men was an insignificantly small fraction of an army, although seeming very numerous to their victims.

A regularly authorized body of foragers, in charge of a commissioned officer, never gave way to excesses like those I have mentioned. Their task was usually well defined. It was to go out with wagons in quest of the contents of smoke-houses or barns or corn-barns ; and if a flock of fowls or a few swine chanced to be a part of the live-stock of the farms visited, the worse for the live-stock and Secessia, and the better for the Union army. The usual plunder secured by regular foraging parties was hams, bacon sides, flour, sweet potatoes, corn-meal, corn on the cob, and sometimes corn-shooks as they were called, that is, corn-leaves stripped from the stalks, dried and bundled, for winter fodder. The neat cattle in the South get the most of their living in the winter by browsing, there being but little hay cured.

In traversing fresh territory, the army came upon extensive quantities of corn in corn-ricks. At Wilcox's Landing, on the James River, where we crossed in June, 1864, the

Rebel Wilcox, who had a splendid farm on the left bank
of the river, had hundreds of bushels of corn, I should
judge, which the forage trains took aboard before they
crossed over; and on the south side of the James, east from
Petersburg, where Northern troops had never before pene-

A CORN-BARN AND HAY-RICK.

trated, many such stores of corn were appropriated to feed
the thousands of loyal quadrupeds belonging to Uncle Sam.

In this section, too, and in the territory stretching from
the Wilderness to Cold Harbor, immense quantities of tobacco were found in the various stages of curing. The
drying-houses were full of it. These houses were rude
structures, having water-tight roofs, but with walls built of
small logs placed two or three inches apart, to admit a free
circulation of air. On poles running across the interior
hung the stalks of tobacco, root upwards. Then, in other
buildings were hogsheads pressed full of the "weed," in
another stage of the curing. It is well known that Petersburg is the centre of a very extensive tobacco-trade, and in
that city are large tobacco-factories. But the war put a
summary end to this business for the time, by closing northern markets and blockading southern ports, so that this
article of foreign and domestic commerce accumulated in the
hands of the producers to the very great extent found by
the army when it appeared in that vicinity. Every soldier

who had a liking for tobacco helped himself as freely as he pleased, with no one caring to stay his hand. But I believe that the experts in smoking and chew- ing preferred the black navy plug of the sutler, at a dol- lar and a quarter, to this unprepared but purer article to be had by the taking.

TOBACCO-DRYING HOUSES.

While the army lay at Warrenton Sulphur Springs, after Gettysburg in '63, a detail of men was made from my company daily to take scythes from the "Battery Wagon," and, with a six-mule team, go off and mow a load of grass wherever they could find it within our lines, to eke out the government forage. The same programme was enacted by other batteries in the corps.

As Sherman's Bummers achieved a notoriety as foragers *par excellence*, some facts regarding them will be of interest in this connection. Paragraphs 4 and 6 of Sherman's *Spe- cial Field Orders* 120, dated Nov. 9, 1864, just before start- ing for Savannah, read as follows : —

"4. The army will forage liberally on the country during the march. To this end each brigade commander will organ- ize a good and sufficient foraging party under the command of one or more discreet officers, who will gather, near the route travelled, corn or forage of any kind, meat of any kind, vegetables, corn-meal or whatever is needed by the command, aiming at all times to keep in the wagons at least ten days' provisions for his command, and three days' forage. Soldiers must not enter the dwellings of the inhab- itants or commit any trespass; but during a halt or camp they may be permitted to gather turnips, potatoes, and other vegetables, and to drive in stock in sight of their camp. To regular foraging parties must be intrusted the gathering of provisions and forage at any distance from the road travelled."

"6. As for horses, mules, wagons, etc., belonging to the inhabitants, the cavalry and artillery may appropriate freely and without limit; discriminating, however, between the rich, who are usually hostile, and the poor and industrious, usually neutral or friendly. Foraging parties may also take mules or horses, to replace the jaded animals of their trains or to serve as pack-mules, for the regiments or brigades. In all foraging of whatever kind, the parties engaged will refrain from abusive or threatening language, and may, where the officer in command thinks proper, give written certificates of the facts, but no receipts; and they will endeavor to leave with each family a reasonable portion for their maintenance."

As Sherman was among the commanders who believed most heartily in having those who provoked the conflict suffer the full measure of their crime, the above instructions seem certainly very mild and humane. On page 182, Vol. II., of his Memoirs, and also on pages 207–8, in a letter to Grant, describing the march, he presents a summary of the working of the plan. His brigade foraging parties, usually comprising about fifty men, would set out before daylight, knowing the line of march for the day, and, proceeding on foot five or six miles from the column, visit every farm and plantation in range. Their plunder consisted of bacon, meal, turkeys, ducks, chickens, and whatever else was eatable for man or beast. These they would load into the farm-wagon or family carriage, and rejoin the column, turning over their burden to the brigade commissary. "Often," says Sherman, "would I pass these foraging parties at the roadside, waiting for their wagons to come up, and was amused at their strange collections — mules, horses, even cattle packed with old saddles, and loaded with hams, bacon, bags of corn-meal, and poultry of every description. . . .

No doubt, many acts of pillage, robbery, and violence were committed by these foragers, usually called 'bummers'; for I have since heard of jewelry taken from women, and the plunder of articles that never reached the commissary; but these acts were exceptional and incidental." Sherman further states that his army started with about five thousand head of cattle and arrived at the sea with about ten thousand, and that the State of Georgia must have lost by his operations fifteen thousand first-rate mules. As to horses, he says that every one of the foraging party of fifty who set out daily on foot invariably returned mounted, accompanying the various wagon-loads of provisions and forage seized, and, as there were forty brigades, an approximation to the number of horses taken can be made.

But this travelling picnic of the Western armies was unique. There is nothing like it elsewhere in the history of the war. Certainly, the Army of the Potomac could not present anything to compare with it. As a matter of fact, there was no other movement in the war whose nature justified such a season of riotous living as this one. But it illustrates in a *wholesale* way the kind of business other armies did on a *retail* scale.

There was no arm of the service that presented such favorable opportunities for foraging as did the cavalry, and none, I may add, which took so great an advantage of its opportunity. In the first place, being the eyes and the ears of the army, and usually going in advance, cavalrymen skimmed the cream off the country when a general movement was making. Then when it was settled down in camp they were the outposts and never let anything in the line of poultry, bee-hives, milk-houses, and apple-jack, not to enumerate other delicacies which outlying farm-houses afforded, escape the most rigid inspection. Again, they were frequently engaged in raids through the country, from the nature of which they were compelled to live in large measure off southern products, seized as they went along;

but infantry and artillery must needs confine *their* quests
for special rations to the homesteads near the line of
march. The cavalry not only could and did search these
when they led the advance, but also made requisitions on all
houses in sight of the thoroughfares travelled, even when
they were two or three miles away, so that, in all probability,
they ate a smaller quantity of government rations, man for
man, than did any other branch of the land-service; but
they did not therefore always fare sumptuously, for now
and then the cavalry too were in a strait for rations.

Next to the cavalry, the infantry stood the best chance of
good living on foraged edibles, as their picket-duty took
them away some distance from the main lines and often into
the neighborhood of farm-houses, from which they would
buy or take such additions to their rations as the premises
afforded. Then, they went out in reconnoitring parties, or,
perhaps, to do fatigue duty, such as the building of bridges,
or the corduroying of roads, which also opened opportunities for them to enlist a few turkeys or chickens in the
Union cause.

Perhaps the most unfortunate natives were those who
chanced to live in a house by the roadside in the direct line
of march of the army, for, from the time the head of the
column struck such a house until the last straggler left it,
there was a continuous stream of officers and men thronging
into and about the premises, all ambitious to buy or beg or
take whatsoever in the line of eatables and drinkables
was to be had by either of these methods. The net result
of this was to leave such families in a starving condition,
and finally begging rations from the army. Those families
by whose premises *both* armies marched were in the depths
of distress, for Confederate soldiers let little in the way of
provisions escape their maws on their line of march, even in
Virginia; so that it was not unusual for such families to
meet the Union advance with tearful eyes, and relate the
losses which they had sustained and the beggary to which

they had been reduced by the seizure of their last cow and last ounce of corn-meal. Sometimes, no doubt, they deceived to ward off impending search and seizure from a new quarter, but as a rule the premises showed their statements to be true.

Sometimes the inhabitants were shrewd and watchful enough to scent danger and secrete the articles most precious to them till the danger was past; but not infrequently they were a little tardy in adopting such a measure, and were overhauled just before they had reached cover, and

SCENE AT A WAYSIDE FARM-HOUSE.

despoiled of the whole or a part of their treasure. The corn-fields of these roadside residents were the saddest of spectacles after the army had passed along in the early fall, for no native-born Southron had a finer appreciation of the excellent qualities of "roasting ears" than the average Yankee soldier, who left no stalk unstripped of its burden. Even the stalks themselves were used, to regale the appetites of the horses and mules.

Volumes might be filled with incidents of foraging. I will relate one or two that came under my own personal observation.

The people of Maryland undoubtedly enjoyed greater exemption from foragers, as a whole, than did those of Virginia, for a larger number of the former than of the latter were supposed to be loyal and were therefore protected. I say *supposed*, for personally I am of the opinion that the Virginians were fully as loyal as the Marylanders. But a large number of the soldiers when fresh and new in the service saw an enemy in every bush, and recognized no white man south of Mason and Dixon's line as other than a "secesh." Very often they were right, but the point I wish to make is that they indulged in foraging to a greater extent probably than troops which had been longer in service. Before my own company had seen any hard service it was located at Poolesville, thirty-eight miles from Washington, where it formed part of an independent brigade, which was included in the defences of Washington, and under the command of General Heintzelman. While we lay there drilling, growling, and feeding on government rations, a sergeant of the guard imperilled his chevrons by leading off a midnight foraging party, after having first communicated the general countersign to the entire party. On this particular occasion a flock of sheep was the object of the expedition. These sheep had been looked upon with longing eyes many times by the men as they rode their horses to water by their pasture, which was, perhaps, half a mile or more from camp.

As soon as the foragers came upon them in the darkness, the sheep cantered away, and their adversaries, who could only see them when near to them, followed in full pursuit. As the chase up and down the enclosure, which was not a very large one, waxed warm, one of the party, more noted for his zeal than his discretion, drew a revolver and emptied nearly every barrel among the flock, doing no bodily injury to the sheep, however, but he *did* succeed in calling down upon his head the imprecations of the sergeant, for his lack of good-sense, and with reason, for in a few minutes the fire of the outer pickets was drawn. This being heard and reported in camp, the long-roll was sounded, calling into line the two regiments of infantry that lay near us, and causing every preparation to be made to resist the supposed attack. The foragers, meanwhile, skulked back to camp by the shortest route, bringing with them two sheep that had been run down by some of the fleeter of the party. But no one save an interested few, inside or outside of the company, ever knew, until the story was told at a reunion of the company in '79 or '80, the cause of all the tumult in camp that dark winter's night.

On another occasion a party of five or six men stole out of camp at midnight, in quest of poultry. They knew of a farm-house where poultry was kept, but to ascertain its exact whereabouts at night was no easy task. On looking around the premises they found that there was no isolated out-building, whereupon they at once decided that the ell to the main house must be the place which contained the "biddies"; but to enter that might rouse the farmer and his family, which they did not care to do. However, a council of war decided to take the risk, and storm the place. Investigation showed the door to be padlocked, but a piece of iron which lay conveniently near, on a window-sill, served to pull out the staple, and the door was open. Meanwhile, guards had been posted at the corners of the house, with drawn revolvers (which they would not have dared to fire), and the captures began. One man entered the ell, and, lighting a match, discovered that he had called at the right house, and that the feathered family were at home. Among them he caught a glimpse of two turkeys, and these, with four fowls taken one at a time by the neck, to control their noise, were passed to another man standing at the door with a pen-knife, who, having performed a successful surgical operation on each, gave them to a third party to put in a bag.

Back of our camp stood the house of a secessionist, — at least, "Black Mary," his colored servant, said he was one, — and in his kitchen and cook-stove, for the sum of twenty-five cents in scrip, having previously dressed and stuffed them, Mary cooked the turkeys most royally, and one commissioned officer of our company, at least, sat down to one of the feasts, blissfully ignorant, of course, as to the source from which the special ration was drawn.

Bee-hives were among the most popular products of foraging. The soldiers tramped many a mile by night in quest of these depositories of sweets. I recall an incident oc-

NO JOKE.

curring in the Tenth Vermont Regiment — once brigaded with my company — when some of the foragers, who had been out on a tramp, brought a hive of bees into camp, after the men had wrapped themselves in their blankets, and, by way of a joke, set it down stealthily on the stomach of the captain of one of the companies, making business quite lively in that neighborhood shortly afterwards.

Foragers took other risks than that of punishment for absence from camp or the column without leave. They were not infrequently murdered on these expeditions. On the 7th of December, 1864, Warren's Fifth Corps was started southward from Petersburg, to destroy the Weldon Railroad still further. On their return, they found some of their men, who had straggled and foraged, lying by the roadside murdered, their bodies stark naked and shockingly mutilated. One of Sherman's men recently related how in the Carolinas one of his comrades was found hanged on a tree, bearing this inscription, "Death to all foragers." A large number of men were made prisoners while away from their commands after the usual fruits of foraging — just how many, no one will ever know; and many of those not killed on the spot by their captors ended their lives in the prison-pens.

During the expedition of the Fifth Corps alluded to, while the column had halted at some point in its march, a few uneasy spirits, wishing for something eatable to turn up, had made off down a hill, ahead of the column, had crossed a stream, and reached the vicinity of a house on the high ground the other side. Here a keen-scented cavalryman from the party had started up two turkeys, which, as the pursuit grew close, flew up on to the top of the smoke-house, whence, followed by their relentless pursuer, they went

THE TURKEY HE DIDN'T CATCH.

still higher, to the ridge-pole of the main house adjoining. Still up and forward pressed the trooper, his "soul in arms and eager for the fray," and as the turkeys with fluttering wings edged away, the hungry veteran, now astride the ridge-pole, hopped along after, when *ping!* a bullet whistled by uncomfortably near him.

"What in thunder are you about!" blurted the cavalry-man, suspecting his comrades of attempting to shoot off his quarry in the moment of victory.

Receiving no satisfactory response from his innocent companions, who had stood interested spectators of his exploit, yet unconscious of what he was exclaiming at, he once more addressed himself to the pursuit when, chuck! a bullet struck a shingle by his leg and threw the splinters in his face. There was no mistaking the mark or the marksman this time, and our trooper suddenly lost all relish for turkey, and, standing not on the order of his going, came sliding and tumbling down off the roof, striking the ground with too much emphasis and a great deal of feeling, where, joined by his comrades, who by this time had taken in the situation, he beat a hasty retreat, followed by the jeers of the Johnnies, and rejoined the column.

A veteran of the Seventh New Hampshire tells of one Charley Swain, who was not only an excellent duty soldier,

A DILEMMA.

but a champion forager. While this regiment lay at St. Augustine, Fla., in 1863, Swain started out on one of his quests for game, and, although it had grown rather scarce, at last found two small pigs penned up in the suburbs of the town. His resolve was immediately made to take them into camp. Securing a barrel, he laid it down, open at one end, in a corner of the pen, and without commotion soon had both grunters inside the barrel, and the barrel standing on end. By hard tugging he lifted it clear of the pen, and, taking it on his back, started rapidly for camp. But his passengers were not long reconciled to such quick and close transit, for he had not proceeded far before grunts developed into squeals, squeals into internal dissensions, to which the bottom of the barrel at last succumbed, and a brace of pigs were coursing at liberty. Here was a poser for the spoilsman. If he caught them again, how should he carry them? While he was attempting to solve this problem the cavalry patrol hove in sight, and Swain made for camp, where, crestfallen and chagrined, he related how he had left to the greedy maws of the provost-guard the quarry which he had hoped to share with his mess that night.

In considering this question of foraging, it has not been my purpose to put the soldiers of the Union armies in an unfair or unfavorable position as compared with their opponents. It has been claimed that Southerners on northern soil were more vindictive and wanton than Northerners on southern soil; and the reason on which this statement is based is that the South hated the Yankees, but the North hated only slavery. Nor is it my intention to charge atrocities upon the best men of either army. They were committed by the few. And I do not wish to be understood as declaring foraging a black and atrocious act, for, as I have shown, it had a legal warrant. I only claim that when the order once goes forth it leads to excesses, which it is difficult to control, and such excesses are likely to seriously affect the unoffending, defenceless women and children with woes out of all proportion with their simple part in bringing on the strife. But so it always has been, and so it probably always will be, till wars and rumors of wars shall cease.

CHAPTER XIII.

CORPS AND CORPS BADGES.

"You'll find lovely fighting
Along the whole line."

KEARNY.

HAT was an army corps? The name is one adopted into the English language from the French, and retains essentially its original meaning. It has been customary since the time of Napoleon I. to organize armies of more than fifty or sixty thousand men into what the French call *corps d'armée* or, as we say, army corps.

It is a familiar fact that soon after the outbreak of the Rebellion Lieutenant-General Scott, who had served with great distinction in the Mexican War, found himself too old and infirm to conduct an active campaign, and so the command of the troops, that were rapidly concentrating in and around Washington, was devolved upon the late General Irvin McDowell, a good soldier withal, but, like every other officer then in the service, without extended war experience. His first work, after assuming command, would naturally have been to organize the green troops into masses that would be more cohesive and effective in action than single undisciplined regiments could be. But this he was not allowed to do. The loyal people of the North were clamoring for something else to be done, and that speedily. The Rebels must be punished for their treason without delay, and President Lincoln was beset night and day to this end.

250

In vain did McDowell plead for a little more time. It could not be granted. If our troops were green and inexperienced, it was urged, so were the Rebels. It is said that because he saw fit to review a body of eight regiments he was charged with attempting to *make a show*, so impatient was public sentiment to have rebellion put down. So having done no more than to arrange his regiments in brigades, without giving them any discipline as such, without an organized artillery, without a commissariat, without even a staff to aid him, McDowell, dividing his force, of about 35,000 men, into five divisions, put four of them in motion from the Virginia bank of the Potomac against the enemy, and the result was — Bull Run, a battle in which brigade commanders did not know their commands and soldiers did not know their generals. In reality, the battle was one of regiments, rather than of brigades, the regiments fighting more or less independently. But better things were in store.

Bull Run, while comparatively disastrous as a battle-field, was a grand success to the North in other respects. It sobered, for a time at least, the hasty reckless spirits who believed that the South would not fight, and who were so unceasingly thorning the President to immediate decisive action. They were not satisfied, it is true, but they were less importunate, and manifested a willingness to let the authorities have a short breathing spell, which was at once given to better preparation for the future.

All eyes seemed now to turn, by common agreement, to General George B. McClellan, to lead to victory, who was young, who had served with distinction in the Mexican War, had studied European warfare in the Crimea, and, above all, had just finished a successful campaign in West Virginia. He took command of the forces in and around Washington July 27, 1861, a command which then numbered about fifty thousand infantry, one thousand cavalry, and six hundred and fifty artillerymen, with nine field batteries, such as they were, of thirty guns. A part of these had belonged to McDowell's Bull Run army, and a part had since arrived from the North. The brigade organization of McDowell was still in force on the Virginia side of the Potomac. I say *in force*. That statement needs qualifying. I have already said that there was originally no cohesion to these brigades; but *since* the battle the army was little better than a mob in the respect of discipline. Officers and men were absent from their commands without leave. The streets of Washington were swarming with them. But I must not wander too far from the point I have in mind to consider. I only throw in these statements of the situation to give a clearer idea of what a tremendous task McClellan had before him. In organizing the Army of the Potomac he first arranged the infantry in *brigades* of four regiments each. Then, as fast as new regiments arrived — and at that time, under a recent call of the President for five hundred thousand three years' volunteers, they were coming in very rapidly, — they were formed into temporary brigades, and placed in camp in the suburbs of the city to await their full equipment, which many of them lacked, to become more efficient in the tactics of "Scott" or "Hardee," and, in general, to acquire such discipline as would be valuable in the service before them, as soldiers of the Union. As rapidly as these conditions were fairly complied with, regiments were permanently assigned to brigades across the Potomac.

After this formation of brigades had made considerable headway, and the troops were becoming better disciplined and tolerably skilled in brigade movements, McClellan began the organization of *Divisions*, each comprising three brigades. Before the middle of October, 1861, eleven of these divisions had been organized, each including, besides the brigades of infantry specified, from one to four light batteries, and from a company to two regiments of cavalry which had been specially assigned to it.

The next step in the direction of organization was the formation of *Army Corps;* but in this matter McClellan moved slowly, not deeming it best to form them until his division commanders had, by experience in the field, shown which of them, if any, had the ability to handle so large a body of troops as a corps. This certainly seemed good judgment. The Confederate authorities appear to have been governed by this principle, for they did not adopt the system of army corps until after the battle of Antietam, in September, 1862. But months had elapsed since Bull Run. Eighteen hundred and sixty-two had dawned. "All quiet along the Potomac" had come to be used as a by-word and reproach. That powerful moving force, Public Sentiment, was again crystallizing along its old lines, and making itself felt, and "Why don't the army move?" was the oft-repeated question which gave to the propounder no satisfactory answer, because to him, with the public pulse again at fever-beat, no answer could be satisfactory. Meanwhile all these forces propelled their energies and persuasions in one and the same direction, the White House; and President Lincoln, goaded to desperation by their persistence and insistence, issued a War Order March 8, 1862, *requiring* McClellan to organize his command into five *Army Corps*. So far, well enough; but the order went further, and specified who the corps commanders should be, thus depriving him of doing that for which he had waited, and giving him officers in those positions not, in his opinion, the best, in all respects, that could have been selected.

But my story is not of the commanders, nor of McClellan, but of the corps, and what I have said will show how they were composed. Let us review for a moment: first, the *regiments*, each of which, when full, contained one thousand and forty-six men; *four* of these composed a *brigade; three brigades* were taken to form a *division*, and *three divisions* constituted a *corps*. This system was not always rigidly adhered to. Sometimes a corps had a *fourth* division, but such a case would be a deviation, and not the regular plan. So, too, a division might have an extra brigade. For example, a brigade might be detached from one part of the service and sent to join an army in another part. Such a brigade would not be allowed to remain independent in that case, but would be at once assigned to some division, usually a division whose brigades were small in numbers.

I have said that McClellan made up his brigades of four regiments. I think the usual number of regiments for a brigade is three. That gives a system of threes throughout. But in this matter also, after the first organization, the plan was modified. As a brigade became depleted by sickness, capture, and the bullet, new regiments were added, until, as the work of addition and depletion went on, I have known a brigade to have within it the skeletons of ten regiments, and even then its strength not half that of the original body. My camp was located at one time near a regiment which had only *thirty-eight men present for duty.*

There were twenty-five army corps in the service, at different times, exclusive of cavalry, engineer, and signal corps, and Hancock's veteran corps. The same causes which operated to reduce brigades and divisions naturally decimated corps, so that some of them were consolidated; as, for example, the First and Third Corps were merged in the Second, Fifth, and Sixth, in the spring of 1864. At about the same time the Eleventh and Twelfth were united to form the Twentieth. But enough of corps for the present. What I have stated will make more intelligible what I shall say about

CORPS BADGES.

What are corps badges? The answer to this question is somewhat lengthy, but I think it will be considered interesting. The idea of corps badges undoubtedly had its origin with General Philip Kearny, but just *how* or exactly *when* is somewhat legendary and uncertain. Not having become a member of Kearny's old corps until about a year after the idea was promulgated, I have no tradition of my own in regard to it, but I have heard men who served under him tell widely differing stories of the origin of the 'Kearny Patch,' yet all agreeing as to the author of the idea, and also in its application being made first to *officers*. General E. D. Townsend, late Adjutant-General of the United States Army, in his "*Anecdotes of the Civil War*," has adopted an explanation which, I have no doubt, is substantially correct. He says: —

"One day, when his brigade was on the march, General Philip Kearny, who was a strict disciplinarian, saw some officers standing under a tree by the roadside; supposing them to be stragglers from his command, he administered to them a rebuke, emphasized by a few expletives. The officers listened in silence, respectfully standing in the 'position of a soldier' until he had finished, when one of them, raising his hand to his cap, quietly suggested that the general had possibly made a mistake, as they none of them belonged to his command. With his usual courtesy, Kearny exclaimed, 'Pardon me; I will take steps to know how to recognize my own men hereafter.' Immediately on reaching camp, he issued orders that all officers and men of his brigade should wear conspicuously on the front of their caps a round piece of red cloth to designate them. This became generally known as the 'Kearny Patch.'"

I think General Townsend is incorrect in saying that Kearny issued orders immediately on reaching camp for all "officers and men" to wear the patch; first, because the testimony of officers of the old Third Corps to-day is that the order was first directed to *officers only*, and this would be in harmony with the explanation which I have quoted; and, second, after the death of Kearny and while his old division was lying at Fort Lyon, Va., Sept. 4, 1862, General D. B. Birney, then in command of it, issued a general order announcing his death, which closed with the following paragraph : —

"As a token of respect for his memory, all the officers of this division will wear crape on the left arm for thirty days, and the colors and drums of regiments and batteries will be placed in mourning for sixty days. To still further show our regard, and *to distinguish his officers as he wished*, each officer will continue to wear on his cap a *piece* of scarlet cloth, or have the top or crown-piece of the cap made of scarlet cloth."

The italics in the above extract are my own ; but we may fairly infer from it : —

First, that up to this date the patch had been required for officers alone, as no mention is made of the rank and file in this order.

Second, that General Kearny did not specify the lozenge as the shape of the badge to be worn, as some claim; for, had such been the case, so punctilious a man as General Birney would not have referred in general orders to a lozenge as " a *piece* of scarlet cloth," nor have given the option of having the crown-piece of the cap made of scarlet cloth if the lamented Kearny's instructions had originally been to wear a lozenge. This being so, General Townsend's quoted description of the badge as "a *round* piece of red cloth " is probably erroneous.

As there were no red goods at hand when Kearny initiated this move, he is said to have given up his own red blanket to be cut into these patches.

Soon after these emblems came into vogue among the officers there is strong traditional testimony to show that the men of the rank and file, *without general orders*, of their own accord cut pieces of red from their overcoat linings, or obtained them from other sources to make patches for themselves ; and, as to the shape, there are weighty reasons for believing that *any* piece of red fabric, of whatsoever shape, was considered to answer the purpose.

These red patches took immensely with the "boys." Kearny was a rough soldier in speech, but a perfect dare-devil in action, and his men idolized him. Hence they were only too proud to wear a mark which should distinguish them as members of *his* gallant division. It was said to have greatly reduced the straggling in this body, and also to have secured for the wounded or dead that fell into the Rebels' hands a more favorable and considerate attention.

There was a special reason, I think, why Kearny should select a *red* patch for his men, although I have never seen it referred to. On the 24th of March, 1862, General McClellan issued a general order prescribing the kinds of flags that should designate corps, division, and brigade head-quarters. In this he directed that the First Division flag should be a red one, six feet by five; the Second Division blue, and the Third Division a red and blue one; — both of the same dimensions as the first. As Kearny commanded the First Division, he would naturally select the same color of patch as his flag. Hence the *red* patch.

The contagion to wear a distinguishing badge extended widely from this simple beginning. It was the most natural thing that could happen for other divisions to be jealous of any innovation which, by comparison, should throw them into the background, for by that time the *esprit de corps*, the pride of organization, had begun to make itself felt. Realizing this fact, and regarding it as a manifestation that might be turned to good account, Major-General Joseph Hooker promulgated a scheme of army corps badges on the 21st of March, 1863, which was the first systematic plan submitted in this direction in the armies. Hooker took command of the Army of the Potomac Jan. 26, 1863. General Daniel Butterfield was made his chief-of-staff, and he, it is said, had much to do with designing and perfecting the first scheme of badges for the army, which appears in the following circular ; —

HEADQUARTERS ARMY OF THE POTOMAC.

Circular.   MARCH 21, 1863.

For the purpose of ready recognition of corps and divisions of the army, and to prevent injustice by reports of straggling and misconduct through mistake as to their organizations, the chief quartermaster will furnish, without delay, the following badges, to be worn by the officers and enlisted men of all the regiments of the various corps mentioned. They will be securely fastened upon the centre of the top of the cap. The inspecting officers will at all inspections see that these badges are worn as designated.

First Corps — a sphere: red for First Division; white for Second; blue for Third.

Second Corps — a trefoil: red for First Division; white for Second; blue for Third.

Third Corps — a lozenge: red for First Division; white for Second; blue for Third.

Fifth Corps — a Maltese cross: red for First Division; white for Second; blue for Third.

Sixth Corps — a cross: red for First Division; white for Second; blue for Third. (Light Division, green.)

Eleventh Corps — a crescent: red for First Division; white for Second; blue for Third.

Twelfth Corps — a star: red for First Division; white for Second; blue for Third.

The sizes and colors will be according to pattern.

By command of
MAJOR-GENERAL HOOKER,
S. WILLIAMS, A.A.G.

Accompanying this order were paper patterns pasted on a fly-leaf, illustrating the size and color required. It will be seen that the badges figured in the color-plates are much reduced in size. Diligent inquiry and research in the departments at Washington fail to discover any of the patterns referred to, or their dimensions; but there are veterans living who have preserved the first badge issued to them in pursuance of this circular, from which it is inferred that the patterns were of a size to please the eye rather than to conform to any uniform scale of measurement. A trefoil which I have measured is about an inch and seven-eighths each way. It is a copy of an original. The stem is straight, turning neither to the right nor left.

The arms of the Fifth Corps badge are often figured as concave, whereas those of a Maltese cross are straight. This is believed to be a deviation from the original in the minds of many veterans who wore them, and they are changed accordingly in the color-plate.

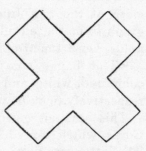

The Sixth Corps wore a St. Andrew's cross till 1864, when it changed to the Greek cross figured in the plate.

That this circular of Hooker's was not intended to be a dead letter was shown in an order issued from Falmouth, Va., May 12, 1863, in which he says : —

ST. ANDREW'S CROSS.

" The badges worn by the troops when lost or torn off must be immediately replaced."

And then, after designating the only troops that are without badges, he adds : —

" Provost-marshals will arrest as stragglers all other troops found without badges, and return them to their commands under guard."

There was a badge worn by the artillery brigade of the Third Corps, which, so far as I know, had no counterpart in other corps. I think it was not adopted until after Gettysburg. It was the lozenge of the corps subdivided into four smaller lozenges, on the following basis : If a battery was attached to the first division, two of these smaller lozenges were red, one white, and one blue ; if to the second, two were white, one red, and one blue ; and if to the third, two were blue, one red, and one white. They were worn on the left side of the cap.

The original Fourth Corps, organized by McClellan, did not adopt a badge, but its successor of the same number wore an equilateral triangle prescribed by Major-General Thomas, April 26, 1864, in General Orders No. 62, Department of the Cumberland, in which he used much the same language as that used by Hooker in his circular, and designated divisions by the same colors.

The badge of the Seventh Corps was a crescent nearly encircling a star. It was not adopted until after the virtual close of the war, June 1, 1865. The following is a paragraph from the circular issued by Major-General J. J. Reynolds, Department of Arkansas, regarding it : —

"This badge, cut two inches in diameter, from cloth of colors red, white, and blue, for the 1st, 2d, and 3d Divisions respectively, may be worn by all enlisted men of the Corps."

This was an entirely different corps from the Seventh Corps, which served in Virginia, and which had no badge. The latter was discontinued Aug. 1, 1863, at the same time with the original Fourth Corps.

The Eighth Corps wore a six-pointed star. I have not been able to ascertain the date of its adoption. There was no order issued.

The Ninth Corps was originally a part of the Army of the Potomac, but at the time Hooker issued his circular it was in another part of the Confederacy. Just before its return to the army, General Burnside issued General Orders No. 6, April 10, 1864, announcing as the badge of his corps, "A shield with the figure nine in the centre crossed with a foul anchor and cannon, to be worn on the top of the cap or front of the hat." This corps had a fourth division, whose badge was green. The corps commander and his staff wore a badge "of red, white, and blue, with gilt anchor, cannon, and green number."

December 23, 1864, Major-General John G. Parke, who had succeeded to the command, issued General Orders No. 49, of which the following is the first section : —

"1. All officers and enlisted men in this command will be required to wear the Corps Badge upon the cap or hat. For the Divisions, the badges will be plain, made of cloth in the shape of a shield — red for the first, white for the second, and blue for the third. For the Artillery Brigade, the shield will be red, and will be worn under the regulation cross cannon."

This order grew out of the difficulty experienced in obtaining the badge prescribed by General Burnside. The cannon, anchor, etc., were made of gold bullion at Tiffany's, New York City, and as it was scarcely practicable for the rank and file to obtain such badges, they had virtually anticipated the order of General Parke, and were wearing the three plain colors after the manner of the rest of Potomac's army. The figures in the color-plate, however, are fashioned after the direction of General Burnside's order. The annexed cut is a fac-simile of one of the original metallic badges worn by

AN ORIGINAL NINTH CORPS BADGE.

a staff officer. This corps had a fourth division from April 19 to Nov. 29, 1864.

The Tenth Corps badge was the trace of a four-bastioned fort. It was adopted by General Orders No. 18 issued by Major-General D. B. Birney, July 25, 1864.

The Eleventh and Twelfth Corps have already been referred to, in General Hooker's circular. On the 18th of April, 1864, these two corps were consolidated to form the Twentieth Corps, and by General Orders No. 62 issued by Major-General George H. Thomas, April

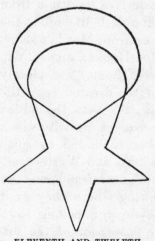

ELEVENTH AND TWELFTH CORPS BADGES COMBINED.

26, "a star, as heretofore worn by the Twelfth Corps," was prescribed as the badge.

The annexed cut shows the manner in which many of the corps combined the two badges in order not to lose their original identity.

The Thirteenth Corps had no badge.

The badge of the Fourteenth Army Corps was an acorn. Tradition has it that some time before the adoption of this badge the members of this corps called themselves *Acorn Boys*, because at one time in their history, probably when they were hemmed in at Chattanooga by Bragg, rations were so scanty that the men gladly gathered large quantities of acorns from an oak-grove, near by which they were camped, and roasted and ate them, repeating this operation while the scarcity of food continued. Owing to this circumstance, when it became necessary to select a badge, the acorn suggested itself as an exceedingly appropriate emblem for that purpose, and it was therefore adopted by General Orders No. 62, issued from Headquarters Department of the Cumberland, at Chattanooga, April 26, 1864.

The badge of the Fifteenth Corps derives its origin from the following incident: — During the fall of 1863 the Eleventh and Twelfth Corps were taken from Meade's army, put under the command of General Joe Hooker, and sent to aid in the relief of Chattanooga, where Thomas was closely besieged. They were undoubtedly better dressed than the soldiers of that department, and this fact, with the added circumstance of their wearing corps badges, which were a novelty to the Western armies at that time, led to some sharp tilts, in words, between the Eastern and Western soldiers. One day a veteran of Hooker's command met an Irishman of Logan's Corps at the spring where they went to fill their canteens. "What corps do you belong to?" said the Eastern veteran, proud in the possession of the distinguishing badge on his cap, which told his story for him. "What corps, is it?" said the gallant son of Erin, straightening his back; "the Fifteenth, to be sure." "Where is your badge?" "My badge, do ye say? There it is!" said

Pat, clapping his hand on his cartridge-box, at his side; " forty rounds. Can you show me a betther?"

On the 14th of February, 1865, Major-General John A. Logan, the commander of this corps, issued General Orders No. 10, which prescribe that the badge shall be "A miniature cartridge-box, one-eighth of an inch thick, fifteensixteenths of an inch wide, set transversely on a field of cloth or metal, one and five-eighths of an inch square. Above the cartridge-box plate will be stamped or worked in a curve ' Forty Rounds.' " This corps had a fourth division, whose badge was yellow, and headquarters wore a badge including the four colors. Logan goes on to say : —

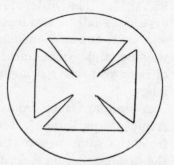

FIRST AND FIFTH CORPS BADGES COMBINED.

" It is expected that this badge will be worn constantly by every officer and soldier in the corps. If any corps in the army has a right to take pride in its badge, surely that has which looks back through the long and glorious line of . . . [naming twenty-nine different battles], and scores of minor struggles ; the corps which had its birth under Grant and Sherman in the darker days of our struggle, the corps which will keep on struggling until the death of the Rebellion."

The following correct description of the badge worn by the Sixteenth Army Corps is given by the assistant-inspector general of that corps, Colonel J. J. Lyon : — " The device is a circle with four Minie-balls, the points towards the centre, cut out of it." It was designed by Brevet Brigadier-General John Hough, the assistant adjutant-general of the corps, being selected out of many designs, submitted by Major-General A. J. Smith, the corps commander, and, in his honor, named the " A. J. Smith Cross." It is easily distinguished from the Maltese cross, in being bounded by curved instead of straight lines. No order for its adoption was issued.

The badge of the Seventeenth Corps, said to have been suggested by General M. F. Ford, and adopted in accordance with General Orders issued by his commander, Major-General Francis P. Blair, was an arrow. He says, "In its swiftness, in its surety of striking where wanted, and its destructive powers, when so intended, it is probably as emblematical of this corps as any design that could be adopted." The order was issued at Goldsboro, N. C., March 25, 1865. The order further provides that the arrow for divisions shall be two inches long, and for corps headquarters one and one-half inches long, and further requires the wagons and ambulances to be marked with the badge of their respective commands, the arrow being twelve inches long.

A circular issued from the headquarters of the Eighteenth Army Corps June 7, 1864, and General Orders No. 108, from the same source, dated August 25, 1864, furnish all the information on record regarding the badge of this body. While both are quite lengthy in description and prescription, neither states what the special design was to be. It was, however, a cross with equi-foliate arms. The circular prescribed that this cross should be worn by general officers, suspended by a tri-colored ribbon from the left breast. Division commanders were to have a triangle in the centre of the badge, but brigade commanders were to have the number of their brigade instead; line officers were to suspend their badges by ribbons of the color of their division, cavalry and artillery officers also were to have distinctive badges. The whole system was quite complex, and somewhat expensive as well, as the badges were to be of metal and enamel in colors. Enlisted men were to wear the plain cross of cloth, sewed to their left breast. This order was issued by General W. F. Smith.

General Orders 108 issued by General E. O. C. Ord

simplified the matter somewhat, requiring line-officers and enlisted men both to wear the plain cross the color of their respective divisions, and enlisted men were required to wear theirs on the front of the hat or top of the cap.

By General Orders No. 11 issued by General Emory Nov. 17, 1864, the Nineteenth Corps adopted " a fan-leaved cross, with an octagonal centre." The First Division was to wear *red,* the Second *blue,* and the Third *white* — the exception in the order of the colors which proved the rule. The badge of enlisted men was to be of cloth, two inches square, and worn on the side of the hat or top of the cap, although they were allowed to supply themselves with metallic badges of the prescribed color, if so minded.

The Twenty-First Corps never adopted a badge.

The Twenty-Second adopted (without orders) a badge quinquefarious in form, that is, opening into five parts, and having a circle in the centre. This was the corps which served in the defence of Washington. Its membership was constantly changing.

The badge adopted by the Twenty-Third Corps (without General Orders) was a plain shield, differing somewhat in form from that of the Ninth Corps, with which it was for a time associated, and which led it to adopt a similar badge.

The following General Order tells the story of the next Corps' badge : —

HEADQUARTERS TWENTY-FOURTH ARMY CORPS,
BEFORE RICHMOND, VA., March 18, 1865.

[General Orders No. 32.]

By authority of the Major-General commanding the Army of the James, the HEART is adopted as the badge of the Twenty-Fourth Army Corps.

The symbol selected is one which testifies our affectionate regard for all our brave comrades — alike the living and the dead — who have braved the perils of the mighty conflict, and our devotion to the sacred cause — a cause which entitles us to the sympathy of every brave and true heart and the support of every strong and determined hand.

The Major-General commanding the Corps does not doubt that soldiers who have given their strength and blood to the fame of their former badges, will unite in rendering the present one even more renowned than those under which they have heretofore marched to battle.

. . . . .

By command of Major-General JOHN GIBBON.
A. HENRY EMBLER, A. A. A. General.

This corps was largely made up of re-enlisted men, who had served nine months or three years elsewhere. Here is another General Order which speaks for itself : —

HEADQUARTERS TWENTY-FIFTH ARMY CORPS,
ARMY OF THE JAMES,
IN THE FIELD, VA., Feb. 20, 1865.

[Orders.]

In view of the circumstances under which this Corps was raised and filled, the peculiar claims of its individual members upon the justice and fair dealing of the prejudiced, and the regularity of the troops which *deserve* those *equal* rights that have been hitherto denied the majority, the Commanding General has been induced to adopt the *Square* as the distinctive badge of the Twenty-Fifth Army Corps.

Wherever danger has been found and glory to be won, the heroes who have fought for immortality have been distinguished by some emblem to which every victory added a new lustre. They looked upon their badge with pride, for to it they had given its fame. In the homes of smiling peace it recalled the days of courageous endurance and the hours of deadly strife — and it solaced the moment of death, for it was a symbol of a life of heroism and self-denial. The poets still sing of the " Templar's Cross," the " Crescent " of the Turks, the " Chalice " of the hunted Christian, and the " White Plume " of Murat, that crested the wave of valor sweeping resistlessly to victory.

Soldiers! to you is given a chance in this Spring Campaign of making this badge immortal. Let History record that on the banks of the James thirty thousand freemen not only gained their own liberty but shattered the prejudice of the world, and gave to the Land of their birth Peace, Union, and Liberty.

GODFREY WEITZEL,
Major-General Commanding.

[Official.]

W. L. GOODRICH,
A. A. A. General.

This corps was composed wholly of colored troops.

In the late fall of 1864, Major-General W. S. Hancock resigned his command of the Second Corps to take charge of the First Veteran Corps, then organizing. The badge adopted originated with Colonel C. H. Morgan, Hancock's chief-of-staff.

The centre is a circle half the diameter of the whole design, surrounded by a wreath of laurel. Through the circle a wide red band passes vertically. From the wreath radiate rays in such a manner as to form a heptagon with concave sides. Seven hands spring from the wreath, each grasping a spear, whose heads point the several angles of the heptagon.

Sheridan's Cavalry Corps had a badge, but it was not generally worn. The device was " Gold crossed sabres on a blue field, surrounded by a glory in silver."

The design of Wilson's Cavalry Corps was a carbine from which was suspended by chains a red, swallow-tail guidon, bearing gilt crossed sabres.

The badge of the Engineer and Pontonier Corps is thus described: " Two oars crossed over an anchor, the top of which is encircled by a scroll surmounted by a castle; the castle being the badge of the U. S. corps of engineers." As a fact, however, this fine body of men wore only the castle designed in brass.

The badge of the Signal Corps was two flags crossed on the staff of a flaming torch. This badge is sometimes represented with a red star in the centre of one flag, but such was not the typical badge. This star was allowed on the headquarters flag of a *very few* signal officers, who were accorded this distinction for some meritorious service performed; but such a flag was rarely seen, and should not be figured as part of the corps badge.

The Department of West Virginia, under the command of General Crook, adopted a spread eagle for a badge, Jan. 3, 1865.

The pioneers of the army wore a pair of crossed hatchets, the color of the division to which they belonged. Then, the Army of the Cumberland have a society badge. So likewise have the Army of the Potomac. There are also medals presented for distinguished gallantry, worn by a few. They are not numerous and are seldom to be seen — for this reason, if for no other, they are of precious value to the owner, and are therefore carefully treasured.

In nearly every corps whose badge I have referred to, the plan was adopted of having the first three divisions take the national colors of red, white, and blue respectively. These corps emblems were not only worn by the men, — I refer now to the Army of the Potomac, — but they were also painted with stencil on the transportation of a corps, its wagons and ambulances. And just here I may add that there was no army which became so devotedly attached to its badges as did the Army of the Potomac. There were reasons for this. They were the first to adopt them, being at least a year ahead of *all* other corps, and more than two years ahead of many. Then, by their use they were brought into sharper comparison in action and on the march, and, as General Weitzel says, "they looked upon their badge with pride, for to it they had given its fame."

These badges can be seen in any parade of the Grand Army, worn on the cap or hat, possibly now and then one that has seen service. I still have such a one in my possession. But at the close of the war many of the veterans desired some more enduring form of these emblems, so familiar and full of meaning to them, and so to-day they wear pinned to the breast or suspended from a ribbon the dear old corps badge, modelled in silver or gold, perhaps bearing the division colors indicated, in enamel or stone, and some of them inscribed with the list of battles in which the bearer participated. What is such a jewel worth to the wearer? I can safely say that, while its intrinsic value may be a mere trifle, not all the wealth of an Astor and a Vanderbilt combined could purchase the experience which it records, were such a transfer otherwise possible.

CHAPTER XIV.

SOME INVENTIONS AND DEVICES OF THE WAR.

A TORPEDO.

THAT "necessity is the mother of invention" nothing can more clearly and fully demonstrate than war. I will devote this chapter to presenting some facts from the last war which illustrate this maxim. As soon as the tocsin of war had sounded, and men were summoned to take the field, a demand was at once made, on both sides of Mason and Dixon's line, for a new class of materials — the materials of war, for which there had been no demand of consequence for nearly fifty years. The arms, such as they were, had been largely sent South before the outbreak. But they were somewhat old-fashioned, and, now that there was a demand for new arms, inventive genius was stimulated to produce better ones. It always has been true, and always will be, that the manufactured products for which there is an extensive demand are the articles which invention will improve upon until they arrive as near perfection as it is possible for the work of human hands to be. Such was the case with the materials of warfare. Invention was stimulated in various directions, but its products appeared most numerous, perhaps, in the changes which the arms, ammunition, and ordnance underwent in their better adaptation to the needs of the hour.

The few muskets remaining in the hands of the government in 1861 were used to equip the troops who left first for the seat of war. Then manufacturing began on an immense scale. The government workshops could not produce a tithe of what were wanted, even though running night and day; and so private enterprise was called in to supplement the need. As one illustration, Grover & Baker of Roxbury turned their extensive sewing-machine workshop into a rifle-manufactory, which employed several hundred hands, and this was only one of a large number in that section. Alger, of South Boston, poured the immense molten masses of his cupolas into the moulds of cannon, and his massive steam-hammers pounded out and welded the ponderous shafts of gunboats and monitors. The descendants of Paul Revere diverted a part of their yellow metal from the mills which rolled it into sheathing for government ships, to the founding of brass twelve-pounders, or Napoleons, as they were called ; and many a Rebel was laid low by shrapnel or canister hurled through the muzzle of guns on which was plainly stamped "Revere Copper Co., Canton, Mass." Plain smooth-bore Springfield muskets soon became Springfield rifles, and directly the process of rifling was applied to cannon of various calibres. Then, muzzle-loading rifles became breech-loading; and from a breech-loader for a single cartridge the capacity was increased, until some of the cavalry regiments that took the field in 1864 went equipped with Henry's sixteen-shooters, a breech-loading rifle, which the Rebels said the Yanks loaded in the morning and fired all day.

I met at Chattanooga, Tenn., recently, Captain Fort, of the old First Georgia Regulars, a Confederate regiment of distinguished service. In referring to these repeating rifles, he said that his first encounter with them was near Olustee, Fla. While he was skirmishing with a Massachusetts regiment (the Fortieth), he found them hard to move, as they seemed to load with marvellous speed, and never to have their fire drawn. Determined to see what sort of fire-arms were opposed to him, he ordered his men to concentrate their fire on a single skirmisher. They did so and laid him low, and afterwards secured his repeating rifle — I think a Spencer's seven or eight shooter — which they carried along, as a great curiosity, for some time afterward.

In the navy Invention made equally rapid strides. When the war broke out, the available vessels were mainly a few ships-of-the-line, frigates and screw steamers; but these could be of little service in such a warfare as was evidently on hand, a warfare which must be carried on in rivers, and

A GUNBOAT.

bays, and coastwise generally, where such clumsy and deep-draught vessels could not be used. So sloops-of-war, gun-boats, mortar-boats, double-enders, and iron-clads came to the front, and the larger old-fashioned craft were used mainly as receiving ships. But with the increase in range and calibre of naval armament came a seeking by Invention for something less vulnerable to their power, and after the encounter of the little "Yankee Cheese Box," so called, and the Rebel Ram "Virginia," the question of what should constitute the main reliance of the navy was definitely settled, and monitors became the idols of the hour. These facts are all matters of well written history, and I refer to them now only to illustrate the truth of the maxim with which I began the chapter.

I wish now to give it still further emphasis by citing some illustrations which the historian has neglected for "nobler game." Some of the inventions which I shall refer to were impractical, and had only a brief existence. Of course your small inventor and would-be benefactor to his kind clearly foresaw that men who were about to cut loose from the amenities of civil life would be likely to spend money freely in providing themselves before their departure with every-

A MORTAR BOAT.

thing portable that might have a tendency to ameliorate the condition of soldier life. With an eye single to this idea these inventors took the field.

One of the first products of their genius which I recall was a combination *knife-fork-and-spoon* arrangement, which was peddled through the state camping-grounds in great numbers and variety. Of course every man must have one. So much convenience in so small a compass must be taken advantage of. It was a sort of soldier's trinity, which they all thought that they understood and appreciated. But I doubt whether this invention, on the average, ever got beyond the first camp in active service.

I still have in my possession the remnants of a *water-filterer* in which I invested after enlistment. There was a metallic mouth-piece at one end of a small gutta-percha tube, which latter was about fifteen inches long. At the other end of the tube was a suction-chamber, an inch long by a half-inch in diameter, with the end perforated, and containing a piece of bocking as a filter. Midway of the tubing was an air-chamber. The tubing long since dried

A DOUBLE-TURRETED MONITOR.

and crumbled away from the metal. It is possible that I used this instrument half a dozen times, though I do not recall a single instance, and on breaking camp just before the Gettysburg Campaign, I sent it, with some other effects, northward.

I remember another filterer, somewhat simpler. It consisted of the same kind of mouth-piece, with rubber tubing attached to a small conical piece of pumice-stone, through which the water was filtered. Neither of these was ever of any practical value.

I have spoken of the rapid improvements made in arms. This improvement extended to all classes of fire-arms alike. Revolvers were no exception, and *Colt's* revolver, which monopolized the field for some time, was soon crowded in the race by *Smith and Wesson*, *Remington*, and others. Thousands of them were sold monthly, and the newly

fledged soldier who did not possess a revolver, either by
his own purchase, or as a present from solicitous relatives,
or admiring friends, or enthusiastic business associates, was
something of a curiosity. Of course a present of this kind
necessitated an outfit of special ammunition, and such was at
once procured. But the personal armory of many heroes was
not even then complete, and a dirk knife — a real " Arkan-
saw toothpick " — was no unusual sight to be seen hanging
from the belt of some of the incipient but blood-thirsty
warriors. The little town of Ashby in Massachusetts, at one
of its earliest war-meetings, voted " that each volunteer
shall be provided with a revolver, a bowie-knife, and a
Bible, and shall also receive ten dollars in money." The
thought did not appear to find lodgement in the brain of the
average soldier or his friends that by the time the government had provided him with what arms, ammunition, and
equipments it was thought necessary for him to have, he would
then be loaded with about all he could bear, without adding
a personal armory and magazine. Nor did he realize that
which afterwards in his experience must have come upon
him with convincing force, that by the time he had
done his duty faithfully and well with the arms which
the government had placed in his hands there would
be little opportunity or need, even if his ambition still
held out, to fall back on his personal arsenal for further
supplies. Members of the later regiments got their eyes
open to this fact either through correspondence with men
at the front, or by having been associated with others
who had seen service. But the troops of '61 and '62
took out hundreds of revolvers only to lose them, give
them away, or throw them away; and as many regiments were forbidden by their colonels to wear them, a
large number were sent back to the North. Revolvers were
probably cheaper in Virginia, in those years, than in any
other state in the Union.

There was another invention that must have been sufficiently popular to have paid the manufacturer a fair rate on his investment, and that was the steel-armor enterprise. There were a good many men who were anxious to be heroes, but they were particular. They preferred to be *live* heroes. They were willing to go to war and fight as never man fought before, if they could only be insured against bodily harm. They were not willing to assume all the risks which an enlistment involved, without securing something in the shape of a drawback. Well, the iron tailors saw and appreciated the situation and sufferings of this class of men, and came to the rescue with a vest of steel armor, worth, as I remember it, about a dozen dollars, and greaves. The latter, I think, did not find so ready a market as the vests, which were comparatively common. These iron-clad warriors admitted that when panoplied for the fight their sensations were much as they might be if they were dressed up in an old-fashioned air-tight stove; still, with all the discomforts of this casing, they felt a little safer with it on than off in battle, and they reasoned that it was the right and duty of every man to adopt all honorable measures to assure his safety in the line of duty. This seemed solid reasoning, surely; but, in spite of it all, a large number of these vests never saw Rebeldom. Their owners were subjected to such a storm of ridicule that they could not bear up under it. It was a stale yet common joke to remind them that in action these vests must be worn behind. Then, too, the ownership of one of them was taken as evidence of faint-heartedness. Of this the owner was often reminded; so that when it came to the packing of the knapsack for departure, the vest, taking as it did considerable space, and adding no small weight to his already too heavy burden, was in many cases left behind. The officers, whose opportunity to take baggage along was greater, clung to them longest; but I think that they were quite generally abandoned with the first important reduction made in the luggage.

One of the first supposed-to-be useful, if not ornamental stupidities, which some of the earlier troops took to themselves by order, was the *Havelock*. True, its invention antedated the time of which I speak. It was a foreign conception, and derived its name from an English general who distinguished himself in the war in India, where they were worn in 1857. It was a simple covering of white linen for the cap, with a cape depending for the protection of the neck from the sun. They may have been very essential to the comfort of the troops in the Eastern climate, but, while whole regiments went South with them, if one of these articles survived active service three months I have yet to hear of it.

A HAVELOCK.

Then there were fancy patent-leather haversacks, with two or three compartments for the assortment of rations, which Uncle Sam was expected to furnish. But those who invested in them were somewhat disgusted at a little later stage of their service, when

A HAVERSACK AND DIPPER.

they were ordered to throw away all such "high-toned" trappings and adopt the regulation pattern of painted cloth. This was a bag about a foot square, with a broad strap for the shoulder, into which soldiers soon learned to bundle all their food and table furniture, which, I think I have elsewhere stated, after a day's hard march were always found in such a delightful hodge-podge.

Now and then an invention was to be found which was a real convenience. I still have in my possession such a one, an article which, when not in use, is a compact roll eight and one-half inches long and two inches in diameter, and designed to hold pens, ink, and paper. Unrolled, it makes a little tablet of the length given and five and one-half inches wide, which was my writing-desk when no better was to be had.

The Turkish fez, with pendent tassel, was seen on the heads of some soldiers. Zouave regiments wore them. They did very well to lie around camp in, and in a degree marked their owner as a somewhat conspicuous man among his fellows, but they were not tolerated on line; few of them ever survived the first three months' campaigning.

A ZOUAVE.

And this recalls the large number of the soldiers of '62 who did not wear the forage cap furnished by the government. They bought the "McClellan cap," so called, at the hatters' instead, which in most cases faded out in a month. This the government caps did not do, with all their awkward appearance. They may have been coarse and unfashionable to the eye, but the colors would stand. Nearly every man embellished his cap with the number or letter of his company and regiment and the appropriate emblem. For infantry this emblem is a bugle, for artillery two crossed cannons, and for cavalry two crossed sabres.

One other item occurs to me, not entirely germane to the chapter, yet interesting enough to warrant its insertion. This was the great care exercised to have all equipments prominently marked with the regiment, company, and State to which the owner belonged. For example, on the back of the knapsack of every man in a regiment appeared in large lettering something like this: Co. B, 33d New York Regiment; or, if it was light artillery, this, 10th Mass. Battery. Nor did the advertising stop here, for the haversacks and canteens were often similarly labelled, and yet, at the time, it seemed necessary to somebody that it should be done. At any rate, nobody found any fault with it; and if it had been thought desirable that each article of apparel should be similarly placarded, there would have been a general acquiescence on the part of the untutored citizen soldiery, who were in the best of humor, and with Pope (Alexander not John) seemed to agree that "Whatever is is right." But how many of these loudly marked equipments survived the strife? Perhaps not one. The knapsack may have been thrown aside in the first battle, and a simple roll composed of the woollen and rubber blanket substituted for it. The haversacks and canteens were soon lost, and new ones took their place; and they lasted just as long and were just as safe as if conspicuously marked. One of the comical sights of the service was to see Rebel prisoners brought in having strapped on their backs knapsacks bearing just such labelling as that which I have quoted. Of course, these were trophies which they had either taken from prisoners or had picked up on some battlefield or in the wake of the Union army, and appropriated to their own use.

Light-artillerymen went to the front decorated with brass scales on their shoulders, but, finding an utter absence of such ornaments on the persons of soldiers who had been in action, and feeling sensitive about being known as recruits, these decorations soon disappeared. Theoretically, they were worn to ward off the blows of a sabre aimed by cavalrymen at the head; practically, it is doubtful whether they ever served such a purpose.

A SPENCER RIFLE

CHAPTER XV.

THE ARMY MULE.

"Two teamsters have paused, in the shade of the pool,
Rehearsing the tricks of the old army mule;
 They have little to say
 Of the blue and the gray,
Which they wore when the garments meant shedding of blood —
They're discussing the mule and 'Virginia mud.'"

I T has often been said that the South could not have been worsted in the Rebellion had it not been for the steady re-enforcement brought to the Union side by the mule. To just what extent his services hastened the desired end, it would be impossible to compute; but it is admitted by both parties to the war that they were invaluable.

It may not be generally known that Kentucky is the chief mule-producing State of the Union, with Missouri next, while St. Louis is perhaps the best mule-market in the world; but the entire South-west does something at mule-raising. Mules vary more in size than horses. The largest and best come from Kentucky. The smaller ones are the result of a cross with the Mexican mustang. These were also extensively used. General Grant says, in his Memoirs (vol. 1. p. 69), that while Taylor's army was at Matamoras, contracts were made for mules, between American traders and Mexican smugglers, at from eight to eleven dollars each. But the main source of supply for the Western States, where they are very generally used, for the South, and for the government, during war time, was Kentucky. When the war broke out, efforts were made by Governor Magoffin of that State — or rather by the Legislature, for the Governor was in full sympathy with the Rebels — to have that commonwealth remain neutral. For this reason when the general government attempted to purchase mules there in 1861, they were refused; but in the course of a few weeks the neutrality nonsense was pretty thoroughly knocked out of the authorities, Kentucky took its stand on the side of the

A SIX-MULE TEAM.

Union, and the United States government began and continued its purchase of mules there in increasing numbers till the close of the war.

What were these mules used for? Well, I have related elsewhere that, when the war broke out, thousands of soldiers came pouring into Washington for its defence, and afterwards went by thousands into other sections of Rebeldom. To supply these soldiers with the necessary rations, forage, and camp equipage, and keep them supplied, thousands of wagons were necessary. Some of the regiments took these wagons with them from their native State, but most did not. Some of the wagons were drawn by mules already owned by the government, and more mules were purchased from time to time. The great advantage possessed by these animals over horses was not at that period fully appreciated, so that horses were also used in large numbers. But the magnitude of the Rebellion grew apace. Regiments of cavalry, each requiring twelve hundred horses, and light batteries one hundred and ten, were now rapidly organizing, calling for an abundance of horse-flesh. Then, disease, exposure, and hard usage consumed a great many more, so that these animals naturally grew scarcer as the demand increased. For certain kinds of work horses *must* be had, mules would not do. The horse was good for any kind of service, as a beast of burden, up to the limits of his endurance. Not so his half-brother the mule. The latter was more particular as to the kind of service he performed.

A MULE EATING AN OVERCOAT.

Like a great many *bipeds* that entered the army, he preferred to do military duty in the safe rear. As a consequence, if he found himself under fire at the front, he was wont to make a stir in his neighborhood until he got out of such inhospitable surroundings.

This nervousness totally unfitted him for artillery or cavalry service ; he must therefore be made available for draft in the trains, the ammunition and forage trains, the supply and bridge trains. So, as rapidly as it could conveniently be done, mules took the place of horses in all the trains, six mules replacing four horses.

Aside from this nervousness under fire, mules have a great advantage over horses in being better able to stand hard usage, bad feed, or no feed, and neglect generally. They can travel over rough ground unharmed where horses would be lamed or injured in some way. They will eat brush, and not be very hungry to do it, either. When forage was short, the drivers were wont to cut branches and throw before them for their refreshment. One m. d. (mule driver) tells of having his army overcoat partly eaten by one of his team — actually chewed and swallowed. The operation made the driver *blue*, if the diet did not thus affect the mule.

In organizing a six-mule team, a large pair of heavy animals were selected for the pole, a smaller size for the swing, and a still smaller pair for leaders. There were advantages in this arrangement; in the first place, in going through a miry spot the small leaders soon place themselves, by their quick movements, on firm footing, where they can take hold and pull the pole mules out of the wallow. Again, with a good heavy steady pair of wheel mules, the driver can restrain the smaller ones that are more apt to be frisky and reckless at times, and, assisted by the brake, hold back his loaded wagon in descending a hill. Then, there was more elasticity in such a team when well trained, and a good driver could handle them much more gracefully and dexterously than he could the same number of horses.

It was really wonderful to see some of the experts drive these teams. The driver rides the near pole mule, holding in his left hand a single rein. This connects with the bits of the near lead mule. By pulling this rein, of course the brutes would go to the left. To direct them to the right one or more short jerks of it were given, accompanied by a sort of gibberish which the mule-drivers acquired in the business. The bits of the lead mules being connected by an iron bar, whatever movement was made by the near one directed the movements of the off one. The pole mules were controlled by short reins which hung over their necks.

The driver carried in his right hand his *black snake*, that is, his black leather whip, which was used with much effect on occasion.

When mules were brought to the army they were enclosed in what was called a *corral*. To this place the driver in quest of a mule must repair to make and take his selection, having the proper authority to do so. I will illustrate how it was done. Here is a figure representing a corral, having on the inside a fence running from A to C. AD and BE are pairs of bars. The driver enters the yard, mounted, and, having selected the mule he wants, drives him toward BE. The bars at AD be-

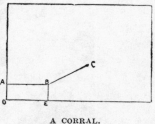

A CORRAL.

ing up, and those at BE being down, the mule advances and the bars BE are put up behind him. He is now enclosed in the small space indicated by ABDE. The mule-driver then mounts the fence, bridles the brute of his choice, lets down the bars at AD, and takes him out. Why does he bridle him from the fence? Well, because the mule is an uncertain animal.

In making his selection the driver did not always draw a prize. Sometimes his mule would be kind and tractable, and sometimes not. Of course he would saddle him, and start to ride him to camp; but the mule is not always docile under the saddle. He too often has a mind of his own. He may go along all right, or, if he is tricky, he may suddenly pause, bracing his forefeet and settling down on his hind ones, as if he had suddenly happened to think of the girl he left behind him, and was debating whether or not to go back after her. It is when the mule strikes such an attitude as this, I suppose, that Josh Billings calls him " a stubborn fact." But the driver! Well, if at that moment he was off his guard, he would get off without previous preparation, as a man sometimes sits down on ice, and look at

the mule. If, however, he was on the alert, and well prepared, the mule, in the end, would generally come off second
best. I have referred to the *Black Snake.* It was the badge
of authority with which the mule-driver enforced his orders.
It was the panacea for all the ills to which mule-flesh was
heir. It was a common sight to see a six-mule team, when

DISMOUNTED.

left to itself, get into an entanglement, seeming inextricably
mixed, unless it was unharnessed; but the appearance of the
driver with his black wand would change the scene as if by
magic. As the heel-cord of Achilles was his only vulnerable
part, so the ears of the mule seemed to be the development
through which his reasoning faculties could be the most
quickly and surely reached, and one or two cracks of the
whip on or near these little monuments, accompanied by the
driver's very expressive ejaculation in the mule tongue,
which I can only describe as a kind of cross between an
unearthly screech and a groan, had the effect to disentangle
them unaided, and make them stand as if at a "present" to
their master. When off duty in camp, they were usually
hitched to the pole of their wagon, three on either side, and
here, between meals, they were often as antic as kittens or
puppies at play, leaping from one side of the pole to the

other, lying down, tumbling over, and biting each other,
until perhaps all six would be an apparently confused heap
of mule. If the driver appeared at such a crisis with his
black " ear-trumpet," one second was long enough to dis-
solve the pile into its original mule atoms, and arrange them
again on either side of the pole, looking as orderly and innocent as if on inspection.

An educated mule-driver was, in his little sphere, as competent a disciplinarian as the colonel of a regiment.   Nor

OATS FOR SIX.

did he always secure the prompt and exact obedience above
described by applications of the Black Snake alone, or even
when accompanied by the sternest objurgations delivered in
the mule dialect. He was a terror to his subjects in yet
another way : and old soldiers will sustain me in the asser-
tion that the propulsive power of the mule-driver was
increased many fold by the almost unlimited stock of profanity with which he greeted the sensitive ears of his muleship when the latter was stubborn. I have seen mules, but
now most obdurate, jump into their collars the next moment

with the utmost determination to do their whole duty when
one of these Gatling guns of curses opened fire upon them.
Some reader may prefer to adjudge as a reason for this good
behavior the fear of the Black Snake, which was likely to
be applied close upon the volley of oaths; but I prefer to
assign as a motive the mule's interest in the advancement of
good morals.

In all seriousness, however, dealing only with the fact,
without attempting to prove or deny justification for it, it
is undoubtedly true that the mule-drivers, when duly
aroused, could produce a deeper cerulean tint in the surrounding atmosphere than any other class of men in the
service. The theory has been advanced that if all of these
professional m. d.'s in the trains of the Army of the Potomac could have been put into the trenches around Petersburg and Richmond, in the fall of 1864, and have been
safely advanced to within ear-shot of the enemy, then, at a
signal, set to swearing simultaneously at their level-*worst*,
the Rebels would either have thrown down their arms and
surrendered then and there, or have fled incontinently to
the fastnesses of the Blue Ridge. There may have been
devout mule-drivers in Sherman's army, but I never saw one
east. They may have been pious on taking up this important work. They were certainly impious before laying it
down. Nevertheless, in these later days, when they are
living better lives, any twinge of conscience which they
may occasionally feel must be relieved by the knowledge
that General Grant has given them credit for being able to
swear a mule-team out of the mud when it could not be
moved by any other process.

I have stated that the mule was uncertain; I mean as to
his intentions. He cannot be trusted even when appearing
honest and affectionate. His reputation as a kicker is world-
wide. He was the Mugwump of the service. The mule
that will not kick is a curiosity. A veteran relates how,
after the battle of Antietam, he saw a colored mule-driver

approach his mules that were standing unhitched from the wagons, when, presto! one of them knocked him to the ground in a twinkling with one of those unexpected instantaneous kicks, for which the mule is peerless. Slowly picking himself up, the negro walked deliberately to his wagon, took out a long stake the size of his arm, returned with the same moderate pace to his muleship, dealt him a stunning blow on the head with the stake, which felled him to the ground. The stake was returned with the same deliberation. The mule lay quiet for a moment, then arose, shook his head, a truce was declared, and driver and mule were at peace and understood each other.

Here is another illustration of misplaced confidence. On the road to Harper's Ferry, after the Antietam campaign in 1862, the colored cook of the headquarters of the Sixtieth New York Regiment picked up a large and respectable looking mule, to whom, with a cook's usual foresight and ambition, he attached all the paraphernalia of the cook-house together with his own personal belongings, and settled himself down proudly on his back among them. All went on serenely for a time, the mule apparently accepting the situation with composure, until the Potomac was reached at Harper's Ferry. On arriving in the middle of the pontoon bridge upon which the army was crossing, from some unexplained reason — perhaps because, on looking into the water, he saw himself as others saw him — the mule lifted up his voice in one of those soul-harrowing brays, for which he is famous — or *in*famous — and, lifting his hind legs aloft, in the next moment tossed his entire burden of cook and cookhouse into the river, where, weighted down with mess-kettles and other utensils of his craft, the cook must have drowned had not members of the regiment come to his rescue. Not at all daunted by this experience, the cookey harnessed the mule again as before, led him across the remaining portion of the bridge, where he remounted and settled himself among his household goods once more, where all was well till the Shenandoah was reached. Here, with another premonitory blast of his nasal trumpet, the mule once more dumped his load into the rapid rolling river,

DUMPED INTO THE POTOMAC.

when the cook lost all confidence in mules as beasts of burden, and abandoned him.

Josh Billings says somewhere that if he had a mule who would neither kick nor bite he would watch him dreadful "cluss" till he found out where his malice *did* lay. This same humorist must have had some experience with the mule, for he has said some very bright and pat things concerning him. Here are a few that I recall : —

"To break a mule — begin at his head."

"To find the solid contents of a mule's hind leg, feel of it clussly."

"The man who wont believe anything he kant see aint so wise az a mule, for they will kick at a thing in the dark."

"The only thing which makes a mule so highly respectable is the great accuracy of his kicking."

"The mule is a sure-footed animal. I have known

him to kick a man fifteen feet off ten times in a second."

These are a few samples, most all of which have reference to his great ability as a kicker. Unquestionably he had no equal in this field of amusement — to him. His legs were small, his feet were small, but his ambition in this direction was large. He *could* kick with wonderful accuracy, as a matter of fact. Mule-drivers tell me he could kick a fly off his ear, as he walked along in the team, with unerring accuracy. This being so, of course larger objects were never missed when they were within range. But the distance included within a mule's range had often to be decided by two or three expensive tests. One driver, whom I well knew, was knocked over with a mule's hind foot while standing *directly in front of him.* This shows something of their range.

I have remarked, in substance, that the mule was conquered only by laying hold of or striking his ears. It may be asked how he was shod if he was such a kicker. To do this, one of two methods was adopted; either to sling him up as oxen are slung, then strap his feet; or walk him into a noose, and cast him, by drawing it around his legs. Of course, he would struggle violently for a while, but when he gave in it was all over for that occasion, and he was as docile under the smith's hands as a kitten. Being surer-footed and more agile than a horse, of course he gets into fewer bad places or entanglements; but once in, and having made a desperate struggle for his relief, and failing, he seems utterly discouraged, and neither whip nor persuasion can move him. Then, as in the shoeing, the driver can handle him with the utmost disregard of heels; but when once on his feet again, stand aside! He has a short memory. He lives in the future, and his heels are in business, as usual, at the old stand.

I need not comment on the size of the mule's ears. Of course, everybody who has seen them knows them to be abnormal in size. But disproportionately large though they may be, there is one other organ in his possession which surpasses them; that is his voice. This is something simply tremendous. That place which the guinea-fowl occupies among the feathered bipeds of the barn-yard in this respect, the mule holds *facile princeps* among the domestic quadrupeds. The poets who lived in the same time with Pericles said of the latter that "he lightened, thundered, and agitated all Greece," so powerful was his eloquence. So, likewise, when

THE REAR GUARD OF THE REGIMENT.

the mule raised his voice, all opposition was silent before him, for nothing short of rattling, crashing thunder, as it seemed, could successfully compete for precedence with him.

In addition to his great usefulness in the train, he was used a good deal under a pack-saddle. Each regiment usually had one, that brought up the rear on the march, loaded with the implements of the cook-house — sometimes with nothing to be seen but head and tail, so completely was he covered in. They were generally convoyed by a colored man. Sometimes these strong-minded creatures, in crossing a stream, would decide to lie down, all encumbered as they were, right in the middle, and down they would settle in spite of the ludicrous opposition and pathetic protests of the convoy. Of course, it was no balm to his wound to have the passing column of soldiers keep up a running fire of banter. But there was no redress or relief to be had until his muleship got ready to move, which was generally after every ounce of his burden had been stripped off and placed on terra firma.

When the army was lying in line of battle in such close proximity to the enemy that the ammunition wagons could not safely approach it, two boxes were taken and strapped on a mule, one on each side, "to keep his balance true," and thus the troops were supplied when needed.

At the terrible battle of Spottsylvania, May 12, 1864, a steady line of pack-mules, loaded with ammunition, filed up the open ravine, opposite the captured salient, for nearly twenty hours, in that way supplying our forces, who were so hotly engaged there.

Rations were furnished in the same manner under similar circumstances. But now and then a mule would lie down under his burden, and refuse to budge.

Grant says (vol. i. p. 106): "I am not aware of ever having used a profane expletive in my life, but I would have the charity to excuse those who may have done so if they were in charge of a train of Mexican pack-mules at the time," alluding to an experience in the Mexican War.

I believe I have stated that the mule much preferred to do military duty in the safe rear; but if there was anything which the war proved with the utmost clearness to both Yanks and Rebs, it was that there was surely no safe rear. This being so, the vivacious mule did not always have a plain and peaceful pilgrimage as a member of the wagon-train. I vividly recall the enjoyment of my company, during Lee's final retreat, whenever our guns were unlimbered, as they were again and again, to be trained on the columns of retreating wagon-trains. The explosion of a shell or two over or among them would drive the long-ears wild, and render them utterly unmanageable, and the driver's best and often his *only* recourse was to let them go if there was room ahead. But one demoralized, disorganized six-mule team would sometimes so effectively block the way, when the road was narrow, and the pursuit close, as to cause the capture of that part of the train behind it. Were any ex-Johnny m. d. to read this chuckling over the misfortunes of his craft, and not quite appreciate my enjoyment, I

MULES LOADED WITH AMMUNITION.

should at once assure him that there are some Yank m. d.'s who can heartily sympathize with him, having had a like experience.

From what I have stated, it will be seen that the mule would be very unreliable in cavalry service, for in action he would be so wild that if he did not dismount his rider he would carry even the most valiant from the scene of conflict, or, what was just as likely, rush madly into the ranks of the enemy. The same observations would suit equally well as objections to his service with artillery. On the 5th of April, 1865, during the retreat of Lee, we came upon a batch of wagons and a battery of steel guns, of the Armstrong pattern, I think, which Sheridan's troopers had cut out of the enemy's retreating trains. The guns had apparently never been used since their arrival from England. The harnesses were of russet leather and equally new; but the battery was drawn by a sorry-looking lot of horses and mules, indiscriminately mingled. My explanation for finding the mules thus tackled was that horses were scarce, and that it was not expected to use the guns at present, but simply to get them off safely; but that if it became necessary to use them they could do so with comparative safety to the mules as the guns were of very long range.

I should have pronounced these particular mules safe anywhere, even under a hot fire, if extreme emaciation had been a sure index of departed strength and nerve in this variety of brute. But that is not mule at all. The next day, at Sailor's Creek, my corps (Second), after a short, sharp contest, made a capture of thirteen flags, three guns, thirteen hundred prisoners, and over two hundred army wagons, with their mules. And such mules! the skinniest and boniest animals that I ever saw still retaining life, I sincerely believe. For a full week they had been on the go, night and day, with rare and brief halts for rest or food. Just before their capture they would seem to have gone down a long hill into a valley, a literal Valley of Humiliation as it proved, for there they were compelled to stay and surrender, either from inability to climb the opposite hill and get away, or else because there was not opportunity for them to do so before our forces came upon them. And yet, in spite of the worn and wasted state of those teams, it is doubtful if their kicking capacity was materially reduced by it.

The question frequently raised among old soldiers is, What became of all the army mules? There are thousands of these men who will take a solemn oath that they never saw a dead mule during the war. They can tell you of the carcasses of *horses* which dotted the line of march, animals which had fallen out from exhaustion or disease, and left by

the roadside for the buzzards and crows. These they can
recall by hundreds; but not the dimmest picture of a single
dead mule, and they will assure you that, to the best of their
knowledge and belief, the government did not lose one of
these animals during the war. I recently conversed with an
old soldier who remembered having once seen, on the
march, the *four hoofs* of a mule — those and nothing more;
and the conclusion that he arrived at was that the mule,
in a fit of temper, had kicked off his hoofs and gone up.

"BUT THE NOBLEST THING THAT PERISHED THERE,
WAS THAT OLD ARMY MULE."

Another soldier, a mule-driver, remembers of seeing a mule-
team which had run off the corduroy road into a mire of
quicksand. The wagon had settled down till its body
rested in the mire, but nothing of the team was visible
save the ear-tips of the off pole mule.

As a fact, however, the mules, though tough and hardy,
died of disease much as did the horses. Glanders took off a
great many, and black tongue, a disease peculiar to them,
caused the death of many more. But, with all their outs,
they were of invaluable service to the armies, and well
deserve the good opinions which came to prevail regarding
their many excellent qualities as beasts of burden. Here is
an incident of the war in which the mule was the hero of
the hour : —

On the night of Oct. 28, 1863, when General Geary's Division of the Twelfth Corps repulsed the attacking forces of Longstreet at Wauhatchie, Tennessee, about two hundred mules, affrighted by the din of battle, rushed in the darkness into the midst of Wade Hampton's Rebel troops, creating something of a panic among them, and causing a portion of them to fall back, supposing that they were at

CHARGE OF THE MULE BRIGADE.

tacked by cavalry. Some one in the Union army, who knew the circumstances, taking Tennyson's "Charge of the Light Brigade" as a basis, composed and circulated the following description of the ludicrous event: —

CHARGE OF THE MULE BRIGADE.

> Half a mile, half a mile,
> Half a mile onward,
> Right through the Georgia troops
> Broke the two hundred.

   ' Forward the Mule Brigade!
    Charge for the Rebs!" they neighed.
    Straight for the Georgia troops
     Broke the two hundred.

  " Forward the Mule Brigade!"
    Was there a mule dismayed?
    Not when the long ears felt
     All their ropes sundered.
    Theirs not to make reply,
    Theirs not to reason why,
    Theirs but to make Rebs fly.
    On! to the Georgia troops
     Broke the two hundred.

    Mules to the right of them,
    Mules to the left of them,
    Mules behind them
     Pawed, neighed, and thundered.
    Breaking their own confines,
    Breaking through Longstreet's lines
    Into the Georgia troops,
     Stormed the two hundred.

    Wild all their eyes did glare,
    Whisked all their tails in air
    Scattering the chivalry there,
     While all the world wondered.
    Not a mule back bestraddled,
    Yet how they all skedaddled —
    Fled every Georgian,
    Unsabred, unsaddled,
     Scattered and sundered!
    How they were routed there
     By the two hundred!

    Mules to the right of them,
    Mules to the left of them,
    Mules behind them
     Pawed, neighed, and thundered;
    Followed by hoof and head
    Full many a hero fled,
    Fain in the last ditch dead,
    Back from an ass's jaw
    All that was left of them, —
     Left by the two hundred.

When can their glory fade?
Oh, the wild charge they made!
  All the world wondered.
Honor the charge they made!
Honor the Mule Brigade,
  Long-eared two hundred!

The following plaint in behalf of this veteran quadruped will close this sketch: —

THE ARMY MULE IN TIME OF PEACE.

"That men are ungrateful can plainly be seen
In the case of that mule standing out on the green.
His features are careworn, bowed down is his head,
His spirit is broken: his hopes have all fled.
He thinks of the time when the battle raged sore,
When he mingled his bray with the cannon's loud roar;
When Uncle Sam's soldiers watched for him to come,
Hauling stores of provisions and powder and rum;
When his coming was greeted with cheers and huzzas,
And the victory turned on the side of the stars.

"These thoughts put new life into rickety bones—
He prances just once, then falls over and groans.
A vision comes over his poor mulish mind,
And he sees Uncle Sam, with his agents behind,
Granting pensions by thousands to all who apply,
From the private so low to the officer high;
To the rich and the poor, the wise man and fool,
But, alas! there is none for the 'poor army mule.'"

CHAPTER XVI.

HOSPITALS AND AMBULANCES.

HE sketch embodied in this chapter is an attempt in a limited space to give the public a more adequate idea of the medical department of the army, what it was, how it grew up, and something of what it accomplished. I enter upon it with a quasi-apology for its incompleteness, understanding fully how inadequate any mere sketch must be regarded by those whose labors in this department made its record one of the most remarkable in the history of the war; yet, like all the other topics treated in this volume, it must undergo abridgment, and I can only hope that what is presented will, in some degree, do justice to this much neglected but very interesting theme in the Rebellion's annals.

At the time of the battle of Bull Run there was no plan in operation by which the wounded in that battle were cared for. Before this engagement took place, while the troops were lying in and around Washington, general hospitals had been established to provide for the sick. For this purpose five or six hotels, seminaries, and infirmaries, in Washington and Georgetown, and two or three in Alexandria, had been taken possession of, and these were all the hospital accommodations to be found at the end of the first three months. So general was the opinion that the war would be speedily ended no one thought of such a thing as building permanent structures for hospital purposes.

But this condition of affairs soon after changed. Preparations for war were made on a grander scale. The Army of the Potomac, under the moulding hands of McClellan, was assuming form, and the appointment by him, Aug. 12, 1861, of Surgeon Charles S. Tripler as medical director of that army indicated a purpose of having a medical department set on foot and put in completeness for active service. Let us pause and glance at the situation as he found it, and we may, perhaps, the better appreciate the full magnitude of the task which he had before him.

Army Regulations were the written law to which it was attempted to have everything conform as far as possible. But when these regulations were drafted, there was no expectation of such a war as finally came upon us, and to attempt to confine so large an army as then existed to them as a guide was as impossible and absurd as for the full-grown man to wear the suit of clothes he cast off at ten years.

" New times demand new measures and new men,"

and so in certain directions Army Regulations had to be ignored. For example, they provided only for the establishment of regimental and general hospitals. A regimental hospital is what its name indicates — the hospital of a particular regiment. But if such a hospital became full or received some patients whose ailments were not likely to submit readily to treatment, such cases were sent to a *General Hospital*, that is, one into which patients were taken regardless of the regiment to which they belonged. But in these early war times, in the absence of a system, any patient who was able could, at his pleasure, leave one general hospital and go to another for any reason which seemed sufficient to him, or he could desert the service entirely.

By general orders issued from the war department May 25, 1861, governors of States were directed to appoint a surgeon and assistant surgeon for each regiment. The men appointed were for the most part country physicians, many of them with little practice, who, on reaching the field, were, in some respects, as ignorant of their duties under the changed conditions as if they had not been educated to the practice of medicine ; and the medical director of the army found his hands more than full in attempting to get them to carry out his wishes. So, to simplify his labors and also to increase the efficiency of his department, brigade hospitals were organized about the beginning of 1862, and by general orders from the war department brigade surgeons were appointed, with the rank of major, and assigned to the staffs of brigadier-generals. These brigade surgeons had supervision of the surgeons of their brigades, and exercised this duty under the instructions of the medical director.

The regimental hospitals in the field were sometimes tents, and sometimes dwellings or barns near camp. It was partly to relieve these that brigade hospitals were established. The latter were located near their brigade or division.

The hospital tent I have already described at some length. I may add here that those in use for hospital purposes before the war were 24 feet long by 14 feet 6 inches wide, and 11 feet 6 inches high, but, owing to their great bulk and weight, and the difficulty of pitching them in windy weather, the size was reduced, in 1860, to 14 feet by 14 feet 6 inches, and 11 feet high in the centre, with the walls 4 feet 6 inches, and a "fly" 21 feet 6 inches by 14 feet. Each of these was designed to accommodate eight patients comfortably. Army Regulations assigned three such tents to a regiment, together with one Sibley and one Wedge or A tent.

The Sibley tent I have likewise quite fully described. I will only add here that, not having a "fly," it was very hot in warm weather. Then, on account of its centre pole and the absence of walls, it was quite contracted and inconvenient. For these reasons it was little used for hospital purposes, and not used at all after the early part of the war.

The hospital tents in the Army of the Potomac were heated, for the most part, by what was called, for some reason, the *California Plan.* This consisted of a pit, dug just outside of the hospital door, two and a half feet deep, from which a trench passed through the tent, terminating outside the other end in a chimney, built of barrels, or in such a manner as I have elsewhere described. This trench was covered throughout its entire extent with iron plates, which were issued by the quartermaster's department for that purpose. The radiation of the heat from the plates kept the tent very comfortable.

The honor of organizing the first field hospital in tents is said to belong to Dr. B. J. D. Irwin, U. S. A., of the Army of the Ohio. It occurred at the battle of Shiloh. While establishing a hospital near the camp of Prentiss' division of that army, which had been captured the day before, the abandoned tents still standing suggested themselves to him as a convenient receptacle for his wounded. He at once appropriated the camp for this purpose, and laid it out in systematic form. It was clearly shown by this and succeeding experiences during the war that the wounded treated under canvas did better and recovered more rapidly than those treated in permanent hospitals.

As fast as they could be procured, hospital tents were furnished, three to a regiment, in accordance with the provision of Army Regulations referred to. Each regiment provided its own nurses and cooks. In general hospitals one nurse was allowed to ten patients, and one cook to thirty.

The capacity of a regimental hospital tent, like a stage-coach, varied according to the demand for room. I have said they were designed to accommodate eight. An old army surgeon says, "Only six can be comfortably accommodated in one of them, three on each side." But when the surgeons were crowded with the wounded, it was a common practice to set two long narrow boards edgewise through the centre

of the tent, about twenty inches apart. If boards were wanting, two good-sized *poles* were cut and used instead. Between these was the passage for the surgeons and nurses.
Behind the boards or poles a filling of straw or fine boughs
was made and covered with blankets. On these latter could
be placed twenty patients, ten on either side; but they were
crowded. When six single cots were put in one of these
tents, three on each side, ample space was afforded to pass
among them.

In the latter part of 1861, the government, realizing its pressing needs, began to build general hospitals for the comfort

A TWO-WHEELED AMBULANCE.

and accommodation of its increasing thousands of sick and
wounded, continuing to build, as the needs increased, to the
very last year of the war, when they numbered two
hundred and five.

Before the civil war, the government had never been
supplied with carriages to convey the sick and wounded.
Only two years before, a board, appointed by the secretary
of war, had adopted for experiment a four-wheeled and a
two-wheeled carriage. The four-wheeled vehicle was tried in
an expedition sent into New Mexico, and was favorably
reported on; the two-wheeled was never tested, but was
judged to be the best adapted to badly wounded men

(though the contrary proved to be the fact), and so the board reported in favor of adopting these carriages in the ratio of five two-wheeled to one four-wheeled.

When Surgeon Tripler took charge, he found several of these two-wheeled carriages in Washington, but they were used chiefly as pleasure-carriages for officers, or for some other private purpose. This was stopped, for a time at least, and an order was issued, leaving one to a regiment and requiring the rest to be turned over to the quartermaster's department. But the perversion of ambulances from their proper use, I will add in passing, continued, to a greater or less extent, till the end of the war. This very year McClellan issued an order for them not to be used except for the transportation of the sick and wounded, unless by authority of the brigade commander, the medical director, or the quartermaster in charge, and the provost-marshal was ordered to arrest officers and confine non-commissioned officers and privates for violation of the order.

The most important steps taken towards organizing the medical department, and placing it on that thorough basis which distinguished it in the later years of the war, were the result of the foresight, energy, and skilful management of Dr. Jonathan Letterman, who was made medical director of the Army of the Potomac on the 19th of June, 1862. His labor was something enormous. It was during the progress of the Peninsular Campaign. All was confusion. Medical supplies were exhausted. Thousands of sick and wounded men were dying for want of proper care and medicine. Yet this campaign, so disastrous in its results to our army from a military point of view, was a valuable teacher in many respects, and one of its most pointed and practical lessons was the necessity shown of having the ambulances organized and under a competent head. It remained for Dr. Letterman to appreciate this need, and effect an organization which remained practically unchanged till the close of the war. Here is the substance of the plan which he drew up, and which General McClellan approved, and published to the army in orders, Aug. 2, 1862, and which General Meade reissued, with some additions and slight changes, a little more than a year later.

AMBULANCE CORPS.

All of the ambulances belonging to an army corps were to be placed under the control of the medical director of that corps, for now, in addition to a medical director of the army, there was a subordinate medical director for each army corps. Such an ambulance corps was put into the hands of a captain as commandant. This corps was divided and subdivided into division, brigade, and regimental trains, corresponding to the divisions of the army corps to which it belonged, having a first lieutenant in charge of a division, a second lieutenant in charge of a brigade, and a sergeant in charge of a regimental detachment. Besides these, three privates, one of them being the driver, were to accompany each ambulance on the march and in battle. The duties of all these men, both officers and privates, were very carefully defined, as well for camp as for the march and battle. Besides the ambulances, there accompanied each corps one medicine-wagon and one army wagon to a brigade, containing the requisite medicines, dressings, instruments, hospital stores, bedding, medical books, small furniture (like tumblers, basins, bed-pans, spoons, vials, etc.).

In addition to the foregoing articles, which were carefully assorted both as to quantity and quality, each ambulance was required to carry in the box beneath the driver's seat, under lock and key, the following articles: —

Three bed-sacks, six 2-pound cans beef-stock, one leather bucket, three camp kettles (assorted sizes), one lantern and candle, six tin plates, six table-spoons, six tin tumblers; and, just before a battle, ten pounds hard bread were required to be put into the box.

There was another scheme, which was conceived and carried into execution by Dr. Letterman, which deserves mention in this connection. This was the establishment of Field Hospitals, "in order that the wounded might receive the most prompt and efficient attention during and after an engagement, and that the necessary operations might be performed by the most skilful and responsible surgeons, at the earliest moment." Under Surgeon Tripler, there had been rendezvous established in rear of the army, to which all the wounded were taken for immediate attention, before

A FOUR-WHEELED AMBULANCE.

being sent to general hospitals. But there was no recognized system and efficiency in regard to it. Just before an engagement, a field hospital for each division was established. It was made by pitching a suitable number of hospital tents. The location of such a hospital was left to the medical director of the corps. Of course, it must be in the rear of the division, out of all danger and in a place easily reached by the ambulances. A division hospital of this description was under the charge of a surgeon, who was selected by the surgeon-in-chief of the division. With him was an assistant surgeon, similarly appointed, whose duty it was to pitch the tents, provide straw, fuel, water, etc., and, in general, make everything ready for the comfort of the wounded. For doing this the hospital stewards and nurses of the division were placed under his charge, and special details made from the regiments to assist. A kitchen or cook-tent must be at once erected and the cooks put in possession of the articles mentioned as carried in the ambulance boxes and hospital-wagons, so that a sufficient amount of nourishing food could be prepared for immediate use.

Another assistant surgeon was detailed to keep a complete record of patients, with name, rank, company, and regiment, the nature of their wound, its treatment, etc. He was also required to see to the proper interment of those who died, and the placing of properly marked head-boards at their graves.

Then, there were in each of these division hospitals three surgeons, selected from the whole division, " without regard to rank, but solely on account of their known prudence, judgment, and skill," whose duty it was to perform all important operations, or, at least, be responsible for their performance. Three other medical officers were detailed to assist these three. Nor was this all, for the remaining medical officers of the division, except one to a regiment, were also required to report at once to the hospital, to act as dressers of wounds and assistants generally. In addition to these, a proper number of nurses and attendants were detailed to be on hand. The medical officers left with regiments were required to establish themselves during the fighting in the rear of their respective organizations, at such a distance as not to unnecessarily expose themselves, where they could give such temporary aid to the wounded as they should stand in need of.

I have said that these hospitals were to be located out of all danger. That statement needs a little modifying. In case the tide of battle turned against our army and it was compelled to retreat, what was before a safe place might at once be converted into a place of great danger. But a hospital could not be struck and its patients moved at a moment's or even a day's warning, as a rule, and so it was made the duty of the medical director of a corps to select a sufficient number of medical officers, who, in case a retreat was found necessary, should remain in charge of the wounded. When the Rebels captured such a hospital, it was their general practice to *parole* all the inmates — that is, require them to give their word of honor that they would not bear arms again until they had been properly exchanged

A MEDICINE WAGON.

as prisoners of war. Our government established what were known as parole camps, where such prisoners were required to remain until duly exchanged.

I think it can now be readily understood, from even this fragmentary sketch, how the establishment of these field hospitals facilitated the care of the wounded, and, by their systematic workings, saved hundreds of lives. With a skilful, energetic man as medical director of the army, giving his orders to medical directors of corps, and these carefully superintending surgeons-in-chief of divisions, who, in turn, held the surgeons and assistant surgeons and officers of ambulance corps to a strict accountability for a careful performance of their duties, while the latter fortified themselves by judicious oversight of *their* subordinates, the result was to place this department of the army on a footing which endured, with the most profitable of results to the service, till the close of the war.

I vividly remember my first look into one of these field hospitals. It was, I think, on the 27th of November, 1863, during the Mine Run Campaign, so-called. General French, then commanding the Third Corps, was fighting the battle of Locust Grove, and General Warren, with the Second Corps, had also been engaged with the enemy, and had driven him from the neighborhood of Robertson's Tavern, in the vicinity of which the terrific Battle of the Wilderness began the following May. Near this tavern the field hospital of Warren's Second Division had been located, and into this I peered while my battery stood in park not far away, awaiting orders. The surgeon had just completed an operation. It was the amputation of an arm about five inches below the shoulder, the stump being now carefully dressed and bandaged. As soon as the patient recovered from the effects of the ether, the attendants raised him to a sitting posture on the operating-table. At that moment the thought of his wounded arm returned to him, and, turning his eyes towards it, they met only the projecting stub. The awful reality dawned upon him for the first time. An arm had gone forever, and he dropped backwards on the table in a swoon. Many a poor fellow like him brought to the operator's table came to consciousness only to miss an arm or a leg which perhaps he had begged in his last conscious moments to have spared. But the medical officers first mentioned decided all such cases, and the patient had only to submit. At Peach-Tree Creek, Col. Thomas Reynolds of the Western army was shot in the leg, and, while the surgeons were debating the propriety of amputating it, the colonel, who was of Irish birth, begged them to spare it, as it was very valuable, being *an imported leg,* — a piece of wit which saved the gallant officer his leg, although he became so much of a cripple that he was compelled to leave the service.

It has been charged that limbs and arms were often use-lessly sacrificed by the operators; that they were especially fond of amputating, and just as likely to amputate for a flesh-wound as for a fractured bone, on the ground that they could do it more quickly than they could dress the wound;

A FOLDING LITTER.

that it made a neater job, thus gratifying professional pride: but how the victim might feel about it or be affected by it then or thereafter did not seem to enter their thoughts. It was undoubtedly true that many flesh-wounds were so ugly the only safety for the patient lay in amputation. A fine fellow, both as a man and soldier, belonging to my company, lost his arm from a flesh-wound — needlessly, as he and his friends always asserted and believed.

A corporal of the First Massachusetts Heavy Artillery suffered a compound fracture of the left knee-joint from a piece of shell by which he was struck at the battle of

A STRETCHER.

Hatcher's Run, Oct. 27, 1864. In the course of time he reached the Lincoln Hospitals (well do I remember them as they stood on Capitol Hill where they were erected just before the bloody repulse at Fredericksburg), where a sur-geon decided that his leg must come off, and, after instruct-ing the nurse to prepare him for the operating-room, left the ward. But the corporal talked the matter over with a wounded cavalryman (this was a year when cavalrymen were wounded quite generally) and decided that his leg must *not* come off ; so, obtaining the loaded revolver of his comrade, he put it under his pillow and awaited the reappearance of the surgeon. He returned not long after, accompanied by two men with a stretcher, and approached the cot.

"What are you going to do ?" asked the corporal.

" My boy, we will have to take your leg off," was the reply of the surgeon.

"Not if I know myself," rejoined the corporal, with determination expressed in both looks and language.

For a moment the surgeon was taken aback by the soldier's resolute manner. But directly he turned to the men and said, " Come, boys, take him up carefully," whereupon the stretcher-bearers advanced to obey the order. At the same instant the corporal drew the revolver from beneath his pillow, cocked it, and, in a voice which carried conviction, exclaimed, " *The man that puts a hand on me dies!*" At this the men stepped back, and the surgeon tried to reason with the corporal, assuring him that in no other way could his life be saved. But the corporal persisted in declaring that if he died it should be with both legs *on*.

At that "Sawbones" (as the men used to call them) lost his temper and sought out the surgeon in general charge, with whom he soon returned to the corporal. This head surgeon, first by threats and afterwards by persuasion, tried to secure the revolver, but, failing to do so, turned away, exclaiming, with an oath, " Let the d—— fool keep it and die !" but a moment after, on second thought, said to the first surgeon that, as they wanted a subject to try the water-cure on, he thought the corporal would meet that want. After obtaining a promise from the surgeon that he would not himself take the leg off or allow any one else to, the corporal assented to the proposition.

A can was then arranged over the wounded knee, in such a manner as to drop water on the cloth which enwrapped it day and night, and a cure was finally effected.

This is the substance of the story as I received it from the lips of the corporal himself, who, let me say in passing, was reduced to the rank of private, and mustered out of the service as such, for daring to keep two whole legs under him. His bravery in the hour of peril — to him — deserved better things from his country than that.

But to return to the field hospital again ; on the ground lay one man, wounded in the knee, while another sat near, wounded in the finger. This latter was a suspicious wound. Men of doubtful courage had a way of shooting off the end of the trigger-finger to get out of service. But

PLACING A WOUNDED MAN ON A STRETCHER.

they sometimes did it in such a bungling manner that they were found out. The powder blown into the wound was often the evidence which convicted them. These men must be proud of such scars to-day.

Three wounded Rebels also lay in the tent, waiting for surgical attention. Of course, they would not be put upon the tables until all of our own wounded were attended to ; they did not expect it. In one part of the tent lay two or three of our men, who were either lifeless or faint from loss of blood. Only a few rods away from the tent were some freshly made graves enclosing the forms of men whose wounds had proved fatal, either having died on their way to the hospital or soon after their arrival. Among these was the gallant Lieutenant-Colonel Theodore Hesser, who was shot

in the head while bravely leading the Seventy-second Pennsylvania Infantry in a charge. The graves were all plainly
marked with small head-boards. A drizzling rain added
gloom to the scene; and my first call at a field hospital, with
its dismal surroundings, was brief.

One regulation made for this department of the service
was never enforced. It provided that no one but the
proper medical officers or the officers, non-commissioned
officers, and privates of the ambulance corps should conduct
sick or wounded to the rear, either on the march or in battle,

CARRYING A WOUNDED MAN TO THE REAR.

but as a matter of fact there were probably more wounded men
helped off the field by soldiers *not* members of the ambulance
corps than by members of that body. There were always
plenty of men who hadn't the interests of the cause so
nearly at heart but what they could be induced, without
much persuasion, when bullets and shells were flying thick,
to leave the front line and escort a suffering comrade to the
rear. Very often such a sufferer found a larger body-guard
than could well make his needs a pretext for their absence from
the line. Then, too, many of these escorts were most unfortunate, and *lost their way*, so that they did not find their regiment again until after the battle was over. A large number
of them would be included among the Shirks and Beats,

whom I have already described. But, in truth, it was not possible for the ambulance corps to do much more in a hot fight than to keep their stretchers properly manned. Each ambulance was provided with two of these, and the severely wounded who could not help themselves must be placed on them and cared for first, so that there was often need for a helping hand to be given a comrade who was quite seriously wounded, yet could hobble along with a shoulder to lean on.

The designating mark of members of the ambulance corps was, for sergeants, a green band an inch and a quarter broad around the cap, and inverted chevrons of the same color on each arm, above the elbow; for privates the same kind of band and a half chevron of the same material. By means of this designation they were easily recognized.

By orders of General Meade, issued in August, 1863, three ambulances were allowed to a regiment of infantry; two to a regiment of cavalry, and one to a battery of artillery, with which it was to remain permanently. Owing to this fact, an artillery company furnished its own stretcher-bearers when needed. I shall be pardoned the introduction of a personal incident, as it will illustrate in some measure the duties and trials of a stretcher-bearer. It was at the battle of *Hatcher's Run*, already referred to, or the *Boydton Plank Road*, as some called it. The guns had been ordered into position near Burgess' Tavern, leaving the caissons and ambulance nearly a half-mile in the rear. Meanwhile, a flank attack of the enemy cut off our communications with the rear for a time, and we thought ourselves sure of an involuntary trip to Richmond; but the way was opened again by some of our advance charging to the rear, and by the destructive fire from our artillery. Soon orders came for the battery to return to the rear. In common with the rest, the writer started to do so when a sergeant asked him to remain and help take off one of our lieutenants, who was lying in a barn near by, severely wounded. So actively had we been engaged that this was my first knowledge of the sad event. But, alas! what was to be done? Our ambulance with its stretchers was to the rear. That could not now avail us. We must resort .to other means. Fortunately, they were at hand. An abandoned army-blanket lay near, and, carefully placing the lieutenant on this, with one man at each corner, we started.

But the wounded officer was heavy, and it was, as can readily be seen, an awkward way of carrying him. Moreover, his wound was a serious one, — mortal as it soon proved, — and every movement of ours tortured him so that he begged of us to leave him there to die. Just then we caught sight of a stretcher on which a wounded Rebel was lying. Some Union stretcher-bearers had been taking him to the rear when the flank attack occurred, when they evidently abandoned him to look out for themselves. It was not a time for sentiment; so, with the sergeant at one end of the stretcher and the narrator at the other, our wounded enemy was rolled off, with as much care as time would allow. With the aid of our other comrades we soon put the lieutenant in his place, and, raising the stretcher to our shoulders, started down the road to the rear. We had gone but a few rods, however, before the enemy's sharpshooters or outposts fired on us, driving us to seek safety in the woods. But it was now dusk, and no easy matter to take such a burden through woods, especially as it rapidly grew darker. Suffice it to know, however, that, after more than an hour's wandering and plunging, our burden was delivered at the ambulance, where another of our lieutenants, also mortally wounded, was afterwards to join him. This fragment of personal experience will well illustrate some of the many obstacles which stretcher-bearers had to contend with, and disclose the further truth that in actual combat the chances for severely wounded men to be taken from the field were few indeed, for at such a time stretcher-bearers, like the proverbial " good men," are scarce.

I omitted to say in the proper connection that the men whose wounds were dressed in the field hospitals were transported as rapidly as convenient to the general hospitals, where the best of care and attention could be given them. Such hospitals were located in various places. Whenever it was possible, transportation was by water, in steamers specially fitted up for such a purpose. There may be seen in the National Museum at Washington, the building in which President Lincoln was assassinated, beautiful models of these steamers as well as of hospital railway trains with all their furnishings of ease and comfort, designed to carry patients by rail to any designated place.

Another invention for the transportation of the wounded from the field was the *Cacolet* or *Mule Litter*, which was borne either by a mule or a horse, and arranged to carry, some one and some two, wounded men. But although it was at first supposed that they would be a great blessing for this purpose, yet, being strapped tightly to the body of the animal, they felt his every motion, thus making them an intensely uncomfortable carriage for a severely wounded soldier, so that they were used but very little.

The distinguished surgeon Dr. Henry I. Bowditch, whose son, Lieut. Bowditch, was mortally wounded in the cavalry fight at Kelly's Ford, voiced, in his "Plea for an Ambulance System," the general dissatisfaction of the medical profession with the neglect or barbarous treatment of our wounded on the battle-field. This was as late as the spring of 1863. They had petitioned Congress to adopt some system without delay, and a bill to that effect had passed the House, but on Feb. 24, 1863, the Committee on Military Affairs, of which Senator Henry Wilson was chairman, reported against a bill "in relation to Military Hospitals and to organize an Ambulance Corps," as an impracticable measure at that time, and the Senate adopted the report, and there, I think, it dropped.

CHAPTER XVII.

SCATTERING SHOTS.

"His coat was e'er so much too short,
His pants a mile too wide,
And when he marched could not keep step
However much he tried."

THE CLOTHING.

ORTY–TWO dollars was the sum allowed by the government to clothe the private soldier for the space of one year. The articles included in his outfit were a cap or hat (usually the former), blouse, overcoat, dress coat, trousers, shirts, drawers, socks, shoes, a woollen and a rubber blanket. This was the wardrobe of the *infantry*. It should be said, however, that many regiments never drew a dress coat after leaving the state, the blouse serving as the substitute for that garment. The *artillery* and *cavalry* had the same except that a jacket took the place of the dress coat, boots that of shoes, and their trousers had a *re-enforce*, that is, an extra thickness of cloth extending from the upper part of the seat down the inside of both legs, for greater durability in the service required of these branches in the saddle.

This outfit was not sufficient to last the year through, for various reasons, and so the quartermaster supplied duplicates of the garments when needed. But whatever was drawn from him beyond the amount allowed by the government was charged to the individual, and deducted from his pay at the end of the year. If, however, a man was so fortunate as not to overdraw his allowance, which rarely happened, he received the balance in cash.

The infantry made way with a large amount of clothing. Much of it was thrown away on the march. A soldier burdened with a musket, from forty to eighty rounds of ammunition, according to circumstances; a haversack stuffed plump as a pillow, but not so soft, with three days rations; a canteen of water, a woollen and rubber blanket, and a half shelter tent, would be likely to take just what more he was obliged to. So, with the opening of the spring campaign, away would go all extra clothing. A choice was made between the dress coat and blouse, for one of these must go. Then some men took their overcoat and left their blanket. In brief, when a campaign was fairly under way the average infantryman's wardrobe was what he had on. Only that and nothing more. At the first start from camp many would burden themselves with much more than the above, but after a few miles tramp the roadside would be sprinkled with the cast-away articles. There seemed to be a difference between Eastern and Western troops in this respect, for reasons which I will not attempt now to analyze, for Grant says (Memoirs, vol. ii., pp. 190–191) : —

" I saw scattered along the road, from Culpeper to Germania Ford, wagon-loads of new blankets and overcoats thrown away by the troops to lighten their knapsacks; an improvidence I had never witnessed before."

It was a way the Army of the Potomac had of getting into light marching order.

When the infantry were ordered in on a charge, they always left their knapsacks behind them, which they might or might not see again. And whenever they were surprised and compelled to fall back hastily, they were likely to throw aside everything that impeded their progress except musket and ammunition. Then, in the heat of battle, again there was a dispensing with all encumbrances that would impair

their efficiency. For these and other reasons, the governmental allowances would not have been at all adequate to
cover the losses in clothing. Recognizing this fact, the government supplied new articles gratis for everything lost in
action, the quartermaster being required to make out a list
of all such articles, and to certify
that they were so lost, before new
ones could be obtained.

But the men who did garrison
duty were not exempt from long
clothing bills more than were those
who were active at the front. I
have in mind the heavy artillerymen
who garrisoned the forts around
Washington. They were in receipt
of visits at all hours in the day from
the most distinguished of military
and civil guests, and on this account
were not only obliged to be efficient
in drill but showy on parade. Hence
their clothing had always to be of
the best. No patched or untidy
garments were tolerated. In the
spring of 1864, twenty-four thousand
of these men were despatched as re-
enforcements to the Army of the

IN HEAVY MARCHING ORDER.　Potomac, and a fine lot of men they
were. They were soldiers, for the
most part, who had enlisted early in the war, and, having had
so safe — or, as the boys used to say, "soft" — and easy a time
of it in the forts, had re-enlisted, only to be soon relieved of
garrison duty and sent to the front as infantry. But while
they were veterans in service in point of time, yet, so far as
the real hardships of war were concerned, they were simply
recruits. I shall never forget that muggy, muddy morning of the 18th of May, when, standing by the roadside

near what was known as the "Brown House," at Spottsylvania, I saw this fine-looking lot of soldiers go by. Their
uniforms and equipments all seemed new. Among the regiments was the First Maine Heavy Artillery.

"What regiment is this?" was inquired at the head of the
column by bystanders.

"First Maine," was the reply.

After the columns had marched by a while, some one
would again ask what regiment it was, only to find it still
the First Maine. It numbered over two thousand strong,
and, never having lost any men in battles and hard
campaigning, its ranks were full. The strength of these
regiments struck the Army of the Potomac with surprise. A single regiment larger than one of their own
brigades!

These men had started from Washington with knapsacks
that were immense in their proportions, and had clung to
them manfully the first day or two out, but this morning in
question, which was of the sultriest kind, was taxing them
beyond endurance, as they plunged along in the mire marching up to the front; and their course could have been followed by the well stuffed knapsacks — or "bureaus," as some
of the old vets called them — that sprinkled the roadside.
It seemed rather sad to see a man step out of the ranks, un-
sling his knapsack, seat himself for a moment to overhaul
its contents, transfer to his pocket some little keepsake,
then, rising, and casting one despairing look at it, hurry on
after the column. Many would not even open their knapsacks, but, giving them a toss, would leave them to fate, and
sternly resume their march. It was the second in the list of
sacrifices that active campaigning required of them. Their
first was made in cutting loose from their comfortable quarters and accumulated conveniences in the forts, which they
had so recently left.

The knapsack, haversack, canteen, and shelter-tent, like
the arms, were government property, for which the com-

manding officer of a company was responsible. At the end
of a soldier's term of service, they were to be turned in or
properly accounted for.

ARMY CATTLE.

An army officer who was reputed to have been of high
and hasty temper, who certainly seemed to have been capa-
ble of rash and inconsiderate remarks, was once overheard
to say of soldiers that they were nothing but cattle, and deserved to be treated only as such. In the short sketch here
submitted on the subject of Army Cattle, I do not include
the variety above referred to, but rather the quadrupedal
kind that furnished food for them.

In the sketch on Army Rations I named fresh beef as one
of the articles furnished, but I gave no particulars as to just
how the army was supplied with it. This I will now endeavor to do.

When there came an active demand for fresh and salt
meat to feed the soldiers and sailors, at once the price
advanced, and Northern farmers turned their attention more
extensively to grazing. Of course, the great mass of the
cattle were raised in the West, but yet even rugged New
England contributed no inconsiderable quantity to swell the
total. These were sent by hundreds and thousands on rail
and shipboard to the various armies. On their arrival, they
were put in a *corral*. Here they were subject, like all supplies, to the disposition of the commissary-general of the
army, who, through his subordinates, supplied them to the
various organizations upon the presentation of a requisition,
signed by the commanding officer of a regiment or other body
of troops, certifying to the number of rations of meat required.

When the army was investing Petersburg and Richmond,
the cattle were in corral near City Point. On the 16th of
September, 1864, the Rebels having learned through their
scouts that this corral was but slightly guarded, and that by

making a wide détour in the rear of our lines the chances were good for them to add a few rations of fresh beef to the bacon and corn-meal diet of the Rebel army, a strong force of cavalry under Wade Hampton made the attempt, capturing twenty-five hundred beeves and four hundred prisoners, and getting off with them before our cavalry could intervene. The beeves were a blessing to them, far more precious and valuable than as many Union prisoners would have been; for they already had more prisoners than they could or would feed. As for us, I do not remember that fresh meat was any the scarcer on account of this raid, for the North, with its abundance, was bountifully supplying the government with whatever was needed, and the loss of a few hundred cattle could scarcely cause even a temporary inconvenience. Had the army been on the march, away from its base of supplies, the loss might have been felt more severely.

Whenever the army made a move its supply of fresh meat went along too. Who had charge of it? Men were detailed for the business from the various regiments, who acted both as butchers and drovers, and were excused from all other duty. When a halt was made for the night, some of the steers would be slaughtered, and the meat furnished to the troops upon presentation of the proper requisitions by quartermasters. The butcher killed his victims with a rifle. The killing was not always done at night. It often took place in the morning or forenoon, and the men received their rations in time to cook for dinner.

The manner in which these cattle were taken along was rather interesting. One might very naturally suppose that they would be driven along the road just as they are driven in any neighborhood; but such was not exactly the case. The troops and trains must use the roads, and so the cattle must needs travel elsewhere, which they did. Every herd had a steer that was used both as a pack animal and a leader. As a pack animal he bore the equipments and cooking utensils of the drovers. He was as docile as an old cow or horse, and could be led or called fully as readily. By day he was preceded in his lead by the herdsman in charge, on horseback, while other herdsmen brought up the rear. It was necessary to keep the herd along with the troops for two reasons — safety and convenience; and, as they could not

LEADING THE HERD.

use the road, they skirted the fields and woods, only a short remove from the highways, and picked their way as best they could.

By night one of the herdsmen went ahead of the herd on foot, making a gentle hallooing sound which the sagacious steer on lead steadily followed, and was in turn faithfully followed by the rest of the herd. The herdsman's course lay sometimes through the open, but often through the woods, which made the hallooing sound necessary as a guide to keep the herd from straying. They kept nearer the road at night than in the day, partly for safety's sake, and partly to take advantage of the light from huge camp-fires which detachments of cavalry, that preceded the army, kindled at intervals to light the way, making them nearer together in woods and swamps than elsewhere. Even then these drovers often had a thorny and difficult path to travel in picking their way through underbrush and brambles.

Such a herd got its living off the country in the summer, but not in the winter. It was a sad sight to see these animals, which followed the army so patiently, sacrificed

THE LAST STEER.

one after the other until but a half-dozen were left. When the number had been reduced to this extent, they seemed to realize the fate in store for them, and it often took the butcher some time before he could succeed in facing one long enough to shoot him. His aim was at the curl of the hair between the eyes, and they would avert their lowered heads whenever he raised his rifle, until, at last, his quick eye brought them to the ground.

From the manner in which I have spoken of these herds, it may be inferred that there was a common herd for the whole army; but such was not the case. The same system prevailed here as elsewhere. For example, when the army entered the Wilderness with three days' rations of hard bread, and three days' rations of meat in their haversacks, the fresh meat to accompany the other three days' rations, which they had stowed in their knapsacks, was driven along in division herds. The remainder of the meat ration which they required to last them for the sixteen days during which it was expected the army would be away from a base of supplies was driven as corps herds. In addition to these there was a general or army herd to fall back upon when necessary to supply the corps herds, but this was always at the base of supplies. Probably from eight to ten thousand head of cattle accompaniéd the army across the Rapidan, when it entered upon the Wilderness Campaign.

THE ARMY HORSE.

I have already stated that the horse was the sole reliance of the artillery and cavalry, and have given the reasons why the mule was a failure in either branch. I have also stated that the mule replaced him, for the most part, in the wagon-trains, six mules being substituted for four horses. I did not state that in the ambulance train the horses were retained because they were the steadier. But I wish now to refer more particularly to their conduct in action and on duty generally.

First, then, I will come directly to the point by saying that the horse was a hero in action. That horses under fire behaved far better than men did under a similar exposure would naturally be expected, for men knew what and whom to fear, whereas a horse, when hit by a bullet, if he could get loose, was fully as likely to run towards the enemy as from him. But not every horse would run or make a fuss when wounded. It depended partly upon the horse and partly upon the character and location of the wound. I have seen bullets buried in the neck or rump of steady-nerved horses without causing them to show more than a little temporary uneasiness. The best illustration of the fortitude

GENERAL HANCOCK AT REAM'S STATION, VA., AUGUST 25, 1864.

of horse-flesh that I ever witnessed occurred on the 25th of August, 1864, at Ream's Station on the Weldon Railroad. In this battle the fifty-seven or eight horses belonging to my company stood out in bold relief, a sightly target for the bullets of Rebel sharpshooters, who, from a woods and corn-field in our front, improved their opportunity to the full. Their object was to kill off our horses, and then, by charging, take the guns, if possible.

It was painfully interesting to note the manner in which our brave limber-horses — those which drew the guns — succumbed to the bullets of the enemy. They stood harnessed in teams of six. A peculiar dull thud indicated that the bullet had penetated some fleshy part of the animal, sounding much as a pebble does when thrown into the mud. The result of such wounds was to make the horse start for a moment or so, but finally he would settle down as if it was something to be endured without making a fuss, and thus he would remain until struck again. I remember having had my eye on one horse at the very moment when a bullet entered his neck, but the wound had no other effect upon him than to make him shake his head as if pestered by a fly. Some of the horses would go down when hit by the first bullet and after lying quiet awhile would struggle to their feet again only to receive additional wounds. Just before the close of this battle, while our gallant General Hancock was riding along endeavoring by his own personal fearlessness to rally his retreating troops, his horse received a bullet in the neck, from the effects of which he fell forward, dismounting the general, and appearing as if dead. Believing such to be the case, Hancock mounted another horse ; but within five minutes the fallen brute arose, shook himself, was at once remounted by the general, and survived the war many years.

When a bullet struck the bone of a horse's leg in the lower part, it made a hollow snapping sound and took him off his feet. I saw one pole-horse shot thus, fracturing the bone. Down he went at once, but all encumbered as he was with harness and limber, he soon scrambled up and stood on three legs until a bullet hit him vitally. It seemed sad to see a single horse left standing, with his five companions all lying dead or dying around him, himself the object of a concentrated fire until the fatal shot finally laid him low. I saw one such brute struck by the seventh bullet before he fell for the last time. Several received as many as five

REAL " HORSE SENSE."

bullets, and it was thought by some that they would average that number apiece. They were certainly very thoroughly riddled, and long before the serious fighting of the day occurred but two of the thirty-one nearest the enemy remained standing. These two had been struck but not vitally, and survived some time longer. We took but four of our fifty-seven horses from that ill-starred fray.

But, aside from their wonderful *heroism*, — for I can find no better name for it, — they exhibited in many ways that sagacity for which the animal is famous. I have already referred to the readiness with which they responded to many of the bugle-calls used on drill. In the cavalry service they knew their places as well as did their riders, and it was a frequent occurrence to see a horse, when his rider had been dismounted by some means, resume his place in line or column without him, seemingly not wishing to be left behind. This quality was often illustrated when a poor, crippled, or generally used-up beast, which had been turned out to die, would attempt to hobble along in his misery and join a column as it passed.

Captain W. S. Davis, a member of General Griffin's staff of the Fifth Corps, rode a horse which had the very singular but horse-sensible habit of sitting down on his haunches, like a dog, after his rider had dismounted. One morning he was missing, and nothing was seen of him for months; but one night, after the corps had encamped, some of the men, who knew the horse, in looking off towards the horizon, saw against the sky a silhouette of a horse sitting down. It was at once declared to be the missing brute, and Captain Davis, on being informed, recovered his eccentric but highly prized animal.

CHAPTER XVIII.

BREAKING CAMP. — ON THE MARCH.

" And now comes 'boots and saddles!' Oh! there's hurrying to and fro,
And saddling up in busy haste — for what, we do not know.
Sometimes 'twas but a false alarm, sometimes it meant a fight;
Sometimes it came in daytime, and sometimes it came at night."

HE subject of this chapter is a very suggestive one to the old soldier. It covers a whole realm of experience which it would be nearly impossible to exhaust. But there is much in this as in other experiences which was common to all long-term veterans, and to this common experience more especially I shall address my attention.

From the descriptions which I have already given of the various kinds of shelter used by the soldiers it will be readily understood that they got the most comfortably settled in their winter-quarters, and that in a small way each hut became a miniature homestead, and for the time being possessed, to a certain extent, all the attractions of home. The bunk, the stools, and other furniture, the army bric-à-brac, whether captured or of home production, which adorned the rough tenement within and without, all came to have a value by association in the soldier's thought, a value which was not fully computed till campaigning impended — that usually direful day, when marching orders came and the boys folded their tents and marched away. This sketch

330

will relate something of army life as it was lived after marching orders were received.

When the general commanding an army had decided upon a plan of campaign, and the proper time came to put it in operation, he at once issued his orders to his subordinate commanders to have their commands ready to take their place in column at a given hour on a given day. These orders came down through the various corps, division, brigade, regimental, or battery headquarters to the rank and file, whose instructions given them on line would be to the effect that at the stated hour they were to be ready to start with three days' rations in their haversacks (this was the usual quantity), the infantry to have forty rounds of ammunition in their cartridge-boxes. This latter quantity was very often exceeded. The Army of the Potomac went into the Wilderness having from eighty to a hundred rounds of ammunition to a man, stowed away in knapsacks, haversacks, or pockets, according to the space afforded, and six days' rations similarly disposed of. When Hooker started on the Chancellorsville Campaign, *eleven days' rations* were issued to the troops.

Sometimes marching orders came when least expected. I remember to have heard the long roll sounded one Saturday forenoon in the camp of the infantry that lay near us in the fall of '63; it was October 10. Our guns were unlimbered for action just outside of camp where we had been lying several days utterly unsuspicious of danger. It was quite a surprise to us; and such Lee intended it to be, he having set out to put himself between our army and Washington. We were not attacked, but started to the rear a few hours afterwards.

Before the opening of the spring campaign a reasonable notice was generally given. There was one orderly from each brigade headquarters who almost infallibly brought marching orders. The men knew the nature of the tidings which he cantered up to regimental headquarters with under his belt.   Very often they would good-naturedly rail at him as he rode into and out of camp, thus indicating their dislike of his errand; but the wise ones went directly to quarters and began to pack up.

When it was officially announced to the men on line at night that marching orders were received, and that at such an hour next morning tents would be struck and the men in

PACKING UP.

place, equipped and provided as already stated, those men who had not already decided the question retired to their huts and took an account of stock in order to decide what to take and what to leave.   As a soldier would lay out two articles on the bunk, of equally tender associations, one could seem to hear him murmur, with Gay,

> "How happy could I be with either
> Were t'other dear charmer away."

as he endeavored to choose between them, knowing too well that both could not be taken.   The "survival of the fittest" was the question, which received deeper and tenderer consideration here in one evening than Darwin has ever given it in the same time. Then, there was the overcoat and the woollen blanket which should be left? Perhaps he finally decided to try taking both along for a while. He will leave the dress-coat and wear the blouse. He has two changes of flannels. He will throw away those he has on, don a clean set and take a change with him. These flannels, by the way, if they were what he drew from the government stores, were often as rough to the skin as coarse sand-paper, which they somewhat resembled in color.

From the head of his bunk he takes a collection of old letters which have accumulated during the winter. These he looks over one by one and commits to the flames with a sigh. Many of them are letters from home ; some are from acquaintances. Possibly he read the *Waverly Magazine*, and may have carried on a correspondence with one or more of the many young women who advertised in it for a "soldier correspondent, who must not be over twenty," with all the virtues namable. There was no man in my company — from old Graylocks, of nearly sixty, down to the callow "chicken" of seventeen — but what felt qualified to fill such a bill, "just for the fun of it, you know." The young woman was generally "eighteen, of prepossessing appearance, good education, and would exchange photographs if desired."

An occasional letter from such a quarter would provoke a smile as the soldier glanced at its source and contents before committing it to the yawn of his army fireplace. This rather unpleasant task completed, he continues his researches and work of destruction. He tucks his little collection of photographs, which perhaps he has encased in rubber or leather, into an inside pocket, and disposes other small keepsakes about his person. If he intends to take his effects in a knapsack, he will at the start have put by more to carry than if he simply takes his blankets (rubber and woollen) rolled and slung over his shoulder. Late in the war this latter was the most common plan, as the same weight could be borne with less fatigue in that manner than in a knapsack, slung on the back.

I have assumed it to be evening or late afternoon when marching orders arrived, and have thus far related what the average soldier was wont to do immediately afterwards. There was a night ahead and the soldiers were wont to "make a night of it." As a rule, there was little sleep to be had, the enforcement of the usual rules of camp being relaxed on such an occasion. Aside from the labor of personal packing and destroying, the rations were to be distributed, and each company had to fall into line, march to the cook-house, and receive their three or more days' allowance of hardtack, pork, coffee, and sugar, all of which they must stow away, as compactly as possible, in the haversack or elsewhere if they wanted them. In the artillery, besides securing the rations, sacks of grain — usually oats — must be taken from the grain-pile and strapped on to the ammunition-chests for the horses; the axles must be greased, good spare horses selected to supply the vacancies in any teams where the horses were unfit for duty; the tents of regimental headquarters must be struck, likewise the cook-tents, and these, with officers' baggage, must be put into the wagons which are to join the trains; — in brief, everything must be prepared for the march of the morrow.

After this routine of preparation was completed, camp-fires were lighted, and about them would gather the happy-go-lucky boys of the rank and file, whose merry din would speedily stir the blood of the men who had hoped for a few hours' sleep before starting out on the morrow, to come out of their huts and join the jovial round; and soon they were as happy as the happiest, even if more reticent. As the fire died down and the soldiers drew closer about it, some comrade would go to his hut, and, with an armful of its furniture, the stools, closets, and tables I have spoken of, reillumine and enliven the scene and drive back the circle of bystanders again.

The conversation, which, with the going down of the fire, was likely to take on a somewhat sober aspect, would again assume a more cheerful strain. For a time conjectures on the plan of the coming compaign would be exchanged. Volumes of wisdom concerning what *ought* to be done changed hands at these camp-fires, mingled with much "I told you so" about the last battle. Alexanders simply swarmed, so

WAITING FOR MARCHING ORDERS.

numerous were those who could solve the Gordian knot of success at sight. It must interest those strategists now, as they read history, to see how little they really knew of what was taking place.

When this slight matter of the proper thing for the army to do was disposed of, some one would start a song, and then for an hour at least "John Brown's Body," "Marching Along," "Red, White, and Blue," "Rally 'round the Flag," and other popular and familiar songs would ring out on the clear evening air, following along in quick succession, and sung with great earnestness and enthusiasm as the chorus was increased by additions from neighboring camp-fires, until tired Nature began to assert herself, when one by one the company would withdraw, each going to his hut for two or three hours' rest, if possible, to partially prepare him for the toils of the morrow. Ah! is not that an all-wise provision of Providence which keeps the future a sealed book, placing it before us leaf by leaf only, as the present? For some of these very men, it may have been, whose voices rang out so merrily at that camp-fire, would lie cold and pale ere the week should close, in the solemn stillness of death.

But morning dawned all too soon for those who gave up most of the night to hilarity, and all were summoned forth at the call of the bugle or the drum, and at a time agreed upon *The General* was sounded.

THE GENERAL.

The above is the General of infantry. That of the artillery was less often used and entirely different.

At this signal, every tent in a regiment was struck. It was quite an interesting sight to see several acres of canvas disappear in a moment, where before it had been the prominent feature in the landscape. As a fact, I believe the General was little used in the latter part of the war. For about two years, when the troops were sheltered by the Sibley, Wedge, and Wall tents, it was necessary to have them struck at an early hour, in order that they might be packed away in the wagon-train. But after the Shelter tent came into use, and each man was his own wagon, the General was seldom heard unless at the end of a long encampment; for, when marching orders came, each man understood that he must be ready at the hour appointed, even if his regiment waited another day before it left camp.

No more provoking incident of army life happened, I believe, than for a regiment to wait in camp long after the hour appointed to march. But such was the rule rather than the exception. Many a man's hearth-stone was then desolate, for if the hour of departure was set for the morning, when morning came and the stockade was vacated, it often suffered demolition to increase the heat of the camp-fires, as previously noted. But as hour after hour wore on, and men still found themselves in camp with nothing to do and plenty of help, they began to wish that they had not been so hasty in breaking up housekeeping and tearing down their shanties, else they might resort to them and make their wait a little more endurable. Especially did they repent if rain came on as they lingered, or if night again overtook them there with their huts untenable, for it would have been the work of only a moment to re-cover them with the Shelter tents. Such waits and their consequences were severe tests to the patience of the men, and sometimes seemed to work more injury to their morals than the average army chaplain could repair in days.

But there is an end to all things earthly, this being no exception. The colors of corps headquarters borne at the heels of the corps commander, and followed by his staff, are at last seen moving into the road. The bugler of the division having the lead sounds the call *Attention*.

ATTENTION.

This call is the Attention of infantry at which the men, already in column, take their places, officers mount, and all await the next call, which is

FORWARD.

At this signal the regiments take "right shoulder shift," and the march begins. Let the reader, in imagination, take post by the roadside as the column goes by. Take a look at corps headquarters. The commander is a major-general. His staff comprises an assistant adjutant-general, an assistant inspector-general, a topographical engineer, a commissary of musters, a commissary of subsistence, a judge-advocate, several aides-de-camp — and perhaps other officers, of varying rank. Those mentioned usually ranked from colonel to captain. In the Union army, major-generals might command either a division, a corps, or an army, but in the Confederate service each army of importance was commanded by a lieutenant-general. Take a look at the corps headquarters flag. Feb. 7, 1863, General Hooker decreed the flags of corps headquarters to be a blue swallow-tail field bearing a white Maltese cross, having in the centre the number of the corps; but, so far as I can learn, this decree was never enforced in a single instance. Mr. James Beale, in his exceedingly valuable and unique volume, "The Union Flags at Gettysburg," shows a nondescript cross on some of the headquarters flags, which some quartermaster may have intended as a compliance with Hooker's order; but though true copies of originals they are monstrosities, which never could have had existence in a well ordered brain, and which have no warrant in heraldry or general orders as far as can be ascertained. When the army entered upon the Wilderness Campaign, each corps headquarters floated a blue swallow-tailed flag bearing its own particular emblem in white, in the centre of which was the figure designating the corps, in red.

Here comes the First Division. At the head rides its general commanding and staff. Behind him is the color-bearer, carrying the division flag. If you are familiar with the corps badges, you will not need to ask what corps or division it is. The men's caps tell the story, but the flags are equally plain-spoken.

This flag is the first *division* color. It is *rectangular* in shape. The corps emblem is red in a white field; the *second* has the emblem white in a blue field; the *third* has the emblem blue in a white field. The divisions had the lead of the corps on the march by turns, changing each day.

But here comes another headquarters. The color-bearer carries a *triangular* flag. That is a *brigade* flag. May 12, 1863, General Hooker issued an order prescribing division flags of the pattern I have described, and also designated what the brigade flags should be. They were to be, first of all, *triangular* in shape; the brigades of the first division should bear the corps symbol in *red* in the centre of a *white* field, but, to distinguish them, the first brigade should have no other mark; the second should have a *blue* stripe next the staff, and the third a *blue* border four and one-half inches wide around the flag.

The brigades of the second division had the corps symbol in *white* in the centre of a *blue* field, with a *red* stripe next the staff to designate the second brigade, and a *red* border the third.

The third division had its brigades similarly designated, with the symbol *blue*, the field *white*, and the stripes *red*.

Whenever there was a fourth brigade, it was designated by a triangular block of color in each corner of the flag.

The chief quartermaster of the corps and the chief of artillery had each his appropriate flag, as designated in the color-plate, but the arrangement of the colors in the flag of the chief quartermasters differed in different corps.

This scheme of Hooker's, for distinguishing corps, division, and brigade headquarters remained unchanged till the end of the war.

The brigades took turns in having the lead — or, as military men say, the *right* — of the division, and regiments had the right of brigades by turns.

There goes army headquarters yonder — the commanding general, with his numerous staff — making for the head of the column.   His flag is the simple star-spangled banner. The stars and stripes were a common flag for army headquarters.   It was General Meade's headquarters flag till Grant came to the Army of the Potomac, who also used it for that purpose.   This made it necessary for Meade to change, which he did, finally adopting a lilac-colored swallow-tail flag, about the size of the corps headquarters flags, having in the field a wreath enclosing an eagle, in gold.

You can easily count the regiments in column by their United States colors.   A few of them, you will notice, have a battle-flag, bearing the names of the engagements in which they have participated.   Some regiments used the national colors for a battle-flag, some the state colors. I think the volunteers did not adopt the idea early in the war.   Originally battles were only inscribed on flags by authority of the secretary of war, that is, in the regular army.   But the volunteers seemed to be a law unto themselves, and, while many flags in existence to-day bear names of battles inscribed by order of the commanding general, there are some with inscriptions of battles which the troops were hardly in hearing of.   The Rebel battle-flag was a blue spangled saltier in a red field, and originated with General Joe Johnston after the first Bull Run.

You will have little difficulty in deciding where a regiment begins or ends. It begins with a field officer and ends with a mule. Originally it ended with several army wagons; but now that portion of regimental headquarters baggage which has not gone to the wagon-train is to be found stowed about the mule, that is led along by a contraband. Yes, the head, ears, and feet which you see are the only visible externals of a mule. He is "clothed upon" with the various materials necessary to prepare a "square meal" for the colonel and other headquarters officers. His trappings would, seemingly, fit out a small family in household goods of a kind. There is a mess-kettle, a fry-pan, messpans, tent-poles, a fly (canvas), a valise, a knapsack and haversack, a hamper on each side, a musket, and other matter which goes to make the burden at least twice the size of the animal. Four mules were regarded as having the carrying capacity of one army wagon. At the end of the brigade you will see two or three of these mules burdened with the belongings of brigade headquarters.

The mule had other company than the negro ofttimes. That man who seems to be flour and grease from head to heels, who needs no shelter nor rubber blanket because he is waterproof already, perhaps, *inside* and out, whose shabby, well-stuffed knapsack furnishes the complement to the mule's lading, who shuffles along with "no style about him," is the cook, perhaps, for the regiment, probably for headquarters, certainly not for Delmonico. It is singular, but none the less true, that if a man made a slovenly, indifferent soldier he was fully as likely to get a berth in the cook-house as to have any other fate befall him. This remark applies to men who *drifted* into the business of "army caterer" after trying other service, and not those who entered at once upon it.

Here comes a light battery at the rear of the division. Possibly it is to remain with this part of the corps for the campaign. Such was sometimes the case, but later a battery was often used anywhere within the limits of a corps that it could be of advantage. This battery has six brass Napoleons, 12-pounders. They are very destructive at short range. It is followed by a battery of steel guns. They are Parrots, three-inch rifles; best for long range, but good anywhere. Not so safe for close action, however, as the Napoleons.

Yonder you can see the Second Division moving across the fields, made up like the one just passed. It will close in upon the rear of this division farther up the road. What an interesting spectacle it presents, the bright sunlight glinting from the thousands of polished muskets, the moving masses of light and dark blue inching along over the uneven ground, the various flags streaming proudly in the air, marking off the separate brigades and regiments. The column is moving at a moderate pace. It takes some time for a corps to get under way. If we wait long enough, the Third Division, made up like the others, will pass by us, unless it has gone on a parallel road.

It is growing warmer. The column has now got straightened out, and for the last hour has moved forward quite rapidly. The road is evidently clear of all obstructions, but the heat and speed begin to tell on the men. Look at the ground which that brigade has just vacated after its brief halt for rest. It is strewn with blankets, overcoats, dress-coats, pantaloons, shirts — in fact, a little of everything from the outfit of the common soldier. As the Second Corps advanced into the Wilderness on the morning of May 4, 1864, I saw an area of an acre or more almost literally covered with the articles above named, many of them probably extras, but some of them the sole garment of their kind, left by the owners, who felt compelled, from the increasing weight of their load, to lighten it to the extent of parting with the blankets which they would need that very night for shelter. This lightening of the load began before the columns had been on the road an hour. A soldier who had been through the mill would not wait for a general halt to occur before parting with a portion of his load, if it oppressed him; but a recruit would hang to his until he bent over at an angle of 45° from a vertical, with his eyes staring, his lower jaw hanging, and his face dripping with moisture. If you were to follow the column after, say, the first two miles, you would find various articles scattered along at intervals by the roadside, where a soldier quietly stepped out of the ranks, sat down, unslung his knapsack or his blanket-roll, took out what he had decided to throw away, again equipped himself, and, thus relieved, hastened on to overtake the regiment. It did not take an army long to get into light marching order after it was once fairly on the road.

A FOOTSORE STRAGGLER.

I have been dealing with the *first* day out of settled camp. On subsequent days, of course the same programme would not be enacted. And, again, if a man clung to his effects till noon, he was likely to do so for the day, as after noon the thought of shelter for the night nerved him to hold on. But men would drop out in the afternoon of the first day for another reason. They blistered or chafed their feet and sat down at the first stream to bathe them, after which, if the weather admitted, they could be seen plodding along barefooted, their pantaloons rolled up a few inches, and their shoes dangling at the end of their musket-barrel.

Then, this very crossing of a stream often furnished an interesting scene in the march of the column. A river broad and deep would be spanned by a pontoon bridge, but the common creeks of the South were crossed by fording. Once in a while (in warm weather) the men would take off most of their clothing and carry it with their equipments across on their heads. It was no uncommon experience for them to ford streams waist-deep, even in cool weather. If the bottom was a treacherous one, and the current rapid, a line of cavalry-men was placed across the river just below the column to pick up such men as should lose their footing. Many were the mishaps of such a crossing, and, unless the enemy was at hand, the first thing to be done after reaching shore was to strip and wring out such clothing as needed it. With those who had slipped and fallen this meant *all they had on* and what was in their knapsack besides, but with most it included only trousers, drawers, and socks.

After the halt which allowed the soldiers time to perform this bit of laundry work had ended, and the column moved along, it was not an uncommon sight to see muskets used as clothes-lines, from which depended socks, shoes, here and there a shirt, perhaps a towel or handkerchief. But if the weather was cool the wash did not hang out in this way. When it became necessary to cross a stream in the night, huge fires were built on its banks, with a picket at hand, whose duty it was to keep them burning until daylight, or until the army had crossed. A greater number of mishaps occurred in fording by night than by day even then. During Meade's retreat from Culpeper, in the fall of 1863, — it was the night of October 11, — my company forded the Rappahannock after dark, and went into camp a few rods

away from the ford; and I remember what a jolly night the
troops made of it when they came to this ford. At short
intervals I was awakened from slumber by the laughter or
cheers of the waders, as they made merry at the expense of
some of their number, who came out after immersion using
language which plainly indicated their disbelief in that kind
of baptism. Here was the field for the tired, **overloaded**

"HEADQUARTERS" IN TROUBLE.

headquarters mule to display his obstinacy to a large and
changing audience, by getting midway of the stream and
refusing to budge. I can see the frenzied Ethiopian in
charge, now, waist-deep in water, wild with despair at the
situation, alternating reasoning with pulling and beating,
while the brute lies down in the stream all encumbered with
the baggage, the passing column jeering poor Sambo, and
making the adjacent woodland echo with their loud guffaws
at his helpless yet laughable condition.

That was a noisy night, and it has always been a matter of
wonder to me that we remained undisturbed, with the enemy
less than three miles up the river, as General Birney, with
whom we then were, has left on record. There was no stopping to wring out. But "close up!" was the order after

crossing, and the dull rattle made by the equipments, the striking of the coffee dipper on the canteen or buckles, as the column glided along in the darkness, or the whipping-up of belated mule-teams, was heard until the gray of morning appeared.

The army on the march in a rain-storm presented some aspects not seen in fair weather. As soon as it began to rain, or just before, each man would remove his rubber blanket from his roll or knapsack, and put it over his shoulders, tying it in front. Some men used their shelter tent instead — a very poor substitute, however. But there was no fun in the marching business during the rain. It might settle the dust. It certainly settled about everything else. An order to go into camp while the rain was in progress was not much of an improvement, for the ground was wet, fence-rails were wet, one's woollen blanket was likely also to be wet, hardtack in the haversack wet — in fact, nothing so abundant and out of place as water. I remember going into camp one night in particular, in Pleasant Valley, Md., on a side-hill during a drenching rain, such as mountain regions know, and lying down under a hastily pitched shelter, with the water coursing freely along beneath me. I was fresh as a soldier then, and this experience, seeming so dreadful then, made a strong impression. Such situations were too numerous afterwards to make note of even in memory.

Then, the horses! It made them ugly and vicious to stand in the pelting rain at the picket-rope. I think they preferred being in harness on the road. But they were likely to get subdued the next day, when sloughs and mire were the rule. If two corps took the same road after a storm, the worse for the hindermost, for it found deep ruts and mud-holes in abundance; and as it dragged forward it would come upon some piece of artillery or caisson in the mire to the hubs, doomed to stay, in spite of the shoutings and lashings of the drivers, the swearing of the officers, and the lifting and straining of mud-bedraggled cannoneers, until six more horses were added to extricate it. Anon the corps would arrive at a place utterly impassable, when down would go the fence by the roadside, if there was one, and out would go the column into the field skirting the road, returning again beyond the mire. At another slough, a staff officer might be found posted to direct the artillery where to make a safe passage.

Such places by night were generally lighted by fires built for that purpose. I remember such a spot in particular — a

THE FLANKERS.

reminiscence of the Mine Run Campaign; I think it was the night of Dec. 4, 1863. My battery was then attached to the Third Division of the Third Corps. By the edge of the slough in question sat General J. B. Carr, the division commander, with a portion of his command near by, and, as a caisson went down in the mire, he called in his "Blue Diamonds" to lift it out, which they did right manfully. There was no turning into fields that night, for, while the roads were soft, the fields were softer, and worse travelling I believe the Army of the Potomac never saw, unless on the "Mud March."

When the army was expecting to run against the enemy

in its advance, *flankers* were thrown out on either side of the column. These flankers were a single file of soldiers, who marched along a few feet apart parallel to the column, and perhaps ten or twelve rods distant from it in open country, but not more than half that distance when it was marching through woods. In the event of an attack, the flankers on that side became the skirmish line in action.

It was an interesting sight to see a column break up when the order came to halt, whether for rest or other reason. It would melt in a moment, dividing to the right and left, and scattering to the sides of the road, where the men would sit down or lie down, lying back on their knapsacks if they had them, or stretching at full length on the ground. If the latter was wet or muddy, cannoneers sat on their carriages and limber-chests, while infantrymen would perhaps sit astride their muskets, if the halt was a short one. When the halt was expected to continue for some considerable time the troops

A HALT.

of a corps or division were massed, that is, brought together in some large open tract of territory, when the muskets would be stacked, the equipments laid off, and each man rush for the "top rail" of the nearest fence, until not a rail remained. The coffee would soon begin to simmer, the pork to sputter in the flames, and, when the march was resumed, the men would start off refreshed with rest and rations.

But if the halt was for a few minutes only, and the marching had not been relieved by the regular rests usually allowed, the men stiffened up so much that, with their equipments on, they could hardly arise without assistance, and, goaded by their stiffened cords and tired muscles and swollen or chafed feet, made wry faces for the first few rods after the column started. In this manner they plodded on until ordered into camp for the night, or perhaps double-quicked into line of battle.

During that dismal night retreat of the Army of the Potomac from Chancellorsville, a little event occurred which showed what a choleric man General Meade was on occasion, and to what an exhausted bodily condition the rigors of a campaign often reduced men. While the general was sitting with General Warren at one of those camp-fires always found along the line of march after nightfall, a poor jaded, mud-bedraggled infantrymen came straggling and stumbling along the roadside, scarcely able, in his wet and wearied condition, to bear up under his burden of musket and equipments. As he staggered past the camp-fire, he struck, by the merest accident, against General Meade, who jumped immediately to his feet, drew his sabre, and made a lunge at the innocent offender, which sent him staggering to the ground. There he lay motionless, as if dead. At once Meade began to upbraid himself for his hasty temper, and seemed filled with remorse for what he had done. Whereat General Warren made efforts to calm his fears by telling him it was probably not as serious as he supposed, and thereupon began to make investigation of the nature of the injury done the prostrate veteran. To General Meade's great gratification, it was found that while his sabre had cut through the man's clothing, it had only grazed his side without drawing blood, but so completely worn out had the soldier become through the exactions of the recent campaign that matter dominated mind, and he lay in a double sense as if dust had returned to dust.

CHAPTER XIX.

ARMY WAGON-TRAINS.

"That every man who swears once drove a mule
Is not believed by any but a fool;
But whosoe'er drove mules and did not swear
Can be relied on for an honest prayer."

EFORE giving a history of the wagon-trains which formed a part, and a *necessary* part, of every army, I will briefly refer to what was known as "Grant's Military Railroad," which was really a railroad built *for* the army, and used solely by it. When the Army of the Potomac appeared before 'Petersburg, City Point, on the James River, was made army headquarters and the "base of supplies," that is, the place to which supplies were brought from the North, and from which they were distributed to the various portions of the army. The Lynchburg or Southside Railroad enters Petersburg from the west, and a short railroad, known as the City Point Railroad, connects it with City Point, ten miles eastward. The greater portion of this ten miles fell within the Union lines after our army appeared before Petersburg, and, as these lines were extended westward after the siege was determined upon, Grant conceived the plan of

running a railroad inside our fortifications to save both time and mule-flesh in distributing supplies along the line. It was soon done. About five miles of the City Point road were used, from which the new road extended to the south-west, perhaps ten miles, striking the Weldon Railroad, which had been wrested from the enemy. Down this the trains ran three miles; then a new branch of about two miles more to the west took them to the left of the Union lines.

Of course, there were stations along this road at which supplies were left for those troops near by. These stations were named after different generals of the army. *Meade* and *Patrick* stations are two names which yet linger in my memory, near each of which my company was at some time located. The trains on this road were visible to the enemy for a time as they crossed an open plain in their trips, and brought upon themselves quite a lively shelling, resulting in no damage, I believe, but still making railroading so uncom-fortable that a high embankment of earth was thrown up, which completely covered the engine and cars as they rolled along, and which still stands as a monument to the labors of the pick-and-shovel brigade. This railroad was what is known as a surface road, by which is meant that there were no cuts made, the track being laid on the natural surface of the ground. When a marsh was met with, instead of filling, the engineers built a trestling. The effect of such railroad-ing to the eye was quite picturesque, as a train wound its serpentine course along the country, up hill and down dale, appearing much as if it had jumped the track, and was going across lots to its destination.

But *the* trains of the army were *wagon*-trains, and so little has been written about them in histories of the war that a limited sketch in this volume will have interest for many readers.

The trains belong to what is known in French as the *matériel* of the army, in distinction from the *personnel*, the

men employed.   In Roman history we frequently find the bag-
gage-trains of the army alluded to as the *impedimenta*.   The
matériel, then, or *impedimenta*, of our armies has, very
naturally, been ignored by the historian ; for the *personnel*,
the actors, are of so much *more* consequence, they have

A MULE DRIVER.

absorbed the interest of both
writers and readers.   I say
the persons are of much more
consequence, but I must not
be understood as belittling
the importance of the trains.
An army without its varied
supplies, which the trains
care for and provide, would
soon be neither useful nor
ornamental.   In fact, an army
is like a piece of machinery,
each part of which is indispensable to every other part.

I presume every one of
mature years has an idea of
what army wagons look like.
They were heavy, lumbering
affairs at best, built for hard
service, all, apparently, after
the same pattern, each one having its tool-box in front,
its feed trough behind, which, in camp, was placed lengthwise of the pole ; its spare pole suspended at the side ; its
wooden bucket for water, and iron " slush-bucket " for
grease, hanging from the hind axle ; and its canvas cover,
which when closely drawn in front and rear, as it always
was on the march, made quite a satisfactory " close carriage."   As a pleasure carriage, however, they were not
considered a success.   When the Third Corps was winter-
ing at Brandy Station in 1863–4 the concert troupe, which
my company boasted was engaged to give a week of evening

entertainments not far from Culpeper, in a large hex-agonal stockade, which would seat six or seven hundred persons, and which had been erected for the purpose by one Lieutenant Lee, then on either General French's or General Birney's staff — I cannot now say which. To convey us thither over the intervening distance of four or five miles, as I now remember, we hired a mule-driver with his army wagon. More than twenty-three years have since elapsed, but those twelve or fourteen rides, after dark, across the rough country and frozen ground around Brandy Station were so thoroughly jolted into my memory that I shall never forget them. The seven dollars apiece per night which we received for our services was but a trifling compen-sation for the battering and mellowing we endured *en route*, and no more than paid for wear and tear. No harder vehicle can be found to take a ride in than an army wagon.

By some stroke of good luck, or, perhaps, good manage-ment, many of the regiments from New England took their transportation along with them. It consisted, in many cases, of twenty-five wagons, two for each company, and five for regimental headquarters. These were drawn at first by four horses, but afterwards by six mules. A light battery had three such wagons. They were designed to carry the baggage of the troops, and when a march was ordered they were filled with tents, stoves, kettles, pans, chairs, desks, trunks, valises, knapsacks, boards, — in fact, whatever con-veniences had accumulated about the camps.

General Sherman, in his Memoirs (vol. i. p. 178), describes very graphically the troops he saw about Washington in '61, as follows : —

" Their uniforms were as various as the states and cities from which they came; their arms were also of every pattern and calibre; and they were so loaded down with overcoats, haversacks, knapsacks, tents, and baggage, that it took from twenty-five to fifty wagons to move the camp of a regiment

from one place to another, and some of the camps had bakeries and cooking establishments that would have done credit
to Delmonico."

General Sherman might have seen much the same situation near Washington even in '62 and '63. Every company in
a regiment located in the defences of the capital city had
one or more large cook-stoves with other appointments to
match, and when they moved only a few miles they took all
their *lares* and *penates* with them. This could then be done
without detriment to the service. It was only when they
attempted to carry everything along in active campaigning
that trouble ensued.

In October, 1861, McClellan issued an order which contained the following provisions : —

" 1. No soldiers shall ride in loaded baggage-wagons under
any circumstances, nor in empty wagons unless by special instructions to that effect.

" 2. Knapsacks shall not be carried in the wagons except
on the written recommendation of the surgeon, which shall
be given in case of sickness.

" 3. Tent-floors shall not be transported in public wagons,
and hereafter no lumber shall be issued for tent-floors except
upon the recommendation of the medical director for hospital
purposes."

This order was issued before the corps were organized,
while the wagons were yet with their regiments, and while
the men yet had their big knapsacks, which they were
always ready to ride with or toss into a wagon when the
regiment moved. This was the time of transporting tent-
floors, the luxurious fault-finding period before carpets,
feather-beds, and roast beef had entirely lost their charm ;
when each man was, in his own way and belief, fully the
size of a major-general ; when the medical director of the
army had time, unaided as yet by subordinates, to decide
the question of tent-floors *versus* no tent-floors for individuals.
Ah, the freshness and flavor of those early war days come back

to me as I write — each day big with importance, as our letters, yet preserved to us, so faithfully record.

Not many months elapsed before it became apparent that the necessities of stern warfare would not permit and should not have so many of the equipments of civil life, when the shelter tent, already described, took the place of the larger varieties; when camp-fires superseded the stoves, and many cther comfortable but unnecessary furnishings disappeared from the baggage. Not how *little* but how *much* could be dispensed with then became the question of the hour. The trains must be reduced in size, and they must be moved in a manner not to hamper the troops, if possible; but the war was more than half finished before they were brought into a satisfactory system of operation.

The greater number of the three-years regiments that arrived in Washington in 1861 brought no transportation of any kind. After McClellan assumed command, a *depot of transportation* was established at Perryville on the Susquehanna; by this is meant a station where wagons and ambulances were kept, and from which they were supplied.

From there Captain Sawtell, now colonel and brevet brigadier general U. S. A., fitted out regiments as rapidly as he could, giving each *six* wagons instead of twenty-five, one of which was for medical supplies. Some regiments, however, by influence or favor at court, got more than that. A few wagons were supplied from the quartermaster's depot at Washington. A quartermaster is an officer whose duty it is to provide quarters, provisions, clothing, fuel, storage, and transportation for an army. The chief officer in the quartermaster's department is known as the quartermaster-general. There was a chief quartermaster of the army, and a chief quartermaster to each corps and division; then, there were brigade and regimental quartermasters, and finally the quartermaster-sergeants, all attending in their appropriate spheres to the special duties of this department.

During the march of the army up the Peninsula in 1862, the fighting force advanced by brigades, each of which was followed by its long columns of transportation. But this plan was very unsatisfactory, for thereby the army was extended along forest paths over an immense extent of country, and great delays and difficulties ensued in keeping the column closed up; for such was the nature of the roads that after the first few wagons had passed over them they were rendered impassable in places for those behind. At least a quarter of each regiment was occupied in escorting its wagons, piled up with ammunition, provisions, tents, etc.; and long after the head of the column had settled in bivouac could be heard the loud shouting of the teamsters to their jaded and mire-bedraggled brutes, the clatter of wagon and artillery wheels, the lowing of the driven herds, the rattling of sabres, canteens, and other equipments, as the men strode along in the darkness, anxious to reach the spot selected for their uncertain quantity of rest.

At times in this campaign it was necessary for the wagon-trains to be massed and move together, but, for some reason, no order of march was issued, so that the most dire confusion ensued. A struggle for the lead would naturally set in, each division wanting it and fighting for it. Profanity, threats, and the flourishing of revolvers were sure to be prominent in the settling of the question, but the train which could run over the highest stumps and pull through the deepest mud-holes was likely to come out ahead.

The verdancy which remained after the first fall of the Union army at Bull Run was to be utterly overshadowed by the baptism of woe which was to follow in the Peninsular Campaign; and on arriving at Harrison's Landing, on the James, McClellan issued the following order, which paved the way for better things: —

Allowance of Transportation, Tents, and Baggage.

Head-Quarters, Army of the Potomac.

Camp near Harrison's Landing, Va., August 10, 1862.

General Orders,
   No. 153.

I. The following allowance of wagons is authorized:

For the Head-Quarters of an Army Corps . . . . *Four*
   "   "   a Division or Brigade   . . . . . . *Three*
For a Battery of Light Artillery, or Squadron of Cavalry   . . . *Three*
For a full regiment of Infantry   . . . . *Six*

This allowance will in no case be exceeded, but will be reduced to correspond as nearly as practicable with the number of officers and men actually present. All means of transportation in excess of the prescribed standard will be immediately turned in to the depot, with the exception of the authorized supply trains, which will be under the direction of the Chief Quartermasters of Corps. The Chief Quartermaster of this Army will direct the organization of the supply trains.

II. The Army must be prepared to bivouac when on marches away from the depots. The allowance of tents will therefore be immediately reduced to the following standard, and no other accommodations must be expected until a permanent depot is established:

For the Head-Quarters of an Army Corps, Division, or Brigade, one wall tent for the General Commanding, and one to every *two* officers of his staff.

To each full regiment, for the Colonel, Field and Staff officers, three wall tents.

For all other commissioned officers, *one* shelter tent each.

For every two non-commissioned officers, soldiers, officers' servants, and camp followers, as far as they can be supplied, *one* shelter tent.

One hospital tent will be allowed for office purposes at Corps Head-Quarters, and *one* wall tent at Division and Brigade Head-Quarters.

All tents in excess of this allowance will be immediately turned in to the depots.

Tents of other patterns required to be exchanged for shelter tents will be turned in as soon as the latter can be obtained from the Quartermaster's department. Under no circumstances will they be allowed to be carried when the Army moves.

III. The allowance of officers' baggage will be limited to blankets, a *small* valise or carpet bag, and a reasonable mess-kit. All officers will at once reduce their baggage to this standard. The men will carry no baggage except blankets and shelter tents. The Chief Quartermaster will provide storage on the transports for the knapsacks of the men and for the officers' surplus baggage.

IV. Hospital tents must not be diverted from their legitimate use, except for offices, as authorized in paragraph II.

V. The wagons allowed to a regiment or battery must carry nothing but forage for the teams, cooking utensils for the men, hospital stores, small rations, and officers' baggage. One of the wagons allowed for a regiment will be used *exclusively* for hospital stores, under the direction of the regimental surgeon. The wagon for regimental Head-Quarters will carry grain for the officers' horses. At least *one and a half* of the wagons allowed to a battery or squadron will carry grain.

VI. Hospital stores, ammunition, Quartermaster's Stores, and subsistence stores in bulk will be transported in special trains.

VII. Commanding officers will be held responsible that the reduction above ordered, especially of officers' baggage, is carried into effect at once, and Corps commanders are specially charged to see that this responsibility is enforced.

VIII. On all marches, Quartermasters will accompany and conduct their trains, under the orders of their commanding officers, so as never to obstruct the movement of troops.

IX. All Quartermasters and Commissaries of Subsistence will attend in person to the receipt and issue of supplies for their commands, and will keep themselves constantly informed of the situation of the depots, roads, etc.

By command of Major General McClellan:

S. WILLIAMS,
Assistant Adjutant General.

Official :

Aide-de-Camp.

This order quite distinctly shows some of the valuable lessons taught by that eventful campaign before Richmond, more especially the necessity of limiting the amount of camp equipage and the transportation to be used for that purpose. But it further outlines the beginnings of the *Supply Trains*, and to these I wish to direct special attention.

I have thus far only referred to the transportation provided for the *camp equipage ;* but *subsistence* for man and beast must be taken along; *clothing*, to replace the wear and tear of service, must be provided; *ammunition* in quantity and variety must be at ready command; *intrenching tools* were indispensable in an active campaign, — all of which was most forcibly demonstrated on the Peninsula. Some effort, I believe, was made to establish these trains before that campaign began, but everything was confusion when compared with the system which was now inaugurated by Colonel (now General) Rufus Ingalls, when he became Chief Quartermaster of the Army of the Potomac. Through his persevering zeal, trains for the above purposes were organized. All strife for the lead on the march vanished, for every movement was governed by orders from army headquarters under the direction of the chief quartermaster. He prescribed the roads to be travelled over, which corps trains should lead and which should bring up the rear, where more than one took the same roads. All of the corps trains were massed before a march, and the chief quartermaster of some corps was selected and put in charge of this consolidated train. The other corps quartermasters had charge of their

WAGON-TRAIN CROSSING THE RAPPA-
HANNOCK ON A PONTOON BRIDGE.
FROM A PHOTOGRAPH.

respective trains, each in turn having his division and brigade quartermasters, subject to his orders. "There never was a corps better organized than was the quartermaster's corps with the Army of the Potomac in 1864," says Grant in his Memoirs.

Let us see a little more clearly what a corps train included. I can do no better than to incorporate here the following order of General Meade : —

Head-Quarters, Army of the Potomac.

General Orders, }   *August 21, 1863.*
      No. 83. }

In order that the amount of transportation in this Army shall not in any instance exceed the maximum allowance prescribed in General Order, No. 274, of August 7, 1863, from the War Department, and to further modify and reduce baggage and supply trains, heretofore authorized, the following allowances are established and will be strictly conformed to, viz.:

1. The following is the maximum amount of transportation to be allowed to this Army in the field:

To the Head-Quarters of an Army Corps, 2 wagons or 8 pack mules.

To the Head-Quarters of a Division or Brigade, 1 wagon or 5 pack mules.

To every three company officers, when detached or serving without wagons, 1 pack mule.

To every 12 company officers, when detached, 1 wagon or 4 pack mules.

To every 2 staff officers not attached to any Head-Quarters, 1 pack mule.

To every 10 staff officers serving similarly, 1 wagon or 4 pack mules.

The above will include transportation for all personal baggage, mess chests, cooking utensils, desks, papers, &c. The weight of officers' baggage in the field, specified in the Army Regulations, will be reduced so as to bring it within the foregoing schedule. All excess of transportation now with Army Corps, Divisions, Brigades, and Regiments, or Batteries, over the allowances herein prescribed, will be immediately turned in to the Quartermaster's Department, to be used in the trains.

Commanding officers of Corps, Divisions, &c., will immediately cause inspections to be made, and will be held responsible for the strict execution of this order.

Commissary stores and forage will be transported by the trains. Where these are not conveniemt of access, and where troops act in detachments, the Quartermaster's Department will assign wagons or pack animals for that purpose; but the baggage of officers, or of troops, or camp equipage, will not be permitted to be carried in the wagons or on the pack animals so assigned. The assignment for transportation for ammunition, hospital stores, subsistence, and forage will be made in proportion to the amount ordered to be carried. The number of wagons is hereinafter prescribed.

The allowance of spring wagons and saddle horses for contingent wants, and of camp and garrison equipage, will remain as established by circular, dated July 17, 1863.

2. For each full regiment of infantry and cavalry, of 1000 men, for baggage, camp equipage, &c., 6 wagons.

For each regiment of infantry less than 700 men and more than 500 men, 5 wagons.

For each regiment of infantry less than 500 men and more than 300 men, 4 wagons.

For each regiment of infantry less than 300 men, 3 wagons.

3. For each battery of 4 and 6 guns — for personal baggage, mess chests, cooking utensils, desks, papers, &c., 1 and 2 wagons respectively.

For ammunition trains the number of wagons will be determined and assigned upon the following rules:

1st. Multiply each 12 pdr. gun by 122 and divide by 112.

2d. Multiply each rifle gun by 50 and divide by 140.

3d. For each 20 pdr. gun, 1½ wagons.

4th. For each siege gun, 2½ wagons.

5th. For the general supply train of reserve ammunition of 20 rounds to each gun in the Army, to be kept habitually with Artillery Reserve, 54 wagons.

For each battery, to carry its proportion of subsistence, forage, &c., 2 wagons.

4. The supply train for forage, subsistence, quartermaster's stores, &c., to each 1000 men, cavalry and infantry, 7 wagons.

To every 1000 men, cavalry and infantry, for small arm ammunition, 5 wagons.

To each 1500 men, cavalry and infantry, for hospital supplies, 3 wagons.

To each Army Corps, except the Cavalry, for entrenching tools, &c., 6 wagons.

To each Corps Head-Quarters for the carrying of subsistence, forage and other stores not provided for herein, 3 wagons.

To each Division Head-Quarters for similar purpose as above, 2 wagons.

To each Brigade Head-Quarters for similar purpose as above, 1 wagon.

To each Brigade, cavalry and infantry, for commissary stores for sales to officers, 1 wagon.

To each Division, cavalry and infantry, for hauling forage for ambulance animals, portable forges, &c., 1 wagon.

To each Division, cavalry and infantry, for carrying armorer's tools, parts of muskets, extra arms and accoutrements, 1 wagon.

It is expected that each ambulance, and each wagon, whether in the baggage, supply or ammunition train, will carry the necessary forage for its own team.

By command of Major General Meade:

S. WILLIAMS,
Assistant Adjutant General.

Official:

Ass't Adj't Gen'l.

As the transportation was reduced in quantity, the capacity of what remained was put to a severer test. For example, when the Army of the Potomac went into the Wilderness in 1864, each wagon was required to carry five days forage for its animals (600 pounds), and if its other freight was rations it might be six barrels of salt pork and four

barrels of coffee, or ten barrels of sugar. Forty boxes of
hardtack was a load, not so much because of its weight as
because a wagon would hold no more. It even excluded
the forage to carry this number. In the final campaign
against Lee, Grant allowed for baggage and camp equipage
three wagons to a regiment of over seven hundred men,
two wagons to a regiment of less than seven hundred and
more than three hundred, and one wagon to less than three
hundred. One wagon was allowed to a field battery. But,
notwithstanding the reductions ordered at different times,
extra wagons were often smuggled along. One captain, in
charge of a train, tells of keeping a wagon and six mules of
his own more than orders allowed, and whenever the inspecting officer was announced as coming, the wagon, in
charge of his man, Mike, was driven off under cover and
not returned till the inspection was completed. This
enabled him to take along quite a personal outfit for himself and friends. But his experience was not unique.
There were many other "contraband" mule-teams smuggled along in the same way for the same object.

In leaving Chattanooga to advance into Georgia, General
Sherman reduced his transportation to one baggage-wagon
and one ambulance for a regiment, and a pack-horse or
mule for the officers of each company. His supply trains
were limited in their loads to food, ammunition, and clothing; and wall tents were forbidden to be taken along,
barring one for each headquarters, the gallant old veteran
setting the example, by taking only a tent-fly, which was
pitched over saplings or fence rails. The general has
recorded in his "Memoirs" that his orders were not strictly
obeyed in this respect, Thomas being the most noted exception, who could not give up his tent, and "had a big wagon,
which could be converted into an office, and this we used to
call 'Thomas's circus.'" In starting on his "march to the
sea," Sherman issued Special Field Orders No. 120; paragraph
3 of this order reads as follows: —

"There will be no general train of supplies, but each corps will have its ammunition train and provision train distributed habitually as follows: Behind each regiment should follow one wagon and one ambulance; behind each brigade should follow a due proportion of ammunition-wagons, provision-wagons and ambulances. In case of danger each corps commander should change this order of march, by having his advance and rear brigades unencumbered by wheels. The separate columns will start habitually at 7 A. M., and make about fifteen miles per day, unless otherwise fixed in orders."

I presume the allowance remained about the same for the Wilderness Campaign as that given in Orders No. 83. General Hancock says that he started into the Wilderness with 27,000 men. Now, using this fact in connection with the general order, a little rough reckoning will give an approximate idea of the size of the train of this corps. Without going into details, I may say that the total train of the Second Corps, not including the ambulances, could not have been far from 800 wagons, of which about 600 carried the various supplies, and the remainder the baggage — the camp equipage of the corps.

When the army was in settled camp, the supply trains went into park by themselves, but the baggage-wagons were retained with their corps, division, brigade, or regimental headquarters. When a march was ordered, however, these wagons waited only long enough to receive their freight of camp equipage, when away they went in charge of their respective quartermasters to join the corps supply train.

I have alluded to the strength of a single corps train. But the Second Corps comprised only about one-fifth of the Union army in the Wilderness, from which a little arithmetic will enable one to get a tolerably definite idea of the *impedimenta* of this one army, even after a great reduction in the original amount had been made. There were probably over 4000 wagons following the Army of the Potomac into the Wilderness. An idea of the ground such a train would cover may be obtained by knowing that a six-mule team took up on the road, say, forty feet, but of course they did not travel at close intervals. The nature of the country determined, in some degree, their distance apart. In going up or down hill a liberal allowance was made for balky or headstrong mules. Colonel Wilson, the chief commissary of the army, in an interesting article to the *United Service* magazine (1880), has stated that could the train which was requisite to accompany the army on the Wilderness Campaign have been extended in a straight line it would have spanned the distance between Washington and Richmond, being about one hundred and thirty miles. I presume this estimate includes the ambulance-train also. On the basis of three to a regiment, there must have been as many as one hundred and fifty to a corps. These, on ordinary marches, followed immediately in the rear of their respective divisions.

When General Sherman started for the sea, his army of sixty thousand men was accompanied by about twenty-five hundred wagons and six hundred ambulances. These were divided nearly equally between his four corps, each corps commander managing his own train. In this campaign the transportation had the roads, while the infantry plodded along by the roadside.

The supply trains, it will now be understood, were the travelling depot or reservoir from which the army replenished its needs. When these wagons were emptied, they were at once sent back to the base of supplies, to be reloaded with precisely the same kind of material as before; and empty wagons had always to leave the road clear for loaded ones. Unless under a pressure of circumstances, all issues except of ammunition were made at night. By this plan the animals of the supply consumed their forage at the base of supplies, and thus saved hauling it.

It was a welcome sight to the soldiers when rations drew low, or were exhausted, to see these wagons drive up to the lines. They were not *impedimenta* to the army just then.

It has sometimes been thought that the wagon-train was a glorious refuge from the dangers and hard labors endured at the front, but such was not the case. It was one of the

COMMISSARY DEPOT AT CEDAR LEVEL. — FROM A PHOTOGRAPH.

most wearing departments of the service. The officers in immediate charge were especially burdened with responsibility, as the statement above illustrates. They were charged to have their trains at a given point at or before a specified time. It *must* be there. There was no "if convenient" or "if possible" attached to the order. The troops must have their rations, or, more important still, the ammunition must be at hand in case of need. Sometimes they would accomplish the task assigned without difficulty, but it was the exception. Of course, they could not start until the army had got out of the way. Then, the roads, already cut up somewhat by the artillery, were soon rendered next to impassable by the moving trains. The quartermaster in charge of a train would be called upon to extricate a wagon here that was blocking the way, to supply the place of a worn-out horse or mule there; to have a stalled wagon unloaded and its contents distributed among other wagons; to keep the train well closed up; to keep the right road even by night, when, of necessity, much of their travelling was done. And if, with a series of such misfortunes befalling him, the quartermaster reached his destination a few hours late, his chances were very good for being roundly sworn at by his superior officers for his delinquency.

During the progress of the train, it may be said, the quartermaster would ease his nervous and troubled spirit by swearing at careless or unfortunate mule-drivers, who, in turn, would make the air blue with profanity addressed to their mules, individually or collectively, so that the anxiety to get through was felt by all the moving forces in the train. A large number of these drivers were civilians early in the war, but owing to the lack of subordination which many of them showed, their places were largely supplied later by enlisted men, upon whom Uncle Sam had his grip, and who could not resign or "swear back" without penalty.

The place of the trains on an advance was in the rear of the army; on the retreat, in front, as a rule. If they were passing through a dangerous section of country, they were attended by a guard, sometimes of infantry, sometimes cavalry. The strength of the guard varied with the nature of the danger expected. Sometimes a regiment, sometimes a brigade or division, was detailed from a corps for the duty. The nature of Sherman's march was such that trains and troops went side by side, as already referred to. The colored division of the Ninth Corps served as train-guard for the transportation of the Army of the Potomac from the Rapidan to the James in 1864.

When ammunition was wanted by a battery or a regiment in the line of battle, a wagon was sent forward from the train to supply it, the train remaining at a safe distance in the rear. The nearness of the wagon's approach was governed somewhat by the nature of the ground. If there was cover to screen it from the enemy, like a hill or a piece of woods, it would come pretty near, but if exposed it would keep farther away. When it was possible to do so, supplies both of subsistence and ammunition were brought

up by night when the army was in line of battle, for, as
I have said elsewhere, a mule-team or a mule-train under fire
was a diverting spectacle to every one but the mule-drivers.

A MULE-TEAM UNDER FIRE.

One of the most striking reminiscences of the wagon-train
which I remember relates to a scene enacted in the fall of
'63, in that campaign of manœuvres between Meade and
Lee. My own corps (Third) reached Centreville Heights
before sunset — in fact, was, I think, the first corps to
arrive. At all events, we had anticipated the most of the
trains. At that hour General Warren was having a lively
row with the enemy at Bristoe Station, eight or nine miles
away. As the twilight deepened, the flash of his artillery
and the smoke of the conflict were distinctly visible in the
horizon. The landscape between this stirring scene and our
standpoint presented one cf the most animated spectacles
that I ever saw in the service. Its most attractive feature
was the numerous wagon-trains, whose long lines, stretching
away for miles over the open plain, were hastening forward
to a place of refuge, all converging towards a common
centre — the high ground lying along the hither side of
Bull Run. The officers in charge of the trains, made somewhat nervous by the sounds of conflict reaching them from

the rear, impatiently urged on the drivers, who, in turn, with lusty lungs uttered vigorous oaths at the mules, punctuated by blows or cracks of the black snake that equalled in volume the intonations of a rifle; and these jumped into their harnesses and took the wagons along over stumps and through gullies with as great alacrity as if the chief strain and responsibility of the campaign centred in themselves. An additional feature of animation was presented by the columns of infantry from the other corps, which alternated in the landscape with the lines of wagons, winding along into camp tired and footsore, but without apparent concern. I do not now remember any other time in my experience when so large a portion of the *matériel* and *personnel* of the army could have been covered by a single glance as I saw in the gathering twilight of that October afternoon.

The system of designating the troops by corps badges was extended to the transportation, and every wagon was marked on the side of the canvas covering with the corps badge, perhaps eighteen inches in diameter, and of the appropriate color to designate the division to which it belonged. In addition to this, the number of its division, brigade, and the nature of its contents, whether rations, forage, clothing, or ammunition,— and, if the latter, the kind, whether artillery or musket, and the calibre,— were plainly stencilled in large letters on the cover. All this and much more went to indicate as perfect organization in the trains as in the army itself, and to these men, who were usually farthest from the fray, for whom few words of appreciation have been uttered by distinguished writers on the war, I gladly put on record my humble opinion that the country is as much indebted as for the work of the soldiers in line. They acted well their part, and all honor to them for it.

A regular army officer, who had a large experience in charge of trains, has suggested that a bugler for each brigade or division train would have been a valuable auxiliary for starting or halting the trains, or for regulating the camp duties as in artillery and cavalry. It seems strange that so commendable a proposition was not thought of at the time.

In 1863, while the army was lying at Belle Plain after the memorable Mud March, large numbers of colored refugees came into camp. Every day saw some old cart or antiquated wagon, the relic of better days in the Old Dominion, unloading its freight of contrabands, who had thus made their entrance into the lines of Uncle Sam and Freedom. As a large number of these vehicles had accumulated near his headquarters, General Wadsworth, then commanding the first division of the First Corps, conceived the novel idea of forming a supply train of them, using as draft steers, to be selected from the corps cattle herd, and broken for that purpose. His plan, more in detail, was to load the carts at

THE "BULL TRAIN."

the base of supplies with what rations they would safely carry, despatch them to the troops wherever they might be, issue the rations, slaughter the oxen for fresh beef, and use the wagons for fuel to cook it. A very practical scheme, at first view, surely. A detail of mechanics was made to put the wagons in order, a requisition was drawn for yokes, and Captain Ford of a Wisconsin regiment, who had had experience in such work, was detailed to break in the steers to yoke and draft.

The captain spent all winter and the following spring in perfecting the " Bull Train," as it was called. The first serious set-back the plan received resulted from feeding the steers with unsoaked hard bread, causing several of them to swell up and die; but the general was not yet ready to give up the idea, and so continued the organization. Chancellorsville battle came when all the trains remained in camp. But the day of trial was near. When the army started on the Gettysburg campaign, Captain Ford put his train in rear of the corps wagon-train, and started, with the inevitable result.

The mules and horses walked right away from the oxen, in spite of the goading and lashing and yelling of their drivers. By nightfall they were doomed to be two or three miles behind the main train — an easy prey for Mosby's guerilla band. At last the labor of keeping it up and the anxiety for its safety were so intense that before the Potomac was reached the animals were returned to the herd, the supplies were transferred or issued, the wagons were burned, and the pet scheme of General Wadsworth was abandoned as impracticable.

Quite nearly akin to this Bull Train was the train organized by Grant after the battle of Port Gibson. His army was east of the Mississippi, his ammunition train was west of it. Wagon transportation for ammunition must be had. Provisions could be taken from the country. He says: " I directed, therefore, immediately on landing, that all the vehicles and draft animals, whether horses, mules, or oxen, in the vicinity should be collected and loaded to their capacity with ammunition. Quite a train was collected during the 30th, and a motley train it was. In it could be found fine carriages, loaded nearly to the top with boxes of cartridges that had been pitched in promiscuously, drawn by mules with plough-harness, straw collars, rope lines, etc.; long-coupled wagons with racks for carrying cotton-bales, drawn by oxen, and everything that could be found in the way of transportation on a plantation, either for use or pleasure." [Vol. i., p. 488.]

Here is another incident which will well illustrate the trials of a train quartermaster. At the opening of the campaign in 1864, Wilson's cavalry division joined the Army of the Potomac. Captain Ludington (now lieutenant-colonel, U. S. A.) was chief quartermaster of its supply train. It is a settled rule guiding the movement of trains that the cavalry supplies shall take precedence in a move, as the cavalry itself is wont to precede the rest of the army. Through some oversight of the chief quartermaster of the army, General Ingalls, the captain had received no order of march, and after waiting until the head of the infantry supply trains appeared, well understanding that his place was ahead of them on the march, he moved out of park into the road. At once he encountered the chief quartermaster of the corps train, and a hot and wordy contest ensued, in which vehement language found ready expression. While this dispute for place was at white heat, General Meade and his staff rode by, and saw the altercation in progress without halting to inquire into its cause. After he had passed some distance up the road, Meade sent back an aid, with his compliments, to ascertain what train that was struggling for the road, who was in charge of it, and with what it was loaded. Captain Ludington informed him that it was Wilson's cavalry supply train, loaded with forage and rations. These facts the aid reported faithfully to Meade, who sent him back again to inquire particularly if that really was Wilson's cavalry train. Upon receiving an affirmative answer, he again carried the same to General Meade, who immediately turned back in his tracks, and came furiously back to Ludington. Uttering a volley of oaths, he asked him what he meant by throwing all the trains into confusion. "You ought to have been out of here hours ago!" he continued. "I have a great mind to hang you to the nearest tree. You are not fit to be a quartermaster." In this manner General Meade rated the innocent captain for a few moments, and then rode away. When he had gone, General Ingalls dropped back from the staff a moment, with a laugh at the interview, and, on learning the captain's case, told him to remain where he was until he received an order from him. Thereupon Ludington withdrew to a house that stood not far away from the road, and, taking a seat on the veranda, entered into conversation with two young ladies who resided there. Soon after he had thus comfortably disposed himself, who should appear upon the highway but Sheridan, who was in command of all the cavalry with the army. On discovering the train at a standstill, he rode up and asked : —

"What train is this?"

"The supply train of Wilson's Cavalry Division," was the reply of a teamster.

"Who's in charge of it?"

"Captain Ludington."

"Where is he?"

"There he sits yonder, talking to those ladies."

"Give him my compliments and tell him I want to see him," said Sheridan, much wrought up at the situation, apparently thinking that the train was being delayed that its quartermaster might spend further time "in gentle dalliance" with the ladies. As soon as the captain approached, the general charged forward impetuously, as if he would ride the captain down, and, with one of those "terrible oaths" for which he was famous, demanded to know what he was there for, why he was not out at daylight, and on after his division. As Ludington attempted to explain, Sheridan cut him off by opening his battery of abuse again, threatening to have him shot for his incompetency and delay, and ordering him to take the road at once with his train. Hav-

GENERAL MEADE AND THE QUARTERMASTER.

ing exhausted all the strong language in the vocabulary, he
rode away, leaving the poor captain in a state of distress
that can be only partially imagined. When he had finally
got somewhat settled after this rough stirring-up, he took a
review of the situation, and, having weighed the threatened
hanging by General Meade, the request to await his orders
from General Ingalls, the threatened shooting of General
Sheridan, and the original order of General Wilson, which
was to be on hand with the supplies at a certain specified
time and place, Ludington decided to await orders from
General Ingalls, and resumed the company of the ladies.
At last the orders came, and the captain moved his train,
spending the night on the road in the Wilderness, and when
morning dawned had reached a creek over which it was
necessary for him to throw a bridge before it could be
crossed. So he set his teamsters at work to build a bridge.
Hardly had they begun felling trees before up rode the chief
quartermaster of the Sixth Corps train, anxious to cross.
An agreement was entered into, however, that they should
build the bridge together; and the corps quartermaster set
his pioneers at work with Ludington's men, and the bridge
was soon finished. Recognizing the necessity for the
cavalry train to take the lead, the corps quartermaster
had assented that it should pass the bridge first when
it was completed, and on the arrival of that moment the
train was put in motion, but just then a prompt and determined chief quartermaster of a Sixth Corps *division* train,
unaware of the understanding had between his superior, the
corps quartermaster, and Captain Ludington, rode forward and
insisted on crossing first. A struggle for precedence immediately set in. The contest waxed warm, and language more for-
cible than polite was waking the woodland echoes when who
should appear on the scene again but General Meade. On
seeing Ludington engaged as he saw him the day before,
it aroused his wrath most unreasonably, and, riding up to
him, he shouted, with an oath: "What! are you here again!"

Then shaking his fist in his face, he continued: " I am sorry now that I did not hang you yesterday, as I threatened." The captain, exhausted and out of patience with the trials which he had encountered, replied that he sincerely wished he had, and was sorry that he was not already dead. The arrival of the chief quartermaster of the Sixth Corps, at this time, ended the dispute for precedence, and Ludington went his way without further vexatious delays to overtake his cavalry division.

"OLD CRONIES"

CHAPTER XX.

ARMY ROAD AND BRIDGE BUILDERS.

"A line of black, which bends and floats
On the rising tide, like a bridge of boats."

LONGFELLOW.

F there is one class of men in this country who more than all others should appreciate spacious and well graded highways, or ready means of transit from one section into another, that class is the veterans of the Union Army; for those among them who "hoofed it" from two to four years in Rebeldom travelled more miles across country in that period than they did on regularly constituted thoroughfares. Now through the woods, now over the open, then crossing a swamp, or wading a river of varying depth, here tearing away a fence obstructing the march, there filling a ditch with rails to smooth the passage of the artillery, — in fact, "short cuts" were so common and popular that the men endured the obstacles they often presented with the utmost good-nature, knowing that every rood of travel thus saved meant fewer foot-blisters and an earlier arrival in camp.

But there was a portion of the army which could not often indulge in short cuts, which must "find a way or make it," or have it made for them by others; and as some time and much skill and labor were necessary in laying out and completing such a way in an efficient manner, a body of

377

men was enlisted for the exclusive purpose of doing this kind of work.   Such a body was the *Engineer Corps*, often called the *Sappers and Miners* of the army ; but so little sapping and mining was done, and that little mainly by the fighting forces, I shall speak of this body of men as *Engineers* — the name which, I believe, they prefer.

In the Army of the Potomac this corps was composed of the Fifteenth and Fiftieth New York regiments of volunteers and a battalion of regulars comprising three companies. They started out with McClellan in the Peninsular Campaign, and from that time till the close of the war were identified with the movements of this army.   These engineers went armed as infantry for purposes of self-defence only, for fighting was not their legitimate business, nor was it expected of them.   There were emergencies in the history of the army when they were drawn up in line of battle. Such was the case with a part of them at least at Antietam, Gettysburg, and the Wilderness, but, so far as I can learn, they were never actively engaged.

The engineers' special duties were to make roads passable for the army by corduroying sloughs, building trestle bridges across small streams, laying pontoon bridges over rivers, and taking up the same, laying out and building fortifica-

CORDUROYING.

tions, and slashing.   Corduroying called at times for a large amount of labor, for Virginia mud was such a foe to rapid transit that miles upon miles of this sort of road had to be laid to keep ready communication between different portions of the army. Where the ground was miry, two stringers were laid longitudinally of the road, and on these the corduroy of logs, averaging, perhaps, four inches in diameter, was laid, and a cover of brush was sometimes spread upon it to prevent mules from thrusting their legs through. Where the surface was simply muddy, no stringers were used. It should be said here that by far the greater portion of this variety of work fell to fatigue details from the infantry, as did much more of the labor which came within the scope of the engineers' duties; for the latter could not have accomplished one-fifth of the tasks devolved upon them in time. In fact, if I except the laying and

A TRESTLE BRIDGE, NO. 1.

taking-up of pontoon bridges, and the laying-out and superintending of the building of forts, there were none of the engineers' duties which were not performed by the fighting force to a large extent. I state this not in detraction of the engineers, who always did well, but in justice to the infantry, who so often supplemented the many and trying duties of their own department with the accomplishments of the engineer corps. The quartermaster of the army had a large number of wagons loaded with intrenching tools with which to supply the troops when their services were required as engineers.

The building of trestle bridges called for much labor from the engineers with the Army of the Potomac, for Virginia is gridironed with small streams. These, bear in mind, the troops could ford easily, but the heavily loaded trains must have bridges to cross on, or each ford would soon have been

A TRESTLE BRIDGE, NO. 2.

choked with mired teams. Sometimes the bridges built by the natives were still standing, but they had originally been put up for local travel only, *not* to endure the tramp and rack of moving armies and their thousands of tons of *impedimenta ;* wherefore the engineers would take them in hand and strengthen them to the point of present efficiency. So well was much of this work done that it endures in places to-day as a monument to their thoroughness and fidelity, and a convenience to the natives of those sections.

When a line of works was laid out through woods, much *slashing*, or felling of trees, was necessary in its front. This was especially necessary in front of forts and batteries. Much of this labor was done by the engineers. The trees were felled with their tops toward the enemy, leaving stumps about three feet high. The territory covered by these fallen trees was called *the Slashes*, hence *Slashing*. No large body of the enemy could safely attempt a passage through such an obstacle. It was a strong defence for a weak line of works.

The *Gabions*, being hollow cylinders of wicker-work without bottom, filled with earth, and placed on the earthworks ; the *Fascines*, being bundles of small sticks bound at both ends and intermediate points, to aid in raising batteries, filling ditches, etc.; *Chevaux-de-frise*, a piece of timber

A LARGE GABION.

traversed with wooden spikes, used especially as a defence against cavalry; the *Abatis*, a row of the large branches of trees, sharpened and laid close together, points outward, with the butts pinned to the ground; the *Fraise*, a defence of pointed sticks, fastened into the ground at such an incline as to bring the points breast-high; — all these were fashioned by the engineer corps, in vast numbers, when the army was besieging Petersburg in 1864.

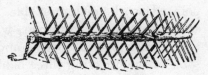

CHEVAUX-DE-FRISE.

But the crowning work of this corps, as it always seemed to me, the department of their labor for which, I believe, they will be the longest remembered, was that of ponton-bridge laying. The word *ponton*, or pontoon, is borrowed from both the Spanish and French languages, which, in turn, derive it from the parent Latin, *pons,*

FASCINES.

meaning a bridge, but it has now come to mean a *boat*, and the men who build such bridges are called by the

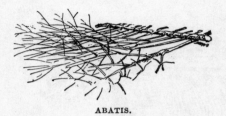

ABATIS.

French *pontoniers*. In fact, the system of ponton bridges in use during the Rebellion was copied, I believe, almost exactly from the French model.

The first ponton bridge which I recall in history was built by Xerxes, nearly twenty-four hundred years ago, across the Hellespont. It was over four thousand feet long. A violent storm broke it up, whereupon the Persian "got square" by throwing two pairs of shackles into the sea and ordering his men to give it three hundred strokes of a whip, while he addressed it in imperious language. Then he ordered all those persons who had been charged with the construction of the bridge to be beheaded. Immediately afterwards he had two other bridges built, "one for the army to pass over, and the other for the baggage and beasts of burden. He appointed workmen more able

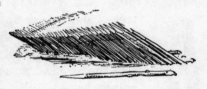

THE FRAISE.

and expert than the former, who went about it in this manner. They placed three hundred and sixty vessels across, some of them having three banks of oars and others fifty oars apiece, with their sides turned towards the Euxine (Black) Sea; and on the side that faced the Ægean Sea they put three hundred and fourteen. They then cast large anchors into the water on both sides, in order to fix and secure all these vessels against the violence of the winds and the current of the water. On the east side they left three passages or vacant spaces, between the vessels, that there might be room for small boats to go and come easily, when there was occasion, to and from the Euxine Sea. After this, upon the land on both·sides, they drove large piles into the earth, with huge rings fastened to them, to which were tied six vast cables, which went over each of the two bridges : two of which cables were made of hemp, and four of a sort of reeds called βιβλος, which were made use of in those times for the making of cordage. Those that were made of hemp must have been of an extraordinary strength and thickness since every cubit in length weighed a talent (42 pounds). The cables, laid over the whole extent of the vessels lengthwise, reached from one side to the other of the sea. When this part of the work was finished, quite over the vessels from side to side, and over the cables just described, they laid the trunks of trees cut for that purpose, and planks again over them, fastened and joined together to serve as a kind of floor or solid bottom ; all which they covered over with earth, and added rails or battlements on each side that the horses and cattle might not be frightened at seeing the sea in their passage."

Compare this bridge of Xerxes with that hereinafter described, and note the points of similarity.

One of the earliest pontons used in the Rebellion was made of India-rubber. It was a sort of sack, shaped not unlike a torpedo, which had to be inflated before use. When thus inflated, two of these sacks were placed side by side, and on this buoyant foundation the bridge was laid. Their extreme lightness was a great advantage in transportation, but for some reason they were not used by the engineers of the Army of the Potomac. They were used in the western army, however, somewhat. General F. P. Blair's division used them in the Vicksburg campaign of 1863.

Another ponton which was adopted for bridge service may be described as a skeleton boat-frame, over which was stretched a cotton-canvas cover. This was a great improvement over the tin or copper-covered boat-frames, which had been thoroughly tested and condemned. It was the variety used by Sherman's army almost exclusively.   In starting for Savannah, he distributed his ponton trains among his four corps, giving to each about nine hundred feet of bridge material.   These pontons were suitably hinged to form a wagon

A CANVAS PONTOON BOAT.   FROM A PHOTOGRAPH.

body, in which was carried the canvas cover, anchor, chains, and a due proportion of other bridge materials.   This kind of bridge was used by the volunteer engineers of the Army of the Potomac.   I recall two such bridges.

One spanned the Rapidan at Ely's Ford, and was crossed by the Second Corps the night of May 3, 1864, when it entered upon the Wilderness campaign.   The other was laid across the Po River, by the Fiftieth New York Engineers, seven days afterwards, and over this Hancock's Veterans crossed — those, at least, who survived the battle of that eventful Tuesday — before nightfall.

But all of the *long* bridges, notably those crossing the Chickahominy, the James, the Appomattox, which now come to my mind, were supported by *wooden* boats of the French pattern.   These were thirty-one feet long, two feet six inches deep, five feet four inches wide at the top, and four feet at the bottom.   They tapered so little at the bows and sterns as to be nearly rectangular, and when afloat the gunwales were about horizontal, having little of the curve of the skiff.

The floor timbers of the bridge, known as *Balks*, were twenty-five and one-half feet long, and four and one-half inches square on the end. Five continuous lines of these were laid on the boats two feet ten inches apart.

The flooring of the bridge, called *chesses*, consisted of boards having a uniform length of fourteen feet, a width of twelve inches, and a thickness of one and a half inches.

To secure the chesses in place, *side-rails* of about the same dimensions as the balks were laid upon them over the outer balks, to which the rails were fastened by cords known as *rack-lashings*.

The distance between the centres of two boats in position is called a *bay*. The distance between the boats is thirteen feet ten inches. The distance between the side-rails is eleven feet, this being the width of the roadway.

An *abutment* had to be constructed at either end of a

AN ANGLE OF FORT HELL (SEDGWICK) SHOWING GABIONS, CHEVAUX-DE-FRISE, ABATIS AND FRAISE. FROM A PHOTOGRAPH.

bridge, which was generally done by settling a heavy timber horizontally in the ground, level with the top of the bridge, confining it there by stakes. A proper approach was then made to this, sometimes by grading, sometimes by corduroying, sometimes by cutting away the bank.

The boats, with all other bridge equipage, were carried upon wagons, which together were known as the Ponton Train. Each wagon was drawn by six mules. A single boat with its anchor and cable formed the entire load for one team. The balks were loaded on wagons by themselves, as were also the chesses, and the side-rails on others. This system facilitated the work of the pontoniers. In camp, the Ponton Train was located near army headquarters. On the march it would naturally be in rear of the army, unless its services were soon to be made use of. If, when the column had halted, we saw this train and its body-guard, the engineers, passing to the front, we at once concluded that there was " one wide river to cross," and we might as well settle down for a while, cook some coffee, and take a nap.

In order to get a better idea of ponton-bridge laying, let us follow such a train to the river and note the various steps in the operation. If the enemy is not holding the opposite bank, the wagons are driven as near as practicable to the brink of the water, unloaded, and driven off out of the way. To avoid confusion and expedite the work, the corps is divided up into the abutment, boat, balk, lashing, chess, and side-rail parties. Each man, therefore, knows just what he has to do. The abutment party takes the initiative, by laying the abutment, and preparing the approaches as already described. Sometimes, when the shore was quite marshy, trestle work or a crib of logs was necessary in completing this duty, but, as the army rarely approached a river except over a recognized thoroughfare, such work was the exception.

While this party has been vigorously prosecuting its special labors, the *boat party*, six in number, have got a ponton afloat, manned it, and ridden to a point a proper distance above the line of the proposed bridge, dropped anchor, and, paying out cable, drop down alongside the abutment, and go ashore. The *balk party* are on hand with five balks, two men to each, and having placed these so that one end projects six inches beyond the outer gunwale of

the boat, they make way for the *lashing party*, who lash
them in place at proper intervals as indicated on the gunwales. The boat is then pushed into the stream the length
of the balks, the hither ends of which are at once made fast
to the abutment.

The *chess party* now step to the front and cover the
balks with flooring to within one foot of the ponton.
Meanwhile the boat-party has launched another ponton,

A WOODEN PONTOON BOAT. FROM A PHOTOGRAPH.

dropped anchor in the proper place, and brought it alongside the first ; the balk party, also ready with another bay of
balks, lay them for the lashing party to make fast; the boat
being then pushed off broadside-to as before, and the free end
of the balks lashed so as to project six inches over the *shore*
gunwale of the first boat. By this plan it may be seen that
each balk and bay of balks completely spans two pontons.
This gives the bridge a firm foundation. The chess party
continue their operations, as before, to within a foot of the
second boat. And now, when the third bay of the bridge is
begun, the *side-rail* party appears, placing their rails on the
chesses over the outside balks, to which they firmly lash them,
the chesses being so constructed that the lashings pass between them for this purpose.

The foregoing operations are repeated bay after bay till
the bridge reaches the farther shore, when the building of

another abutment and its approaches completes the main part of the work. It then remains to scatter the roadway of the bridge with a light covering of hay, or straw, or sand, to protect it from wear, and, perhaps, some straightening here and tightening there may be necessary, but the work is now done, and all of the *personnel* and *matériel* may cross with perfect safety. No rapid movements are allowed, however, and man and beast must pass over at a walk. A guard of the engineers is posted at the abutment, ordering " Route step ! " " Route step ! " as the troops strike the bridge, and sentries, at intervals, repeat the caution further along. By keeping the cadence in crossing, the troops would subject the bridge to a much greater strain, and settle it deeper in the water. It was shown over and over again that nothing so tried the bridge as a column of infantry. The current idea is that the artillery and the trains must have given it the severest test, which was not the case.

In taking up a bridge, the order adopted was the reverse of that followed in laying it, beginning with the end next the enemy, and carrying the chess and balks back to the other shore by hand. The work was sometimes accelerated by weighing all anchors, and detaching the bridge from the further abutment, allow it to swing bodily around to the hither shore to be dismantled. One instance is remembered when this manœuvre was executed with exceeding despatch. It was after the army had recrossed the Rappahannock, following the battle of Chancellorsville. So nervous were the engineers lest the enemy should come upon them at their labors they did not even wait to pull up anchors, but cut every cable and cast loose, glad enough to see their flotilla on the retreat after the army, and more delighted still not to be attacked by the enemy during the operation, — so says one of their number.

One writer on the war speaks of the engineers as grasping " not the musket but the *hammer*," a misleading remark, for not a nail is driven into the bridge at any point,

A PONTOON BRIDGE AT BELLE PLAIN, VA. FROM A PHOTOGRAPH.

When the Army of the Potomac retreated from before Richmond in 1862 it crossed the lower Chickahominy on a bridge of boats and rafts 1980 feet long. This was constructed by three separate working parties, employed at the same time, one engaged at each end and one in the centre. It was the longest bridge built in the war, of which I have any knowledge, save one, and that the bridge built across the James, below Wilcox's Landing, in 1864. This latter was a remarkable achievement in ponton engineering. It was over two thousand feet long, and the channel boats were firmly anchored in thirteen fathoms of water. The engineers began it during the forenoon of June 14, and completed the task at midnight. It was built under the direction of General Benham for the passage of the wagon-trains and a part of the troops, while the rest crossed in steamers and ferry-boats.

But ponton bridges were not always laid without opposition or interference from the enemy. Perhaps they made the most stubborn contest to prevent the laying of the bridges across the Rappahannock before Fredericksburg in December, 1862.

The pontoniers had partially laid one bridge before daylight, but when dawn appeared the enemy's sharpshooters, who had been posted in buildings on the opposite bank, opened so destructive a fire upon them that they were compelled to desist, and two subsequent attempts to continue the work, though desperately made, were likewise brought to naught by the deadly fire of Mississippi rifles. At last three regiments, the Seventh Michigan, and the Nineteenth and Twentieth Massachusetts, volunteered to cross the river, and drive the enemy out of cover, which they did most gallantly, though not without considerable loss. They crossed the river in ponton boats, charged up the steep bank opposite, drove out, or captured the Rebels holding the buildings, and in a short time the first ponton bridge was completed. Others were laid near by soon after.

I think the engineers lost more men here — I mean now in actual combat — than in all their previous and subsequent service combined.

Ponton bridges were a source of great satisfaction to the soldiers. They were perfect marvels of stability and steadiness. No swaying motion was visible. To one passing across with a column of troops or wagons *no* motion was discernible. It seemed as safe and secure as mother earth,

and the army walked them confidence as if they were. while my company was cross- on the bridge laid at Point Webster Atkinson, a can- about six feet and a quarter low, he was afterwards mor- Hatcher's Run, — being well- fatigue of the all-night march walked off the bridge. For-

with the same serene I remember one night ing the Appomattox of Rocks that D. noneer, who stood in boots — dear fel- tally wounded at nigh asleep from the we were undergoing, tunately for him, he

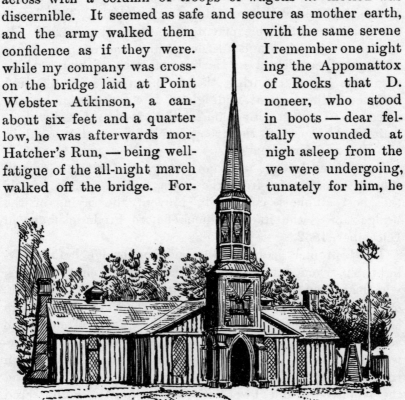

POPLAR GROVE CHURCH.

stepped — not into four or five fathoms of water, but — a ponton. As can readily be imagined, an unexpected step down of two feet and a half was quite an "eye-opener" to him, but, barring a little lameness, he suffered no harm.

The engineers, as a whole, led an enjoyable life of it in the service. Their labors were quite fatiguing while they lasted, it is true, but they were a privileged class when compared with the infantry. But they did well all that was required of them, and there was no finer body of men in the service.

The winter-quarters of the engineers were, perhaps, the most unique of any in the army. In erecting them they gave their mechanical skill full play. Some of their officers' quarters were marvels of rustic design. The houses of one regiment in the winter of '63–4 were fashioned out of the straight cedar, which, being undressed, gave the settlement a quaint but attractive and comfortable appearance.

Their streets were corduroyed, and they even boasted sidewalks of similar construction. Poplar Grove Church, erected by the Fiftieth New York Engineers, a few miles below Petersburg, in 1864, still stands, a monument to their skill in rustic design.

CHAPTER XXI.

TALKING FLAGS AND TORCHES.

"Ho! my comrades, see the signal
Waving through the sky;
Re-enforcements now appearing,
Victory is nigh."

ES, there were flags in the army which talked for the soldiers, and I cannot furnish a more entertaining chapter than one which will describe *how* they did it, *when* they did it, and what they did it for. True, all of the flags used in the service told stories of their own. What more eloquent than " Old Glory," with its thirteen stripes, reminding us of our small beginning as a nation, its blue field, originally occupied by the cross of the English flag when Washington first gave it to the breeze in Cambridge, but replaced later by a cluster of stars, which keep a tally of the number of States in the Union! What wealth of history its subsequent career as the national emblem suggests, making it almost vocal with speech! The corps, division, and brigade flags, too, told a little story of their own, in a manner already described. But there were other flags, whose sole business it was to talk to one another, and the stories they told were immediately written down for the benefit of the soldiers or sailors. These flags were *Signal* flags, and the men who used them and made them talk were known in the service as the *Signal Corps*.

What was this corps for? Well, to answer that question at length would make quite a story, but, in brief, I may say that it was for the purpose of rapid and frequent communication between different portions of the land or naval forces. The army might be engaged with the enemy, on the march, or in camp, yet these signal men, with their flags, were serviceable in either situation, and in the former often especially so; but I will begin at the beginning, and present a brief sketch of the origin of the Signal Corps.

The system of signals used in both armies during the Rebellion originated with one man — Albert J. Myer, who was born in Newburg, N. Y. He entered the army as assistant surgeon in 1854, and, while on duty in New Mexico and vicinity, the desirability of some better method of rapid communication than that of a messenger impressed itself upon him. This conviction, strengthened by his previous lines of thought in the same direction, he finally wrought out in a system of motion telegraphy.*

Recognizing to some extent the value of his system, Congress created the position of Chief Signal Officer of the army, and Surgeon Myer was appointed by President Buchanan to fill it. Up to some time in 1863 Myer was not the *Chief* Signal Officer alone, but the *only* signal officer commissioned as such, all others then in the corps — and there were quite a number — being simply *acting* signal officers on detached service from various regiments.

One of the officers in the regular army, whom Surgeon

* These facts are taken from a small pamphlet written by Lieutenant J. Willard Brown of West Medford, Mass., and issued by the Signal Corps Association. Other facts pertaining to signalling have been derived from "A Manual of Signals," written by General Myer (Old Probabilities) himself, since the war.

Myer had instructed in signalling while in New Mexico, went over to the enemy when the war broke out and organized a corps for them.

From this small beginning of one man grew up the Signal Corps. As soon as the value of the idea had fairly penetrated the brains of those whose appreciation was needed to make it of practical value, details of men were made from the various regiments around Washington, and placed in camps of instruction to learn the use of the " Signal Kit," so called. The chief article in this kit was a series of seven flags, varying from two feet to six feet square. Three of these flags, one six feet, one four feet, and one two feet square, were white, and had each a block of red in the centre one-third the dimensions of the flag; that is, a flag six feet square had a centre two feet square; two flags were black with white centres, and two were red with white centres. When the flags were in use, they were tied to a staff, whose length varied with the size of the flag to be used. If the distance to signal was great, or obstructions intervened, a long staff and a large flag were necessary; but the four-foot flag was the one in most common use.

PLATE 1.

It will be readily inferred that the language of these flags was to be addressed to the eye and not the ear. To make that language plain, then, they must be distinctly seen by the persons whom they addressed. This will explain why they were of different colors. In making signals, the color of flag to be used depended upon the color of background against which it was to appear. For example, a *white* flag, even with its red centre, could not be easily seen against the sky as a background. In such a situation a *black* flag was necessary. With green or dark-colored backgrounds the *white* flag was used, and in fact this was *the* flag of the signal service, having been used, in all probability, nine times out of every ten that signals were made.

Before the deaf and dumb could be taught to

PLATE 2.

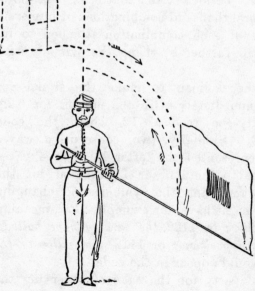

PLATE 3.

talk, certain motions were agreed upon to represent particular ideas, letters, and figures. In like manner, a key, or *code*, was constructed which interpreted the motions of the signal flag, — for it talked by motions,— and in accord with which the motions were made. Let me illustrate these motions by the accompanying cuts.

Plate 1 represents a member of the Signal Corps in position, holding the flag directly above his head, the staff vertical, and grasped by both hands. This is the position from which all the motions were made.

Plate 2 represents the flagman making the numeral " 2 " or the letter " i." This was done by waving the flag to the right and instantly returning it to a vertical position. To make " 1 " the flag was waved to the left, and instantly returned as before. See plate 3. This the code translated as the letter " t " and the word "the." " 5 " was made by waving the flag directly to the front, and returning at once to the vertical.

The signal code most commonly used included but two symbols, which made it simple to use. With these, not only could all the letters of the alphabet and the numerals be communicated, but an endless variety of syllables, words, phrases, and statements besides. As a matter of fact, however, it contained several thousand combinations of numerals with the significance of each combination attached to it. Let me illustrate still further by using the symbols " 2 " and " 1."

Let us suppose the flagman to make the signal for " 1," and follow it immediately with the motion for " 2." This would naturally be read as 12, which the code showed to mean O. Similarly, two consecutive waves to the right, or 22, represented the letter N. Three waves to the right and one to the left, or 2221, stood for the syllable *tion.* So by repeating the symbols and changing the combinations we might have, for example, 2122, meaning *the enemy are advancing;* or 1122, *the cavalry have halted;* or 12211, *three guns in position;* or 1112, *two miles to the left,* — all of which would appear in the code.

Let us join a signal party for the sake of observing the method of communicating a message. Such a party, if complete, was composed of three persons, viz., the signal officer (commissioned) in charge, with a telescope and field-glass; the flagman, with his kit, and an orderly to take charge of the horses, if the station was only temporary. The point selected from which to signal must be a commanding position, whether a mountain, a hill, a tree-top, or a house-top. The station having been attained, the flagman takes position, and the officer sweeps the horizon and intermediate territory with his telescope to discover another signal station, where a second officer and flagman are posted.

Having discovered such a station, the officer directs his man to "call" that station. This he does by signalling the number of the station (for each station had a number), repeating the same until his signal is seen and answered. It was the custom at stations to keep a man on the lookout, with the telescope, for signals, constantly. Having got the attention of the opposite station, the officer sends his message. The flagman was not supposed to know the import of the message which he waved out with his flag. The officer called the numerals, and the flagman responded with the required motions almost automatically, when well practised.

At the end of each word motion "5" was made once; at the end of a sentence "55"; and of a message "555." There were a few words and syllables which were conveyed by a single motion of the flag; but, as a rule, the words had to be spelled out letter by letter, at least by beginners. Skilled signalists, however, used many abbreviations, and rarely found it necessary to spell out a word in full.

So much for the manner of *sending* a message. Now let us join the party at the station where the message is being *received*. There we simply find the officer sitting at his telescope reading the message being sent to him. Should he fail to understand any word, his own flagman signals an interruption, and asks a repetition of the message from the last word understood. Such occurrences were not frequent, however.

The services of the Signal Corps were just as needful and

valuable by night as in daylight ; but, as the flags could not then talk understandingly, *Talking Torches* were substituted for them.   As a "point of reference" was needful, by which to interpret the torch signals made, the flagman lighted a "foot torch," at which he stood firmly while he signalled with the "flying torch."   This latter was attached to a staff of the same length as the flagstaff, in fact, usually the flagstaff itself.   These torches were of copper, and filled with turpentine.   At the end of a message the flying torch was extinguished.

The rapidity with which messages were sent by experienced operators was something wonderful to the uneducated looker-on.   An ordinary message of a few lines can be sent in ten minutes, and the rate of speed is much increased where officers have worked long together, and understand each other's methods and abbreviations.

Signal messages have been sent twenty-eight miles; but that is exceptional.   The conditions of the atmosphere and the location of stations were seldom favorable to such long-distance signalling.   Ordinarily, messages were not sent more than six or seven miles, but there were exceptions.   Here is a familiar but noted one : —

In the latter part of September, 1864, the Rebel army under Hood set out to destroy the railroad communications of Sherman, who was then at Atlanta.   The latter soon learned that Allatoona was the objective point of the enemy. As it was only held by a small brigade, whereas the enemy was seen advancing upon it in much superior numbers, Sherman signalled a despatch from Vining's Station to Kenesaw, and from Kenesaw to Allatoona, whence it was again signalled to Rome.   It requested General Corse, who was at the latter place, to hurry back to the assistance of Allatoona. Meanwhile, Sherman was propelling the main body of his army in the same direction.   On reaching Kenesaw, "the signal officer reported," says Sherman, in his *Memoirs*, "that since daylight he had failed to obtain any answer to his call for Allatoona; but while I was with him he caught a faint glimpse of the tell-tale flag through an embrasure, and after much time he made out these letters

'C' 'R' 'S' 'E' 'H' 'E' 'R'

and translated the message 'Corse is here.' It was a source of great relief, for it gave me the first assurance that General Corse had received his orders, and that the place was adequately garrisoned."

General Corse has informed me that the distance between the two signal stations was about sixteen miles in an air line. Several other messages passed later between these stations, among them this one, which has been often referred to :—

ALLATOONA, Georgia, Oct. 6, 1864 — 2 P. M.
Captain L. M. DAYTON, Aide-de-Camp: —

I am short a cheek-bone and an ear, but am able to whip all h—l yet. My losses are heavy. A force moving from Stilesboro to Kingston gives me some anxiety. Tell me where Sherman is.

JOHN M. CORSE, Brigadier-General.

The occasions which called the Signal Corps into activity were various, but they were most frequently employed in reporting the movements of troops, sometimes of the Union, sometimes of the enemy. They took post on elevated stations, whether a hill, a tall tree, or the top of a building. Any position from which they could command a broad view of the surrounding country was occupied for their purpose. If nature did not always provide a suitable place for lookout, art came to the rescue, and signal towers of considerable height were built for this class of workers, who, like the cavalry, were the "eyes" of the army if not the ears. I remember several of these towers which stood before Petersburg in 1864. They were of especial use there in observing the movements of troops within the enemy's lines, as they stood, I should judge, from one hundred to one hundred and fifty feet high. Although these towers were erected somewhat to the rear of the Union main lines, and were a very open trestling, they were yet a conspicuous target for the enemy's long-range guns and mortar-shells.

Sometimes the nerve of the flagman was put to a very severe test, as he stood on the summit of one of these frail structures waving his flag, his situation too like that of Ma-

homet's coffin, while the Whitworth bolts whistled sociably by him, saying, "Where is he? Where is he?" or, by another interpretation, "Which one? Which one?" Had one of these bolts hit a corner post of the lookout, the chances for the flagman and his lieutenant to reach the earth by a new route would have been favorable, although the engineers who built them claimed that with *three* posts cut away the tower would still stand. But, as a matter of fact, I believe no shot ever seriously injured one of the towers, though tons weight of iron must have been hurled at them. The roof of the Avery House, before Petersburg, was used for a signal station, and the shells of the enemy's guns often tore through

SIGNAL TREE-TOP.

below much to the alarm of the signal men above.

Signalling was carried on during an engagement between different parts of the army. By calling for needed re-enforcements, or giving news of their approach, or requesting ammunition, or reporting movements of the enemy, or noting the effects of shelling, — in these and a hundred kindred ways the corps made their services invaluable to the troops. Sometimes signal officers on shore communicated with others on shipboard, and, in one instance, Lieutenant Brown told me that through the information he imparted to a gunboat off Suffolk, in 1863, regarding the effects of the shot which were thrown from it, General Longstreet had since written him that the fire was so accurate he was compelled to withdraw his troops. The signals were made from the tower of the Masonic Hall in Suffolk, whence they were taken up by another signal party on the river bluff, and thence communicated to the gunboat.

Not long since, General Sherman, in conversation, alluded to a correspondent of the New York "Herald" whom he had threatened to hang, declaring that had he done so his "death would have saved ten thousand lives." The relation of this anecdote brings out another interesting phase of signal-corps operations. It seems that one of our signal officers had succeeded in reading the signal code of the

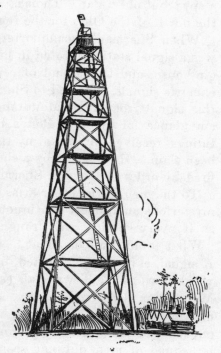

A SIGNAL TOWER BEFORE PETERS-
BURG, VA.

enemy, and had communicated the same to his fellow-officers. With this code in their possession, the corps was enabled to furnish valuable information directly from Rebel headquarters, by reading the Rebel signals, continuing to do so during the Chattanooga and much of the Atlanta campaign, when the enemy's signal flags were often plainly visible. Suddenly this source of information was completely cut off by the ambition of the correspondent to publish all

the news, and the natural result was the enemy changed
the code. This took place just before Sherman's attack on
Kenesaw Mountain (June, 1864), and it is to the hundreds
slaughtered there that he probably refers. General Thomas
was ordered to arrest the reporter, and have him hanged as
a spy; but old "Pap" Thomas' kind heart banished him to
the north of the Ohio for the remainder of the war, instead.

When Sherman's headquarters were at Big Shanty, there
was a signal station located in his rear, on the roof of an old
gin-house, and this signal officer, having the "key" to the
enemy's signals, reported to Sherman that he had translated
this signal from Pine Mountain to Marietta, — "Send an
ambulance for General Polk's body," — which was the first
tidings received by our army that the fighting bishop had
been slain. He was hit by a shell from a volley of artillery
fired by order of General Sherman.

To the men in the other arms of the service, who saw this
mysterious and almost continuous waving of flags, it seemed
as if every motion was fraught with momentous import.
"What could it all be about?" they would ask one another.
A signal station was located, in '61–2, on the top of what
was known as the Town Hall (since burned) in Poolesville,
Md., within a few rods of my company's camp, and, to the
best of my recollection, not an hour of daylight passed without more or less flag-waving from that point. This particular squad of men did not seem at all fraternal, but kept
aloof, as if (so we thought) they feared they might, in an
unguarded moment, impart some of the important secret
information which had been received by them from the
station at Sugar Loaf Mountain or Seneca. Since the war,
I have learned that their apparently excited and energetic
performances were, for the most part, only practice between
stations for the purpose of acquiring familiarity with the
code, and facility in using it.

It may be thought that the duties of the Signal Corps
were always performed in positions where their personal

safety was never imperilled. But such was far from the fact. At the battle of Atlanta, July 22, 1864, a signal officer had climbed a tall pine-tree, for the purpose of directing the fire of a section of Union artillery, which was stationed at its foot, the country being so wooded and broken that the artillerists could not certainly see the position of the enemy. The officer had nailed a succession of cleats up the trunk, and was on the platform which he had made in the top of the tree, acting as signal officer, when the Rebels made a charge, capturing the two guns, and shot the officer dead at his post.

From the important nature of the duties which they performed, the enemy could not look upon them with very tender regard, and this fact they made apparent on every opportunity. Here is an incident which, I think, has never been published : —

When General Nelson's division arrived at Shiloh, Lieutenant Joseph Hinson, commanding the Signal Corps attached to it, crossed the Tennessee and reported to General Buell, after which he established a station on that side of the river, from which messages were sent having reference to the disposition of Nelson's troops. The crowd of stragglers (presumably from Grant's army) was so great as to continually obstruct his view, and in consequence he pressed into service a guard from among the stragglers themselves to keep his view clear, and placed his associate, Lieutenant Hart, in charge. Presently General Grant himself came riding up the bank, and, as luck would have it, came into Lieutenant Hinson's line of vision. Catching sight of a cavalry boot, without stopping to see who was in it, in his impatience, Lieutenant Hart sang out : "Git out of the way there ! Ain't you got no sense ? " Whereupon Grant very quietly apologized for his carelessness, and rode over to the side of General Buell. When the lieutenant found he had been addressing or " dressing " a major-general, his confusion can be imagined. (See frontispiece).

After arriving before Fort McAllister, General Sherman sent General Hazen down the right bank of the Ogeechee to take the fort by assault, and himself rode down the left bank to a rice plantation, where General Howard had established a signal station to overlook the river and watch for vessels. The station was built on the top of a rice-mill. From this point the fort was visible, three miles away. In due time a commotion in the fort indicated the approach of Hazen's troops, and the signal officer discovered a signal flag about three miles above the fort, which he found was Hazen's, the latter inquiring if Sherman was there. He was answered affirmatively, and informed that Sherman expected the fort to be carried before night. Finally Hazen signalled that he was ready, and was told to go ahead. Meanwhile, a small United States steamer had been descried coming up the river, and, noticing the party at the rice-mill, the following dialogue between signal flags ensued : —

"Who are you ? "

" General Sherman."

" Is Fort McAllister taken ? "

" Not yet; but it will be in a minute."

And in a few minutes it *was* taken, and the fact signalled to the naval officers on the boat, who were not in sight of the fort.

During the battle of Gettysburg, or, at least, while Sickles was contending at the Peach Orchard against odds, the signal men had their flags flying from Little Round Top; but when the day was lost, and Hood with his Texans pressed towards that important point, the signal officers folded their flags, and prepared to visit other and less dangerous scenes. At that moment, however, General Warren of the Fifth Corps appeared, and ordered them to keep their signals waving as if a host were immediately behind them, which they did.

General E. P. Alexander, the officer referred to as having organized the Rebel Signal Corps, in an article in the

Century Magazine for January, 1887, describing "Pickett's Charge," says that he was "particularly cautioned, in moving the artillery, to keep it out of sight of the signal-station upon Round Top." In a foot-note referring to this caution he says: —

"This suggests the remark that I have never understood why the enemy abandoned the use of military balloons early in 1863, after having used them extensively up to that time. Even if the observer never saw anything, they would have been worth all they cost, for the annoyance and delays they caused us in trying to keep our movements out of their sight. That wretched little signal-station upon Round Top that day caused one of our divisions to lose over two hours, and probably delayed our assault nearly that long. During that time a Federal corps arrived near Round Top, and became an important factor in the action which followed."

In a note addressed to the historian of the Signal Corps Association, to whom General Alexander has furnished a sketch of the organization of the Rebel Signal Corps, he says: —

"You are more than welcome to the compliment I paid the signal-station on Round Top in my article in the January *Century*. I have forgiven all my enemies now; and though you fellows there were about the last that I did forgive, I took you in several years ago, and concluded to 'let by-gones be by-gones.' "

> " Thy work is done ; along Virginia's river
>   No more thy signal flies ;
>   From Georgia's hills by night no more the quiver
>   Of thy red torch shall rise.

> " There came a noon when from the bastions frowning
>   Of every fort and bay
>   Flung out a banner ; hurrying on and crowning
>   The mountains far away.

" We left undecked no hamlet's little steeple
  That loud with joy-bells rung ;
And from the breasts of a too happy people
  Its passion-flowers were hung.

" We knew its language ; knew our work was over ;
  And hailed, while ours we furled,
The only Flag whose sovereign folds shall cover
  Henceforth our Western world.''